The Americanisation Trade Order

This book provides insights into the world trading order that is informed by power—in particular, the unidirectional norm imparting impact of US foreign trade law and practice on its trading partners and non-State actors. In this context, the recent tensions between the US and China have brought to the fore several fundamental and systemic questions. Underpinning these is the challenge of accommodating economic power under the rule of international economic law, including inculcating responsibility in its engagement.

In the light of the recent US challenges to the world trading order, this timely publication will help us understand how the US will continue to shape the international economic order.

Asif H Qureshi is a Professor and Distinguished Scholar in Residence, Peking University, School of Transnational Law, China.

Routledge Research in International Economic Law

Asian Perspectives on International Investment Law
Edited by Junji Nakagawa

Cost and EU Public Procurement Law
Life-Cycle Costing for Sustainability
Edited by Marta Andhov, Roberto Caranta and Anja Wiesbrock

Promoting and Managing International Investment
Towards an Integrated Policy Approach
Edited by J Anthony VanDuzer and Patrick Leblond

International Investment Law and Gender Equality
Stabilization Clauses and Foreign Investment
Sangwani Patrick Ng'ambi

The Legality of Economic Activities in Occupied Territories
International, EU Law and Business and Human Rights Perspectives
Antoine Duval and Eva Kassoti

International Investment Protection within Europe
The EU's Assertion of Control
Julien Berger

Trade, Migration and Law
Free Movement of Persons in the South African Development Community
Victor Amadi

The Americanization of the World Trade Order
Asif H Qureshi

For more information about this series, please visit https://www.routledge.com/Routledge-Research-in-International-Economic-Law/book-series/INTECONLAW

The Americanisation of the World Trade Order

Asif H Qureshi

Routledge
Taylor & Francis Group
LONDON AND NEW YORK

First published 2022
by Routledge
4 Park Square, Milton Park, Abingdon, Oxon OX14 4RN

and by Routledge
605 Third Avenue, New York, NY 10158

Routledge is an imprint of the Taylor & Francis Group, an informa business

British Library Cataloguing-in-Publication Data
A catalogue record for this book is available from the British Library

Library of Congress Cataloging-in-Publication Data
A catalog record has been requested for this book

ISBN: 978-0-367-49835-1 (hbk)
ISBN: 978-0-367-49836-8 (pbk)
ISBN: 978-1-003-04757-5 (ebk)

DOI: 10.4324/9781003047575

Typeset in Galliard
by Deanta Global Publishing Services, Chennai, India

To
Habib and Mianghi

Contents

Foreword

As the world shifts away from the US towards the Asia-Pacific region, there could be no better guide to US foreign trade law than Professor Dr Asif Qureshi. US trade law is vast and complex, legally, economically, and politically, as is the case with the trade law of other large regions or countries, such as the European Union or China. This book offers a detailed, thorough, and often passionate trip through this maddening 'bramble bush,' to quote Karl Llewellyn's well-known characterisation of law. Thanks to Asif Qureshi's detailed map and sure hand, we readers emerge not only unscathed but also much the wiser for our adventure.

I first met Asif Qureshi many years ago in London. He was then already a leading scholar of international economic law, and we at the London School of Economics called upon his knowledge and expertise for a PhD examination. His teaching, research, and publications have consolidated his worldwide reputation as one of the best scholars in the field. Since our initial meeting, I have substantially relied on and learned so much from his superb analysis of *Interpreting WTO Agreements: Problems and Perspectives* (1st ed. 2006, 2nd ed. 2015) and his basic textbook on *International Economic Law* (with Professor Andreas Ziegler, 2nd ed. 2011, 4th ed. 2019) in teaching World Trade Organization (WTO) law, European Union law, and international food safety law.

The current book brings new perspectives to the study of international trade law in general and of US foreign trade law in particular. First, its critical coverage, with chapters dealing with the constitutional and substantive issues that US hegemony poses for international economic law, US law and policy on intellectual property rights, surveillance of foreign currency exchange, the national security approach to international trade, the conditions for preferential market access by developing countries, and export controls.

Second, its method: Asif Qureshi takes legal texts seriously, but his inquiries do not stop with positive law. On the contrary, the analysis does not use general public international law as the only criterion of assessment. In the spirit of legal pluralism, it also draws very much on WTO law, including the General Agreement on Tariffs and Trade (GATT 1994) and specific agreements such as those on intellectual property (TRIPS) and safeguards (SCM), and also on US constitutional and administrative law, economics, and other facets of American society, such as values.

Third, broadening this method of hermeneutic critique from a more personal viewpoint, the book assesses US foreign trade law against the standards of reciprocity, shared morality, and the general interests of humankind. These, according to the author, are the basic features of the international legal order, which, from his perspective, is based on liberalism and the promotion of trade. Since the late 1940s, they have been inscribed to some extent in the GATT and in the WTO Agreements.

Fourth, the author's standpoint: Asif Qureshi's aim is to promote a shared vision of international economic law, to ensure due respect of the policy spaces of all WTO Members and others, and to protect the interests of the international community as a whole. In other words, contrary to many schools of international politics which inform our knowledge of international trade law, the book seeks to develop and apply an ethical perspective on international trade.

This book by a leading scholar in the field offers a stimulating, critical perspective on US foreign trade law. It is an important contribution to our knowledge of this subject and of international trade law in general, both from the standpoint of public international law and from the perspective of the global south. As the author implicitly suggests, this perspective needs to be further articulated, developed, and applied to other main trading countries, if we wish to elaborate and sustain international trade rules and practices for the benefit of all peoples and the economic, political, and moral sustainability of our planet.

Professor Dr Francis Snyder
CV Starr Professor of Law and Jean Monnet Chair ad personam
Peking University School of Transnational Law, China
Peking University Shenzhen Graduate School, Shenzhen, China
Visiting Professor, College of Europe, Bruges, Belgium (since 1988)
Professor Emeritus, Aix-Marseille University, France
Officier des Palmes Académiques (France)
People's Republic of China Friendship Award 2018
Peking University Friendship Award 2018

Preface

This work is intended essentially as a focus on some of the challenges of accommodating the phenomenon of an economic superpower into a normative framework, for an international trading order the ownership of which rests with the international community. It is not intended as a litany of complaints about US foreign trade legislation as such. The purpose of the exercise is, however, to highlight some of the problematic aspects of US foreign trade legislation. The tenor and flavour of analysis herein is equally relevant and applicable to any other country/economic union that fits the bill. In the emphasis on the US there has been a collateral critique, in parts, of the US scholarship on international trade. But this is inevitable in some measure and an aspect of scholarship. No disrespect is intended. Indeed, just as the challenges of managing the phenomenon of an economic superpower is the legitimate scientific basis of an enquiry, so is a community of scholars whose focus is the US foreign trade.

This work is not exhaustive of the phenomenon of Americanisation in all its manifestations. Thus, it does not cover the issues arising from the transplantation of US trade laws in foreign countries,[1] nor does it trace specifically the imprint of the US in the development of multilateral economic organisations and their substantive codes.[2] There are no sound reasons for this, but it is hoped the seeds for an approach to their analysis have been sown here.

In the same vein, the World Trade Organization (WTO) dispute settlement has a role as a barometer for insights into the Americanisation of the international trading order—both in terms of the number and types of complaints with respect to US trade laws, as well as US complaints of the trade practices of other countries. Until around the end of 2021 there have been a total of 156 complaints

1 See generally for example Jaakko Husa, 'Developing Legal System, Legal Transplants, and Path Dependence: Reflections on the Rule of Law' *The Chinese Journal of Comparative Law* Vol. 6 No. 2 (2018) 129–150.

2 For example, for US involvement in the International Monetary Fund (IMF) see M G De Vries, *IMF History (1972–78)* Volumes 1, 2, and 3 (IMF: 2007) and M G De Vries, *The IMF in a Changing World 1945–85* (IMF: 1986); and for US involvement in the WTO see for example Craig VanGrasstek, *The History and Future of the World Trade Organization* (WTO: 2013).

levelled in the WTO against the United States. This has been by far the highest number of complaints against a member of the WTO and noticeably higher than other major trading countries. A significant majority of the complaints have involved US trade legislation concerned with trade remedies viz., anti-dumping, countervailing, and safeguard measures. In this work US trade legislation concerned with trade remedies has not been specifically focused upon. This is for two reasons. First, trade remedies are mainly defensive measures concerned with cross-border flows of trade into the US and therefore their contribution to the Americanisation of the international trading order as conceived herein is relatively less and indirect. Second, this aspect of US trade legislation has been extensively already analysed in the WTO. Similarly, the US has been a leader in instigating complaints against other members of the WTO—with some 124 complaints made since the inception of the WTO until 2021. The dispute settlement system of the WTO can be a vehicle for underlining the Americanisation of the international trading order. However, it is a system which is intended in the first instance to ensure compliance with the WTO code agreed upon between members of the WTO. In this work the substantive disputes in the WTO between the US and members of the WTO have not been a basis as such for an understanding of the Americanisation of the world trading system. Finally, in this work, because of time constraints, it was not possible to consider the implications of some very recent US legislation, for example, the America COMPETES Act of 2022.

I am grateful to Peking University, School of Transnational Law (STL), China, and Korea University School of Law, South Korea, for facilitating this research. It has been conducted during a period wherein my appointment has straddled both institutions. At STL I am grateful to Professor Mark Feldman for offering his comments on Chapters Five and Six at so short a notice; Professor Francis Snyder for agreeing to write the Foreword to this work; and to my research assistants Li Manyun, Li Zhuangxu, and Hu Minghao for their contribution in proofreading. Much of the research for the first chapter was conducted during my sabbatical from Korea University, at the University of California, School of Law, Irvine, US.

My thanks also to Routledge for giving me the opportunity to publish this work. The proposal for this work was reviewed by several reviewers commissioned by Routledge. Almost all the chapters herein have been reviewed in one form or another by various anonymous reviewers from whose comments I have benefited, and whose dissent I have learnt to tolerate.

Acknowledgements

I am grateful to the following for allowing me to publish work from their journals:

1. 'The World Trade Organization and the Promotion of Effective Dispute Resolution: In Times of a Trade War,' *AIIB Yearbook Of International Law* (Brill, Netherlands: 2019).
2. 'The Americanization of the International Economic Order and its Normative Boundaries,' *Asian Journal of WTO & International Health Law and Policy* (National Taiwan University Press, Taiwan: 2020).
3. 'United States Special 301—A Deeply Flawed Tool for IPR Regulation?' *Journal of World Trade* (Kluwer Law International, Netherlands: 2021).
4. 'US Surveillance of Foreign Currency Exchange & Macroeconomic Practices,' *World Trade Review* (Cambridge University Press, UK: 2021).
5. 'A Public International Law Perspective of Section 232 of the US Trade Expansion Act,' *Kansas Journal of Law and Public Policy* (Kansas, USA: 2021).

Introduction

'Disorganising the World Trade Order—A US privilege?'

There is no denying that the United States (US) has made a positive contribution to the development of the international economic system since the inception of the Bretton Woods institutions post-Second World War. This is despite its contribution to the demise of the Havana Charter for an international trade organisation in 1948; and its subsequent foot-dragging in the establishment of an international trade organisation until 1994, upon the creation of the World Trade Organization (WTO). Under the initiative and support of the US, the international community saw the establishment of the International Monetary Fund (IMF) and the World Bank Group as important pillars of the international economic system. However, as is well known, in the last decade the Trump era brought a sharp focus on the disorganising influence of the US on the world trade order—the weakening of its principal dispute settlement system. Much of the capacity for this disorganising influence was already embedded in US legislation—and not much has been done nor is it likely under the new Biden administration to set the record straight. This genre of foreign trade legislation preserved US authority to unilaterally imprint its interests in the face of an organised world trade order and its rule-oriented trajectory—to which the US itself had hitherto made a commitment. From an international perspective, it is appropriate to query whether the US has the privilege to disorganise the world trade order solely at its behest.

In the same vein, this capacity to disorganise has built-in mechanisms for the Americanisation of the world trade order. Americanisation is not only the process of cultural transplantation through trade in goods and services—it is also the indoctrination of American analysis of foreign trade practices; the imparting of 'American values' as conditions for access to its market; and the integration of American foreign policy with foreign trade. However, Americanisation is not to be equated with globalisation itself; rather it refers to a possible consequence of it. Americans may well have an understandable blind spot about the value of Americanisation. However, both the US and the international community have an obligation to reflect upon its value in a plural world which the international

DOI: 10.4324/9781003047575-1

community so cherishes. Vehicles for Americanisation are not only to be found in US foreign trade law but also through the influence the US has in multilateral organisations. In this brief work, the focus has mainly been on the principal US foreign trade laws, in an endeavour to highlight the normative costs they impose on the international community. Moreover, regardless of whether a State is a developed or a developing one, whether a foreign individual is trading with the US or with a third country—the normative tentacles of 'disorganised Americanisation' have an impact and therefore must be understood alongside the multilateral normative framework in international trade.

Chapter One is titled 'The Americanisation of the International Economic Order and Its Normative Boundaries.' It sets out the underlying themes of this work. In particular, the chapter focuses on the challenges of integrating an economically powerful State in the international economic order (IEO). As such it identifies the process of the Americanisation of the IEO focusing firstly on the relationship between economic power and the rule of international economic law—in decision-making and adjudicative processes in relevant multilateral fora. Secondly, it focuses on the responsibilities that a State has, and/or should have, in the engagement of trade wars. The manner of engagement in decision-making, judicial resolutions, and trade wars partake of legislative processes for the Americanisation of the IEO.

In Chapter Two an international law and policy perspective is applied to the US Special 301 reviews in the management of the normative framework of intellectual property rights of foreign States—with emphasis on the pharmaceutical sector and transfer of technology. In particular, the chapter draws upon the US Special 301 Reports between 2018 to 2020. A critical stance of Special 301 is adopted, given the relative paucity of such a treatment amongst scholars generally. This evaluation is intended to be an input from an international perspective, and equip those who are at the receiving end of the normative impact of the Special 301 reviews. The chapter concludes that Special 301 is lacking in informed, expert, and empirically based inputs in economics, international law, and ethics. Above all it lends itself to being hijacked by the agenda of a political executive without adequate constitutional and due process safeguards for those it is targeted at.

Chapter Three focuses on the way the US identifies the exchange rate and macroeconomic policies of its key trading partners, including the policy advice it gives to them. When according to a US set criteria, its trading partners' exchange rate and macroeconomic policies contribute to a US trade deficit, the US presumes to give policy advice to its trading partners. The chapter concentrates on the US apparatus that is set in two different pieces of legislation concerned essentially with currency manipulation—from the perspective of the WTO and IMF legal regimes. The chapter concludes that the US regime concerning currency manipulation, although implemented to address a compliance void under the IMF and WTO procedures, is despite that justification, flawed.

Chapter Four looks at the impact of US national security concerns, as set out in Section 232 of the US Trade Expansion Act, on imports of goods and services to the United States, from an international perspective. This perspective involves elaborating on the impact of Section 232 on economic interests outside the United States. Much of the current focus on Section 232 has been in terms of its impact on US concerns within the State. Moreover, there is a need to bring to bear not just a WTO analysis of Section 232 but also an analysis within the wider context of public international law and policy generally. In the analysis thus far, Section 232 has been the subject of much American 'navel-gazing' albeit from a scholarly US perspective. However, other than the growing focus on Section 232 from a WTO perspective, given the recent challenges in the WTO with reference to restrictions on steel and aluminum on national security grounds, there is little if any analysis that brings to bear the wider set of principles and concepts that exist in public international law.

Chapter Five sheds light on the conditionality attached in US unilateral trade preference schemes, from the beneficiary countries' standpoint, against the background of international law and policy. It focuses on the very propriety of those conditions, the extent of their normative impact, and the suitability of trade preferential schemes as vehicles for channelling conditionality. This discourse is based on a textual analysis of the US GSP legislation, including insights from an extensive US review in January 2020 of compliance with US conditions, involving certain developing countries. In this manner the chapter highlights the value orientations of the conditions transplanted into another country, and the implications for the self-determination of domestic policy-making.

Finally, Chapter Six comprises a focus on the US Export Control Reform Act 2018 (ECRA). ECRA is a controversial legislation, the setting of which is underpinned by the US and China competition in the economic and military spheres. This chapter concentrates on ECRA from an international law perspective. It argues for a multilateral approach to the management of export controls. The focus on ECRA is set against the background of similar recent EU and China export control legislation.

The chapters are followed by an Annex with extracts of relevant US legislation relied upon in this work.

1 The Americanisation of the International Economic Order and Its Normative Boundaries[1]

'We must reflect about ourselves and our capacity to influence before we inflict ourselves on other societies.'

Introduction

Since the dawn of the Bretton Woods era, discourse in international economic law (IEL) has been preoccupied with international economic organisations. These institutions have been evolving, yet the legal focus has continued with the formal institutions qua institutions, rather than their underlying drivers viz., the principal member State stakeholders in these organisations. Either the perceived realpolitik has been pushed to the realms of international political economy; or there has been a delusional, almost aspirational focus on the institutions qua institutions. Indeed, a consideration of the interface between the legal systems of these member States concerning foreign economic practice has been understood as domestic case studies and therefore either beyond the ambit of public international law, or partaking of comparative law.

In the case of the United States (US) in particular, such characterisation is inappropriate, as it has been a major influence in the development of the international economic order (IEO). A focus on it cannot in terms of IEL be marginalised as a case study, and/or not commanding a public international law analysis. A candid focus that contextualises the role of the US in the development of the IEO as its primary underlying driver is important for clarity, completeness, and addressing the challenges of the specific genre of issues it poses—both constitutional and substantive—for the IEO. Fragmented approaches in legal scholarship have now been discarded and several approaches have pushed at the self-imposed disciplinary boundaries viz., law and policy, law in context, critical legal studies, and interdisciplinary approaches to law.

1 The work on this chapter was done whilst the author was a Visiting Professor at the University of California Irvine Law School Fall 2019. This chapter is based on an article published in the *Asian Journal of WTO & International Health Law and Policy* Vol. 15 No. 1 (2020).

DOI: 10.4324/9781003047575-2

Hitherto there has been some focus on the US law on foreign economic relations and IEL, both from a practical[2] and theoretical perspective.[3] The practical focus touches on both public international law and domestic law aspects of selected international business problems; with an emphasis on trade issues; essentially against the background of US law and US perspective; and mainly locating the public international law and US law alongside each other for a US audience.

One theoretical treatment of note[4] is formulated as 'transnational legal ordering,' and comprises a collective set of norms in which US norms or inputs in their formulation may or may not feature, although they normally do. The emphasis is very much on the issues arising from the processes of reordering of the domestic law of 'other' States, and locates its essential formative process in the transnational space—against the background of US influence. Thus, whilst this focus is concerned with the 'reordering' of the 'other'—it is conspicuously light in deconstructing the underlying propriety of the origins and the nature of the order involved in the reordering. Transnational legal ordering is proposed through rose-tinted spectacles as a desideratum that should be aspired to. Discourse on the origins of this ordering, the processes involved in its formation, the motivations involved in the formation of the order, the impact on the other, and the quality of justice involved in the transnational law cannot be dismissed by the mere assertion that a legal realist perspective is taken 'in which law is constituted by both power and reason, exercising its authority both through coercion and a normativity that is grounded in legal reasoning and process.'[5] The Opium War and the unequal treaties imposed thereafter qualify under this modern day reasoning. In the same vein, it is not enough simply to explain that States 'invest in law precisely to advance their perceptions of their interests and normative goals.' The State 'perceptions of their interests and normative goals' cannot be a given and call for critical scrutiny. However, despite this, the matrix of law and power as an explanation of legal ordering can be persuasive, and this focus on the US ironically partakes of it in some measure. In some measure, as the approach here is one that subjects the US to scrutiny under international law and international policy—as it drives international economic relations in international organisations and foreign States.

2 See for example J Jackson, W Davey & A Sykes, *Cases, Materials and Texts on Legal Problems of International Economic Relations*, 6th ed. (West Academic Publishing: 2013); Harold H Koh, Detlev F Vagts & William S Dodge, *Transnational Business Problems*, 5th ed. (Foundation Press: 2014); Hannah L Buxbaum, Stephen D Cohen, Robert A Blecker & Peter D Whitney, *Fundamentals of U.S. Foreign Trade Policy: Economics, Politics, Laws, and Issues* (Westview Press: 2003); and K Damm, *The Rules of the Global Game: A New Look at U.S. International Economic Policymaking* (University of Chicago Press: 2004).

3 See for example G Shaffer (ed) *Transnational Legal Ordering and State Change* (Cambridge University Press: 2013); and T C Halliday & G Shaffer, *Transnational Legal Orders* (Cambridge University Press: 2015). J Bhagwati & H T Patrick (eds) *Aggressive Unilateralism* (University of Michigan Press: 1990).

4 See Shaffer in Shaffer (ed) 2013 and Halliday & Shaffer (ed) 2015.

5 Halliday & Shaffer, op. cit., Chapter 1.

The recent trade war between China and the US has brought to the fore several fundamental questions concerned with the challenges of reigning in the naked use of economic power. These challenges can be conceived, at a general level, in terms of the relationship between on the one hand economic power, and on the other the rule of law. And at a specific level, the relationship between international disciplines and the use of instruments of economic power (trade/currency wars). Indeed, it is even possible to consider the very thrusting of international trade in goods and services into another market, as manifestations of economic power also—given that goods and services traded also partake of certain values and cultural traits that are introduced into another society. They can be threats to national capacity, values, and culture. In short, there is here the need for a normative analysis of economic capacity. Such an evaluation needs to take on board the fact that normativity and economic power can take different forms.

This normative approach can be contextualised in terms of the US–China trade war, as follows. First and foremost is the relationship between economic power and the rule of IEL. This has been, in one form or another, the subject of much discourse in international relations and legal philosophy; and remains a fundamental challenge in the ordering of disciplines for economic superpowers. Specifically, the processes of decision-making and dispute settlement in international economic organisations, have been the subject of focus hitherto from the perspective of the participation of developing countries in these institutions—but perhaps not enough with reference to the superpower/s in such circumstances. Second, the US–China trade war is premised on the equation between fair trade and parity in trade balances as between countries, along with unemployment concerns. The international trading order has hitherto been underpinned doctrinally by the theory of comparative advantage; whilst trade liberalisation in the World Trade Organization (WTO) has been conceptualised mainly through the negotiation of a reciprocal market access process. The theory of comparative advantage has hitherto blunted the economic power premise under which the parity in the balance of trade argument is premised. Third, the availing of a 'trade war' as a vehicle for bringing about change not only calls into question the legitimacy of the methodology but also invites scrutiny in terms of the responsibilities of the State responsibility during the 'trade war.' Are there international disciplines akin to international humanitarian law (IHL) during such 'wars'? Are there questions of distributive justice that need to be explored? Trade wars call for ethical scrutiny and invite parallels with the way international law has developed in relation to the use of force by States. What have been the failings of the Bretton Woods institutions, if any, in the precipitation of such a state of affairs in the international economic system? Finally, the justification of national security so freely used for the imposition of economic measures in violation of accepted multilateral norms raises not only concerns about the very integrity of international disciplines but also the very nature of the goods and services internationally traded. National security in terms of the WTO has been the subject of only recent WTO litigation. The domestic constitutional setting in which the executive's national mandate is underpinned by national security concerns, calls for more analysis from an international law perspective. Moreover, the national security perspective draws a focus on the intrinsic nature of a good (or service) not only in terms of its national security aspects but also as an express or implicit vehicle of influence and imposition of non-trade values.

In sum, this current episode in the history of international economic relations underscores the Americanisation of the international economic order (IEO). What has been the US contribution to the development of the international economic order? What pictures are the American brushes painting now and what issues do they raise that have a specific American attribute? The US–China trade war, howsoever it pans out, has a dimension that partakes of the Americanisation of the IEO. In this chapter, two strands of this focus on the Americanisation of IEL are followed viz., the relationship between economic power and the rule of IEL; and economic power and the responsibility in its exercise. The objectives in this chapter are modest, namely, to suggest that there is scope for a normative discussion (both *lex lata* and *lex feranda*) here that needs to be taken further.

Americanisation and the Importance of Focusing on it

The description 'Americanisation' has been used in several contexts. Indeed, it has even been used in connection with international law generally;[6] including specifically with reference to certain disciplines in IEL;[7] and legal systems wherein American legal concepts/ideas and laws have been transplanted.[8] Legal discourse, however, is sparse, and not comprehensive in terms of IEL. Some of the analysis is positive, for example attributing American legal transplantation to European Legal Systems to the American lead as an industrialised nation.[9] Some of the analysis is negative, partaking of Marxist analysis of international law.[10] There is, however, a fair amount of non-legal literature that focuses on the *consequences* of

6 Apoorva Anubhuti, 'Americanization of International Laws,' <https://papers.ssrn.com/sol3/papers.cfm?abstract_id=1712286> (last visited September 2019).

7 See for example Roger P Alford, 'The American Influence on International Arbitration,' *The Ohio State Journal on Dispute Resolution* Vol. 19 (2003–2004) 69. Available at <https://scholarship.law.nd.edu/law_faculty_scholarship/562> (last visited September 2019); Wolfgang Alschne, 'Americanization of the BIT Universe: The Influence of Friendship, Commerce and Navigation (FCN) Treaties on Modern Investment Treaty Law,' *Goettingen Journal of International Law* Vol. 5 No. 2 (2003) 455–486.

8 Wolfgang Wiegand, 'Americanization of Law: Reception or Convergence?' in Lawrence M Friedman & Harry N Scheiber (eds) *Legal Culture And The Legal Profession* (Westview Press: 1996) 137; and R Daniel Kelemen & Eric C Sibbitt, 'The Globalization of American Law,' *International Organization* Vol. 58 No. 1 (2004) 103–136R. Daniel Kelemen & Eric C Sibbitt, 'The Americanization of Japanese Law,' *University of Pennsylvania Journal of International Economic Law* Vol. 23 No. 2 (2002).

9 Robert A. Kagan, 'Globalization and Legal Change: The "Americanization" of European Law?' (2007) <https://doi.org/10.1111/j.1748-5991.2007.00009.x>.

10 See for example Anubhuti, 'Americanization of International Laws,' op. cit.

the Americanisation of law and/or globalisation attributing to the US cultural hegemony and the homogenisation of the global economy.[11]

The Americanisation of the IEO involves a consideration of several aspects of US involvement in international economic relations. First, the way changes are brought about by the US in the international economic system that are in the interest of the international economic community in its vision—for example, the US was a key architect of the Bretton Woods institutions which have served the international community for decades now. Second, the US has brought about changes to the IEO that are of specific interest to the US—for example, ensuring only a limited scope for the Special Drawing Rights created under the auspices of the International Monetary Fund (IMF), as an internationally exchangeable currency medium. Third, changes that transplant US domestic practice into the international system, and emulated in the domestic practices of various countries, for example anti-dumping practices in the world trading order under the General Agreement on Tariffs and Trade (GATT) 1947 and then the WTO, which also involved several countries modelling their legislation on the US anti-dumping legislation. Fourth, changes brought about in foreign economic relations through US domestic legislation applying extraterritorially—a classical example here is the extraterritorial application of US anti-trust laws. Fifth, changes brought about bilaterally and regionally—in particular, through trade agreements, for example the US practice set in Section 230 of the Communications Decency Act under which the US provides for permissive regulation, to govern and shield US corporations involved in online platforms such as Facebook, Twitter, and YouTube from litigation abroad.[12] Finally, changes brought about through economic sanctions to achieve non-economic goals but which nevertheless have systemic consequences for the IEO—for example sanctions on Iran. Individually and cumulatively these effects are informed by US ideological political/economic/ cultural and strategic preferences.

This Americanisation of the IEO can be constructed as having two dimensions. First, the internal dimension—a perspective from the recipient country's standpoint. This internal perspective captures the nature of the reception of the Americanisation in foreign countries viz., whether the Americanisation is voluntary, solicited, informed, or 'coerced.' The external dimension focuses on the 'apparatus' of the US, on the way in which it should engage in international

11 See for example M Rupert & M S Solomon, *Globalization and International Political Economy: The Politics of Alternative Futures* (Rowman & Littlefield: 2005); Jones Michael Jaja, 'Globalization or Americanization: Implication for Sub-Saharan Africa,' in Kent G Deng (ed) *Globalization – Today, Tomorrow* (IntechOpen: 2010). Available from: <https://www.intechopen.com/books/globalization--today--tomorrow/globalization-or-americanization-implication-for-sub-saharan-africa>; R Oldenziel, 'Is Globalization a Code Word for Americanization? Contemplating McDonalds, Coca-Cola, and Military Bases,' *TSEG/ Low Countries Journal of Social and Economic History* Vol. 4 No. 3 (2007) 84–106.

12 See for example David McCabe & Ana Swanson, 'U.S. Using Trade Deals to Shield Tech Giants From Foreign Regulators,' *The New York Times* (October 7, 2019).

economic relations involving the Americanisation of the IEO. It addresses questions of responsibility to the international community, introspection, and generally the lenses through which the US apparatus conceives and engages with the rest of the world.

There are several reasons for the importance of the focus on the Americanisation of the international economic order. First, the US is one of the few countries which in the different ways outlined herein, for example, has historically and continually proactively engaged in the shaping of the IEO. This has been possible because of the way its domestic system has developed for this purpose over the years, including the international formal and informal institutions which the US has assisted in crafting. This is to be contrasted with China which has less of such an historical tradition and contribution to the IEO. In the case of the European Union (EU) it has a record of working within the international institutions, with a softer approach and capacity to international economic relations, as a regional grouping.

Second, the size of the US economy, its political stature in international relations, and its increasingly strategic nationally oriented economic endeavours give such weight and notice to the influence of the US that an understanding of the way the IEO is really driven is called for. In this context of note is the fact that the US has publicly declared that it will not allow any other country to be superior to it in the nuclear armaments field.[13] On one view this goes beyond a mere concern with the defence of the country and raises a presumption that the same design underlies its approach to international economic relations This is a shift from an endeavour to create level playing fields for all non-state entities in the global market, to a national strategic endeavour for global dominance in the economic sphere. Moreover, the US has taken the path of a trade war to engage in the deconstruction/construction of the IEO. This *modus operandi* along with its liberal use of the national security justification for imposing trade restrictions is consistent with the characterisation of its ambitions as being not just about fair trade. In this respect, it needs to be acknowledged that similar ambitions of world dominance in the economic sphere have been ascribed to China arising from its 2025 Vision.[14] Indeed, the US is said to be responding to this which further reinforces the point being made here. Certainly, in certain sectors considered strategic the State in both market and non-market planned economies is steering the development of the concerned sectors to the State's advantage thus blurring the distinction between planned and market

13 'We will never allow anybody to have anything even close to what we have,' President Trump statement March 21, 2018. Andrew Osborn & Steve Holland, 'Trump Congratulates Putin on Election, Leaders Look to Meet Soon,' *Reuters* (March 20, 2018). Available at <https://www.reuters.com/article/us-russia-election-usa-trump/trump-congratulates-putin-on-election-leaders-look-to-meet-soon-idUSKBN1GW22C> (last visited February 2022).

14 See for example James McBride & Andrew Chatzky, 'Is "Made in China 2025" a Threat to Global Trade?' *US Council on Foreign Relations* (May 13, 2019). Available at <https://www.cfr.org/backgrounder/made-china-2025-threat-global-trade> (last visited September 2019).

economies. But in any event, whether or not these inferences are persuasive, the critical point here is not whether it is the case but that it is quite possible for a State to have such designs for dominance. Therefore, international discourse must engage with such possibilities, as there are here systemic issues that concern the sustainable design and functioning of the IEO.

Third, from a practical legal perspective, States and private actors need to organise their affairs not only through the formal Bretton Woods institutional lenses but also against the background of what is termed herein the Americanisation of the IEO. Thus, rightly or wrongly, a resident of a State trading in goods and services needs to have an understanding not just of the rights accorded under WTO law, but also those rights as affected by the Americanisation of the IEO. In the same vein, US edicts can be directed at foreign States directly thus requiring State actors to understand US law. For example in 2019 South Korea passed legislation to amend its Distant Waters Fisheries Development Act to combat illegal fishing because the US had designated it as an illegal, unreported, and unregulated fishing country (IUU).[15] Finally, and importantly, by specifically setting the Americanisation of the IEO as such, it is possible to bring to bear a critical eye to the phenomenon of economic hegemony generally—be it American, Chinese, or Russian—so as to ensure its management in a manner that is conducive to the development of the IEO for the interests of the international community as a whole.

Against what background is this phenomenon to be evaluated critically? As a preliminary point, 'critical' here is not to be equated with anti-Americanism. Simply put it calls for an objective unbiased evaluation. It is not anti-American to focus on the Americanisation of the IEO from the perspective of the development of the IEO in the interest of the international community. The background of evaluation is complex involving a variety of considerations that are informed by the spectrum of possibilities and attributes that characterise the global economy and the community it serves. One objective is to trace US influence in relevant decision-making processes; relevant from the viewpoint of the development of an IEO that could nurture diverse possibilities in the attainment of community goals. There are here several definitional and methodological issues. What is meant by development? How is the causal link between the US practice and policy to be discerned? What is meant by the IEO? Be that as it may, such an enquiry implicates economic analysis including tracing contributions towards the achievement of internationally recognised goals, such as sustainable development, freer borders, and the maximisation of individual liberty. More specifically, it involves the extent to which the US involvement creates a democratic deficit or asymmetry in the decision-making for the development of the IEO. This is a human rights and self-determination focus, raising due process and constitutional questions. A second substantive objective

15 See 'US Welcomes Passage of South Korean Bill Aimed at Fighting Illegal Fishing,' *Korea Times* (November 2, 2019). Available at <https://m.koreatimes.co.kr/pages/article.asp?newsIdx=278081> (last visited February 2022).

involves a consideration of the extent to which the US has inculcated 'American traditions and values' in the normativity of the international economic system, and through that further facilitated Americanisation of the global economy. This is the cosmopolitan, cultural (in the wide sense) diversity reflection. A third objective involves a consideration of the extent to which the US involvement has prioritised developed country preoccupations, for example emphasis on trade and intellectual property protection, as opposed to transfer of technology and development of developing countries, in the goals that drive the international economic system. This is about the arrogation of agenda setting by developed States, and the arrogation of the direction of the development of the IEO. A fourth objective focuses on the contributions to the building blocks of the international economic system—systemic and technological—the US has paved the way for, through its long traditions and technological leads including its push for a liberal market system in the global arena. In sum, the canvas for a critical and objective evaluation of the Americanisation of the IEO is wide—indeed, in some respects posing challenges to an objective evaluation.

Inevitably this focus must be somewhat interdisciplinary—economic, political, and legal. It is, however, a focus ultimately intended to facilitate greater legal analysis from the perspective of international law and policy. In some measure this international law perspective partakes of the New Haven School of Law as a process of decision-making.[16] The New Haven School focuses on predicting how relevant decision-makers make decisions. In international economic relations there are grounds for suggesting that there are times when the US is where ultimately the relevant decision-making in international economic relations is taking place. 'In some measure' because this discourse is also steeped in the idea of the rule of law, the sovereign equality of States, the right to self-determination, non-intervention in the internal affairs of another State, and the challenge of designing an international economic order that serves the interest of the international community as a whole delivering on distributive justice objectives.[17] Indeed, in some respects this compendium of principles is antithetical to the New Haven School particularly in its emphasis on the rule of law. The closest theoretical framework to this perspective is a development perspective where development is defined to include the development of all nations—developed and developing. However, a normative approach grounded in any particular paradigm can suffer from dogma and be blinkered. Therefore, an eclectic analytical approach best serves the objectives of this focus. This International Law perspective therefore focuses on where the real decision-making in international economic relations is really set but querying also how the Americanisation of the IEO is compatible with International Law; how the genre of problems associated with a major power in international

16 See for example W Michael Reisman, 'International Law-making: A Process of Communication,' *Faculty Scholarship Series* (1981) 713. Available at <https://digitalcommons.law.yale.edu/fss_papers/713>.

17 John Rawls, *A Theory of Justice* (Belknap: 1971).

economic relations can be addressed; what lessons can be learnt from history and the nature of the potential abusive involvement of a superpower in the IEO. Finally, as a preface to what follows ultimately, power that is overwhelming can only be immediately confronted with difficulty. However, such force can over a continuum be inhibited through a range of 'soft inhibitors', checks and balances, conditioning, education, and mechanisms for the mobilisation of collective pressure. In this chapter they are alluded to but certainly such a consideration is important and needs to be elaborated.

Relationship Between Economic Power and the Rule of IEL

Certainty, predictability and level playing fields in international economic relations at the level of residents of one State, engaging in economic relations with those of another, are critical to the functioning of the IEO. In the same vein, the depoliticisation of economic relations both as between States and its people is important. Such considerations are underlined in the IEO by for example non-discrimination prohibitions in multilateral and bilateral trade and investment agreements, including fundamental principles in international law that protect the sovereign rights of a State over its resources. This implies also that there should not be the interplay of power relations in the economic sphere including the infusion of political considerations in economic relations. In sum, herein is set the rule of law in the framework of the IEO. The application of the rule of law at the international level, however, can be challenging. To some extent this does turn on the meaning of the rule of law in the international context.[18] However, if the fundamental principle of the rule of law is the application of law to all concerned—in IEL there is no exception to this. Thus, in the current trade war the US has not arrogated to itself the power to act arbitrarily. It has on the one hand justified its actions albeit controversially by anchoring them in some legal basis viz., national security. Equally, the US has demanded various reforms in the WTO within but also outside the WTO, such as the reform of the WTO dispute settlement system, and the status of China as a developing country in the WTO. The reality therefore on one view may be understood differently, namely that the US is acting outside the normal bounds of the international normative framework, albeit consistently with its own interests and reform agenda. This is a consequence of the weight the US gives to its stature in international economic relations. It comes from the weight of its economic power, which the existing international economic order has to some extent failed properly to address. Both the WTO and the IMF lack effective mechanisms to manage the US. The IMF has, however, survived an existential threat because of the palliative of the

18 See generally Jeremy Waldron, 'The Rule of International Law,' *Harvard Journal of Law & Public Policy* Vol. 30 No. 1 (2006) 15; Heike Krieger et al., *The International Rule of Law: Rise or Decline?* (Oxford University Press: 2019).

weighted voting system which gives the US a measure of an upper hand. This has not been the case, however, in the WTO.

In the circumstances, there is that perennial question that needs to be addressed, namely how can a normative regime manage a powerful subject without alienating it, or creating an existential threat to its continued existence? This question is considered here in terms of dispute resolution and decision-making in international economic relations. It can also be addressed in terms of the underlying economic rationale of international economic relations and through the raising of consciousness with respect to the impact from the very nature of international trade and investment. The latter considerations are not set in the rule of IEL as such but nevertheless are integral to its subject matter.

Economic Power and Dispute Resolution

Discourse on economic power and effective implementation by the US of its international economic obligations has been ongoing for several years within the US. In fact, two notable US doyens in international trade have surprisingly been defensive. Thus, Robert Hudec has advocated 'honourable disobedience;'[19] and John Jackson with reference to the direct applicability of international agreements in domestic law has been opposed to it, on the basis of the need to safeguard the discretion of a State in entertaining an 'efficient breach.'[20]

The relationship between dispute resolution and economic power has been addressed relatively more recently in 2011, with reference to calls for making the dispute settlement system more effective in the WTO—provocatively and prophetically, by yet another US scholar, as follows:[21]

> Simply put, reforming the system to make it yet more 'legalistic' would be unwarranted, as such proposals would make it too rigid and unaccommodating and might push its more powerful members toward outright bilateralism, eventually causing it to collapse.

Colares argues that the WTO dispute settlement is increasingly judicialised accompanied by judicial activism. Against this background he asserts efforts to strengthen the WTO compliance of judicial determinations would only result in alienating the more powerful players in the system. In Colares's discourse there are two antithetical positions with respect to the strengthening of compliance in the WTO, namely the mainstream who advocate further judicialization of the system, and those who take a more pragmatic diplomacy-oriented approach to dispute resolution. Thus, he observes, that adjudication whilst being an 'egalitarian mode of interaction, is,

19 Robert Hudec, *Essays on the Nature of International Trade Law* (Cameron May: 1999).

20 J Jackson & A Sykes, *Implementing the Uruguay Round* (Oxford University Press: 1997) 462.

21 Juscelino F Colares, 'The Limits of WTO Adjudication: Is Compliance the Problem?' *Journal of International Economic Law* Vol. 14 No. 2 (2011) 403–436.

in principle, unresponsive to the logic of power and the implications resulting from power asymmetries.' A few points need to be made here. First, it is inappropriate to divide the discourse in this manner—branding the mainstream approach as 'legalism' in a pejorative construct. 'Legalism' involves different approaches to improving the system and does not preclude the idea of variegated methods of implementation of judicial decisions, provided the circumstances so warrant. Thus, further time and other flexibilities in the implementation process are not precluded, provided there is a reasonable basis for them. Moreover, in trade law and policy discourse, the precise balance in international trade relations between rule and diplomacy orientation has been in existence for some time.

One concern with Colares's argument is that it has intertwined two strands. On the one hand, it advances alternative methods of implementation viz., greater time for implementation/bilateral negotiations for settlement. On the other, it clearly advances mere power on its own as a reason for preferential treatment in the implementation of judicial decisions. The latter is surely not a rational position. Moreover, on its own terms the ultimate logic of power is anchored in being sustainable for which grounding in the rule of law is indispensable. Thus, despite the realisation of his prophesy, the US has not at any rate overtly justified its position in the impasse on the WTO Appellate Body (AB) currently, on the basis purely of its superpower status as such.

Second, Colares's conclusion of judicial activism in the WTO, whilst cogently argued, is presented as a conclusion objectively arrived at. The fact is that it is difficult to objectively evaluate decisions of the Appellate Body (AB) of the WTO, as evidencing a teleological approach to interpretation, and/or partaking of judicial activism. In the final analysis, this is often a matter of judgement. Indeed, the charge of judicial activism can be the consequence of selective evaluation focussed for the purposes of serving a State's own preoccupations and agenda. Thus, the WTO Dispute Settlement Understanding (DSU) has no reference to whether members can avail of legal representation for themselves in WTO dispute settlement, yet current focus on judicial activism does not refer to cases which have addressed this. Third, there is no mention by Colares as to why the US itself participated in the establishment of a WTO dispute settlement system that for the first time took a leap from diplomacy to a rule-oriented dispute settlement system. Was it because at the time the US perceived certain advantages in the need for such a system, as for example a safeguard for itself and of ensuring disciplines on certain others.[22] In sum, whilst Colares's predictions seem to be

22 See for example Robert E Hudec, 'The New WTO Dispute Settlement Procedure: An Overview of the First Three Years,' *Minnesota Journal of International Law* (1999) 51. 'We expect such views from smaller countries, which usually believe they will fare much better under a rule-based system than they will in a world of ad hoc negotiations where power dictates outcomes. But the GATT's two largest superpowers – the United States and the European Community – also wanted this kind of regulatory system. The perspective that leads large countries to want rule-based regulatory systems is quite complex, but for present purposes it will suffice to cite four advantages. A rule-based system is the most resource-

materialising and his defence resonates with some of the reasons proffered by the Trump administration in the impasse over the WTO AB, this neither exonerates US conduct to the extent it operates outside the bounds of the WTO framework, nor necessarily adds further substance to some of his arguments. The fact of the matter is power is transient as are superpowers. Moreover, justifications for power are not just about power per se, they can often be about a certain kind of power. It is not completely clear if discourse in this manner would take place if China were the superpower. All this said, Colares's prophecy, and the recent undermining of the world trading order, does indeed call for further understanding of how to manage economic power within the bounds of a normative framework. This discussion must be engaged in upfront regardless of which State is involved.

Decision-Making and Economic Power

The manner of decision-making in international economic organisations is central to the accommodation of power in its institutional setting. In economic organisations this has been addressed through the introduction of qualified majorities, weighted voting, and/or consensus decision-making. In the IMF and the World Bank Group, the underlying rationale of this has been the greater contribution made by the member/s involved in the organisation concerned, albeit through criteria established to determine the economic weight generally of the members' involved. Economic power on its own is not directly the reason as such.

Another way in which power is accommodated is through decision-making by consensus. Here, a decision is formed, unless it is formally challenged by a member.[23] Only if a decision cannot be arrived at through consensus is a decision made the subject of voting. In this situation, the knowledge of the voting framework of the organisation, and the economic weight underpinning opinions proffered, can have as potent an effect as, for example, a formal weighted voting system.[24] Moreover, as has been observed[25] that consensus decision-making 'does not provide for equality (in terms of decision and influence) because not every Member has the same ability to maintain vetoes.[26] Thus, the US has been able

efficient way to resolve conflicts with other countries. A rule-based system is also the most effective way to negotiate and capture desired policy changes in achievable incremental steps. A rule-based system creates the most predictable conditions for business decisions. Finally, a rule-based system helps to cement one's own liberal trade policies against the internal political pressures of protectionism.'

23 See for example Art. IX of the Marrakesh Agreement Establishing the World Trade Organization.

24 See Asif H Qureshi & Andreas Ziegler, *International Economic Law*, 4th ed. (Sweet & Maxwell: 2019).

25 Claus-Dieter Ehlermann & L Ehring, 'Decision-Making in the World Trade Organization: Is the Consensus Practice of the World Trade Organization Adequate for Making, Revising and Implementing Rules on International Trade?' *Journal of International Economic Law* Vol. 8 No. 1 (2005) 51–75. See also Qureshi & Ziegler, ibid.

26 Ehlermann & Ehring, ibid.

to sustain its veto of further appointments in the WTO Appellate Body (AB) for some time now. However, this US veto is not without limitations.[27] First, the US blocking of the AB member recruitment process can be considered an 'abuse' of the member's prerogative to participate in the WTO decision-making process. Consensus decision-making in the WTO can be arbitrary, capricious, abusive, and/or unreasonable. The US has not given specific reasons in terms of the decision to appoint or the agreed process involved in appointing a new member. Second, there cannot be an assumption that every minutia of decision-making must be the subject of consensus decision-making (including, for example, date, timing, and the very launching of the recruitment process) such that it unravels an already agreed consensus of having an AB comprising of seven members. Of course, the US could block the appointments of individuals at the time of the decision involving the selection of a candidate, based on the suitability of the candidates in question, consecutively in the selection processes as the vacancies arise. This is in the circumstances the only technically appropriate option for a State taking such a strategy, but one more disruptive and insidious. Third, the membership of the WTO have been deprived of a benefit they were entitled to under the WTO Dispute Settlement Understanding (DSU) viz., access to an appellate process. In the circumstances, the US veto has an impact on the balance of 'benefits' that members are entitled to and likely to cause a nullification or impairment of those benefits. Moreover, the circumstances brought about by egregious abuse of power by a superpower in decision-making and dispute settlement must universally be considered as bringing the whole economic system concerned as having come to an end—a circumstance akin to a material breach. The US veto on the AB appointments can be considered a material breach as it is an abusive exercise of the veto nullifying and impairing the benefits members are entitled to under the WTO. In addition, the DSU provision that all disputes must be settled through the WTO dispute settlement system cannot be operative, since the dispute system itself has been materially paralysed by the US veto. Thus, just as the WTO agreements can be undone by the consensus of the membership, the same process can be triggered in the case when a major stakeholder in the organisation fundamentally refuses to engage materially in the organisation. To some extent, this is *de facto* the case, but what is being advocated here is that this consequence should be openly acknowledged as potentially involving the deconstruction of the whole system—unravelling the possibility of counter-measures by others outside the WTO framework. In the WTO, this is the case given that the dispute settlement system itself has been paralysed. Such an understanding should bring home the message that one breach of such a proportion can be counterproductive to a member who presumes unreasonably to hold hostage the WTO dispute settlement system. This collective acknowledgement has in some

27 What follows derives from Asif H Qureshi, 'The World Trade Organization and the Promotion of Effective Dispute Resolution: In Times of a Trade War,' *AIIB Yearbook of International Law*, op. cit.

measure now manifested itself through the setting up, albeit ad hoc, of another form of an appellate process involving a significant membership of the WTO, excluding the US.[28] In addition, there is a growing chorus formally of members opposed to the US stand.[29]

In this manner, the prospect of the complete deconstruction of the normative system individually or multilaterally considered could have a powerful inhibiting effect on the abusive use of economic power. Finally, given the reform of the DSU was intended to be integral to the totality of any consensus arrived at in the Doha Round, is it permissible that one member can push for one reform in the face of the expressly agreed reform negotiating *modus operandi*? In sum, the veto in consensus decision-making is set within the institutional and normative framework of the WTO. It does not exist in isolation. Indeed, its exercise must be informed by the objects and purposes of the institution and its normative framework.

The dynamics of economic power (contra military power) and its setting in international economic relations cannot be assumed to be beyond the rule of law. Moreover, a sustainable economic power trajectory must engage in the law in an economically interdependent world. The logic of economic power has a limited temporal dimension—more so in the economic sphere. The moral authority of the rule of law has a longer lasting legitimacy and resilience in the long run in civilised societies. Ultimately the logic of power will give ground to the moral authority of the rule of law, before the authority of the rule of law amasses legitimacy through a credible force, for example collective responses to the abusive use of economic power. In sum, the international economic order is not completely devoid of disciplines to address abusive exercises of economic power.

The management of economic powers in an international setting is a function of the IEO. Equally, the negotiations in the formulation of the decision-making processes in such settings, whilst controversial, is ultimately a reflection of the international power structure. However, with the according of some differential power in decision-making, given realpolitik, there is a window of opportunity for the introduction of safeguards. This opportunity, alas, has not been taken. Yet there is a vested interest amongst all, in securing safeguards in such cases of abusive use of that differential decision-making. First, economically powerful States understand that their status is transient (prudential consideration). Second, such States understand that the State at any given time can be hijacked by an unruly executive, and therefore there need to be external checks

28 The multi-party interim appeal arrangement based on Article 25 of the WTO DSU. See *Statement by Ministers, Davos, Switzerland, 24 January 2020* (European Commission: 2020). Available at <https://trade.ec.europa.eu/doclib/docs/2020/january/tradoc_158596.pdf> (last visited February 2022).

29 For the increasing number of alternative proposals within the WTO to resolve the AB impasse, see *Members Adopt Panel Ruling in Australia-Indonesia Paper Duty Dispute* (WTO: 2020). Available at <https://www.wto.org/english/news_e/news20_e/dsb_27jan20_e.htm> (last visited February 2022).

to forestall such an occurrence (external checks). Third, if there is no explicit spelling out of safeguards these could be read into the design of the differential decision-making process. Thus, it would be better to agree upon certain safeguards expressly at the outset to keep control over the scope of the differential decision-making process (safeguarding position). The safeguards could take different forms. For example, the differential and more favourable decision-making could be expressly made subject to such doctrines as ultra vires, *abus de droit*, accountable reasons for the decision, time frameworks for the decision, availability of judicial review of the decision made, and requirements of domestic parliamentary approval of certain executive decisions. In addition, at some time historically it was considered farfetched that men should receive equal opportunities/gender awareness training before they made relevant decisions in domestic situations, for example in employment and promotions cases. Would it be similarly considered farfetched, yet possible, that prospective candidates standing for elections/and or taking oath for office as presidents and prime ministers undergo 'global awareness' training, so as to enrich their decision-making with reference to decisions made in international economic relations, or at the least inhibit abusive use of preferential decision-making rights in international economic relations?

There are two built-in constraints that rein in the excesses of economic power and that are set in in the very nature of international economic relations as they have unfolded in the twenty-first century viz., the contemporary economic foundations underpinning international economic relations; and the modern nature of goods and services traded and invested. Both are non-coercive and embedded in the rational self.

Economic Foundations

First, in international economic doctrine there has never been any scope for abusive use of economic capacity. The theory of comparative advantage calls for international trade even where one State has obvious advantage in all sectors. It is not premised on equality in balances of trade. And it is basic economics that unilaterally imposed trade restrictions and distortions are self-inflicting. There is therefore a built-in inhibition in the abusive use of economic power in the long term. More so in free market democracies where the detriment can translate into voting patterns. The challenge here is how to eliminate and/or lessen the duration of this self-harm that is informed by the capacity to sustain arising from economic power. Ultimately here the focus must be on the domestic decision-making processes in this sphere. To this end already much has been written about the constitutionalisation of IEL.[30] Here in addition to the call for the

30 See for example Marise Cremona, Peter Hilpold, Nikolaos Lavranos, Stefan Staiger Schneider & Andreas Ziegler (eds) *Reflections on the Constitutionalisation of International Economic Law: Liber Amicorum for Ernst-Ulrich Petersmann* (Brill: 2013).

entrenchment of multilateral international agreements there are also lessons to be learnt from the way in which monetary policy by Central Banks has been insulated from political executive pressure in advanced economies. Is there scope for enlarging important policy-making that is insulated from the executive although not necessarily within the domain of the Central Banking authorities? Is there scope for enlarging legislative scrutiny of executive decisions? Should countries be compelled to have independent think-tanks that scrutinise State policies in the economic sphere?

Modern Nature of Trade and Investment

Second, international trade and investment both call for self-scrutiny and self-restraint in the manner of engagement. Most goods/services and foreign investment in this era are not mere transmissions of goods, services, and investment as such. In fact, they encapsulate in varying degrees gender, cultural, environmental, social, aesthetic, religious, technological (including standards), and civilisational values and attributes (non-economic attributes). Few goods and services are not value laden in this manner—those that are least processed and essentially are the building blocks or facilitators for the realisation for others in surviving and developing their own non-economic value aspirations. Another category of economic relations that is non-value laden is where the international trade and investment is made to the order of the receiving State.

To some extent that goods/services and investment have some of these attributes is recognised already in so far as cultural goods and services are concerned in the Convention on the Protection and Promotion of the Diversity of Cultural Expressions (hereafter the Cultural Diversity Convention). The same can be said of the recognition of gender[31] and environmental[32] specific goods and services. Indeed, there are now efforts at determining a list of goods and services that threaten national security falling under a dual user category.[33] This gradual unpacking of the non-economic attributes of goods and services in the real world has come about in a reactive manner and is, moreover, not yet fully shaped in clear legal practice, if at all.

31 See UNCTAD, 'Making Trade Policies Gender-responsive' (2019). Available at <https://unctad.org/en/PublicationsLibrary/ditc2019d1_en.pdf> (last visited November 2019).

32 See <https://www.ictsd.org/sites/default/files/research/2013/12/info_note_list-of-environmental-goods_sugathan.pdf> (last visited November 2019).

33 Ana Swanson, 'Trump Officials Battle Over Plan to Keep Technology Out of Chinese Hands' *The New York Times* (October 23, 2019). Available at <https://www.nytimes.com/2019/10/23/business/trump-technology-china-trade.html?smid=nytcore-ios-share> (last visited November 2019); and see Chapter 6 herein.

The Prime Directive

In the science fiction 'Star Trek'[34] the space explorers from earth were governed by the 'Prime Directive' which prohibited in any way interference in the natural development of other alien civilisations. There are good reasons for the ethos of the 'Prime Directive' to inform at some level the way States and residents of one State engage in economic relations with those of another. The basis for such a contention is already founded in some fundamental principles of international law viz., sovereign equality and independence; non-interference in the internal affairs of another State; the international law regime on indigenous people; the right to development; the right to self-determination and sustainable development. Indeed, where international trade and investment destroys completely native cultures, values, identity, and self-development/determination capacities is there not a case to introduce the vernacular of 'creeping economic genocide,' 'indirect economic genocide'—to borrow from international investment law? Moreover, there is in State practice, both in trade and investment, national legislation that carves out a domain protecting certain national values. This is also reflected in multilateral and bilateral trade and investment agreements that allow for exceptions—albeit at the discretion of States—in the restriction of trade and investment in certain fields. What is reserved for a State as a defence for itself must also in some measure influence that State's engagement with others.

This advocation of a 'Prime Directive' ethos in the framework of international economic relations has echoes of the call for a New International Economic Order by developing countries in the 1970s. However, that call was set against a different set of historical circumstances, and importantly was essentially a reassertion/re-affirmation by those States of their ownership of their natural resources. The call for a 'Prime Directive' has not hitherto featured much in international discourse mainly because historically the nature of trade/investment involved non-processed materials and the rules for international trade generated in that paradigm have continued into this very different era. Historically also international economic engagements partook of conquest and colonialism.

Moreover, the theory of comparative advantage that has dominated economic analysis is mainly focussed on increased productivity. This was reinforced by the realisation that mass production accommodated through larger markets facilitated by the opening of foreign markets led to marginal cost efficiencies. In short, economic theory driven by profit maximisation and efficiency considerations suppressed such discourse, and its realisation in a comprehensive normative framework.

Organising and inculcating a 'Prime Directive' specifically in the engagement of international economic relations requires first as a prerequisite the establishment of an indicia for the calibration of the non-trade attributes of goods/services

34 See <https://www.startrek.com/videos/watch-my-first-contact-with-michael-dorn> (last visited December 2019).

and investment. For example, with respect to goods the degree of processing; the variety of alternatives fulfilling similar functions; the aesthetic ranges of colour and shape that the good could be assimilated to; the likely impact of the good on the environment; safety/social and cultural concerns. Thus, forks and spoons are like chopsticks but a flood of these in the markets of Northeast Asia could have a severe impact on the use of chopsticks. Second, giving more specificity to the 'Prime Directive' against the rich background of existing international legal principles. For example, codes of conduct in different sectors that require manufacturers seeking to extend their market before extending it to reflect on the non-functional attributes of the product and the impact of those on the foreign society in which the market exists. These could become part of the corpus of existing codes inculcating corporate social responsibility. And finally transmitting the 'Prime Directive' ethos at relevant national decision-makers engaged in international trade/investment or its facilitation. Thus, negotiating market access for a certain sector, for example women's apparel of a certain design, into a society with different and set expectations of apparel designs, needs to be approached with some restraint.

Trading of goods/services and the imparting of foreign investment with non-functional attributes are not only informed by those responsible for setting the framework for the international transfer of such items; and those responsible for their manufacture/creation and marketing—but also informed by individual foreign choices. Moreover, the range of non-functional attributes are not set in stone in any society but are the subject of change, development, and evolution depending on the state of knowledge and foreign infusions that different societies undergo because of endogenous/exogenous influences. There is no suggestion here that individual choices should be stifled, or that the state of development of non-functional concerns (culture/environment/art/safety...) should be cast in stone or that the responsibility is only unidirectional. What is being proposed here is that these concerns should feature in the decision making of anyone concerned with imparting/receiving foreign goods/services and investment. All relevant decision-makers need to be aware of the impact of their decisions and choices. Importantly these decisions should be informed and not coerced/under pressure.

How does this specifically engage in the economic power management focus of this discourse? First, it forms an important part of the restraint that is generated from self-awareness self-scrutiny and introspection. It invites the important reflection on the part of relevant decision-makers in the export of goods and services as well as in foreign investment, of the non-economic impact of their economic transactions. Economic capacity empowers and with this empowerment there is responsibility. Second, economic capacity comes from mass production and associated capacity to supply in trade and investment. This economic capacity must facilitate the opening of new markets in a responsible informed and non-coercive manner. Third, with economic capacity comes also the command of a large domestic market which translated in the *modus operandi* of international trade negotiations is instrumental in opening foreign markets. For example, insisting on the opening of the market for aircrafts impacts on environmental questions and travelling habits of foreign individuals.

In sum, the rule of IEL and the underlying nature of the subject matter inform the rule of IEL in the interface between economic power and law.

Economic Power and Responsibility in its Exercise?

IEL allows for a fair degree of autonomy to States. This autonomy is availed and exercised disparately by different States. In a globalised world, engagement in this autonomy by the more powerful can leave a greater imprint on the international economy, indeed sometimes even create tensions with the IEO. One important attribute of economic prowess in this domain is the potential for engaging in trade and currency wars. Both forms of warfare engaged in by economically powerful states can have serious consequences for the international community. In the current state of the development of IEL, what constitutes a trade or a currency war is not clear. This is to the advantage of the powerful States, as it reserves to them the determination as to when a state of such a war exists, when it can be triggered; as well as leaving them a wide measure of discretion in determining when their national security interests are affected. The more powerful a State the more expansive its concern for its national security and its perception of a threat to it—such as to trigger engagement in economic warfare. In this section economic warfare as an aspect of economic power is explored with reference to the responsibilities of the State in such an engagement. State responsibility here includes State responsibility under international law and State responsibility that is set in notions of fairness and justice. The latter is a necessary precursor for the development of international law on State responsibility.

Trade War[35]

A trade war can be understood in terms of the value of the international trade involved; the kind of trading nations implicated, along with the consequential spillover effects on the trade of other countries; or with reference to violations of the world trade disciplines under the WTO, and/or under other international law disciplines? There are sound reasons for addressing this basic question viz., to determine the relevant normative framework and to address the consequences arising from it.

A trade war is not a trade dispute. A trade dispute is specific; it is one that is amenable to being justiciable under an agreed normative framework—very likely under the WTO. However, a trade war may well have its origins in a trade dispute

35 The following four paragraphs on what is a 'trade war' is based on Asif H Qureshi, 'The World Trade Organization and the Promotion of Effective Dispute Resolution: In Times of a Trade War,' *AIIB Yearbook of International Law*, op. cit. This is set out here as a necessary prelude to the further discussion on State responsibility in the context of a trade war.

and in principle trade wars can play out both within and outside the WTO. A trade war within the WTO could involve one or a series of disputes involving 'violations' of the WTO agreements but conducted within the framework of the WTO dispute settlement system. A trade war outside the WTO involves a general disregard of the existing normative framework, with a 'gloves off' approach to achieving certain policy goals. As such it can be purely bilateral but where it undermines the international trading order, and the economic interests of a wider circle of countries involving counter-responses, the trade war can partake of a 'world trade war.' Where this trade war is 'likely to endanger the maintenance of international peace and security' or becomes a 'threat to the peace, breach of the peace, or act of aggression' it could in principle be of interest to the UN Security Council.[36] Where the trade war impacts foreign investment, the investment concerns engendered may be the subject of investor-State arbitration under the conditions set out in applicable bilateral investment agreements. In the circumstances, the nature of a trade war has normative significance, albeit in extreme situations. Recourse to the UN Security Council of course has a political context where the participants in the trade war are members of the Security Council. Be that as it may an international consensus albeit outside the UN Security Council, that the trade war endangers 'peace and security' or is a 'threat to the peace, breach of the peace, or act of aggression' must of itself carry some weight.

From a WTO perspective, its architects seem to have envisaged a spectrum of possible trade grievances involving 'violations' of the WTO disciplines, including 'non-violations' of obligations set in WTO agreements but which nevertheless nullify or impair the benefits a member is entitled to; and grievances arising from the occurrence of a 'situation' known as a 'situation complaint' which affect a member's negotiated benefits.[37] Most disputes between members involve actual violations of provisions of the WTO agreements as such. The full scope of a 'non-violation' and 'situation' complaint is not clear, other than the received wisdom that they are applicable in very limited circumstances involving the undermining of tariff undertakings. This breath of grievances which the WTO dispute settlement mechanism caters for seems to involve all manner of conflicts—from a mere dispute to a situation approximating to a war—but with the important caveat that the grievance should be aired within the framework of the WTO dispute settlement system. In such circumstances, there is some scope for a trade grievance to surface and escalate which is outside the WTO managed substantive rights and obligations as such, but which nevertheless can be resolved within the WTO dispute settlement system, assuming it is justiciable. That said, there are disputes which can fester outside the WTO dispute settlement system, as for example the raising of unbound tariffs between opposite sides; or where the dispute is of a political/ideological nature, as between market-/and State-oriented economic

36 See Chapter IV Article 34 and Chapter VII of the UN Charter.
37 See WTO Dispute Settlement Understanding.

doctrines. Of course, all the parties in such circumstances can have recourse to the political organs of the WTO to bring about desired changes.

Finally, disputes can playout, outside the WTO framework—indeed despite it, as in the Trump era. This is because whilst there is a prohibition in the WTO that disputes should be settled within the WTO dispute settlement system, there are no effective sanctions available within the WTO for enforcing its internalisation of disputes within the WTO, if the parties together choose to engage with each other outside its framework and/or one or both of the parties have the capacity to operate outside the bounds of the WTO. Where, however, only one party acts in the cover of the WTO that party may be authorised to retaliate. However, the authority to retaliate including the quantum of retaliation could be informed by the extent to which there has already been the use of unilateral retaliation outside the WTO. In sum, the capacity of the WTO dispute settlement system to manage 'trade wars' has existed although weakened by the current AB impasse. Members of the WTO have a responsibility to resolve trade disputes within the framework of the WTO dispute settlement system, and/or engage in constructive dialogue within the WTO political organs, namely the General Council and the Ministerial Council. In principle the UN Security Council is also open for this purpose.

Aspects of a trade war can be assimilated to circumstances of an armed conflict where the consequences of the trade war are like those resulting from an armed conflict and/or raise national security concerns, for example of an existential nature. This intellectual leap has already been made in investment arbitration wherein the Argentinian circumstances of economic necessity have been assimilated to that of national security.[38] There is nothing intrinsically different between killing a person through arms and starving to death a person by robbing them of their livelihood or vital medicine. There is nothing different between bombing a hospital and depriving the hospital of vital lifesaving supplies resulting in patient deaths. There is nothing different between degrading civilian treatment that consists of making men walk naked and depriving women of the use of vital sanitary menstrual pads in public. Granted in all such circumstances there is a temporal difference, a methodological difference, and differences in nature and degree of coerciveness. There is, however, certainty and comparability in consequences.

This assimilation of a trade war to a circumstance akin to an armed conflict has not been countenanced in the WTO dispute settlement. Thus, in the recent Russia–Measures Concerning Traffic in Transit[39] a WTO panel ruled, in interpreting the meaning of 'war or other emergency in international relations' in Article XXI of GATT 1994 national security exception, as follows. It equated 'war' with armed conflict and 'other emergency in international relations' as being informed by the genre of war, and thus excluding 'political and economic differences' unless these give rise to 'defence and military interests, or maintenance of law and

38 See for example *LG&E et al v Argentine Rep*, ICSID Case No. ARB/02/1 (Award October 2006).

39 WT/DS512/R (2019).

public order interests.'[40] This WTO panel decision, which has not been the subject of appeal, must be read strictly in terms of the interpretation of Article XXI of GATT 1994, such that it is not open to abusive use as an exception to conformity with WTO rules. Moreover, whilst war is narrowly defined 'other emergency in international relations' does not exclude the possibility of assimilating a circumstance of economic conflict with a war like circumstance, provided it gives rise to 'defence and military interests, or maintenance of law and public order interests.' Certainly, a trade war as conceived herein impacts on 'maintenance of law and public order interests.' Indeed, a trade war impacts the maintenance of international law and international public order interests. Moreover, this narrow interpretation for the purposes of the invocation of the national security defence must be correct, otherwise a wider interpretation would take the regulation of a trade war out of the ambit of the disciplines of the WTO, and indeed pave the way for self-initiated displacement of the application of WTO disciplines.

Questions as to Whether a State Has Responsibilities in the Conduct of a Trade War

States have certain responsibilities in the conduct of a trade war i.e., when a trade war that has significant economic/non-economic consequences that are inflicted intentionally and that are foreseeable. The focus of these responsibilities under international law centre around the very legality of the actions taken and the redress available (on a par to *jus ad bellum*). This responsibility is set essentially in the normative frameworks of the WTO, the IMF, and bilateral investment agreements. These are currently being considered in the WTO dispute settlement system. But what about the responsibility of the State during the conduct of a trade war? The fact that there is no State responsibility under international law, or that it is difficult to substantiate, does not distract from a discourse on the propriety of the State's conduct during the trade war. In other words, the *jus in bello* is not contingent on a demonstration of legality *in jus ad bellum.*

Trade War – jus in bello

There are two normative questions that are not generally discussed or understood but are a more modern challenge that need to be addressed. These two questions are essentially set on a par to *jus in bello*. First, regardless of the legality of the trade war, are there any rules in international law that regulate the conduct of the parties in the way they engage in the trade war? In other words, is there a comparable international humanitarian law here? Or are the principles built in international humanitarian law of relevance here? Second, and related are there any ethical considerations that States need to reflect upon regardless of the law? Thus, there is much ado about a trade war, including the cloaking of such economic

40 Para 7.75.

conflicts as trade wars by the principal participants involved. Such claims must embody responsibility in terms of fair play along with ethical considerations.

The normative framework of international humanitarian law is focused on the conduct of armed conflict. Therefore, in principle it does not have a bearing in circumstances of a trade war. The principles underlying IHL may, however, have a relevance to circumstances of a trade war. The rules of IHL differentiate between civilian and armed combatants. International economic sanctions can distinguish between State operators and civilians although trade wars conducted through tariff responses blur the distinction between State and civilian operators. This is not critical in that the important lesson here is that there are certain rules that need to be followed in times of war albeit differently in terms of civilians. Moreover, the distinction itself is useful in that it points to the possibility of the reduction of the impact of the consequences of a trade war by limiting its impact on State operators alone. Obligations under IHL are owed to the international community. A trade war, especially in a global integrated market, has international repercussions and therefore quite apart from anything else as underpinned by IHL, the international community has a substantive interest in the enforcement of the manner of the conduct of a trade war.

Some fundamental principles underpinning IHL[41] have relevance and/or can be adapted to the circumstances of a trade war viz., the prohibition on the use of indiscriminate measures; the need to confine measures to those that are necessary; the use of only proportionate measures; the prohibition on causing unnecessary suffering and superfluous damage; the prohibition on not causing injury/damage to third States; and finally, the principle of humanity. These are the principles which are discernible in the four Geneva Conventions 1949[42] and are said to reflect customary international law. These principles are of such a nature that it is arguable even outside the framework of IHL they have relevance to comparable situations, in the conduct of a trade war. One other principle in IHL namely the prohibition on certain types of weapons has a bearing in terms of the type of 'weaponisation' in a trade war availed is availed—for example, it may be possible to adapt this by placing a ceiling on the amount of tariffs imposed; the type of trade measures used; or the types of goods and services targeted, or indeed the weaponization of a reserve currency such as the dollar.

Just as international human rights law is not displaced by a circumstance of armed conflict it must follow also that a trade war does not displace the application

41 See for example E Crawford & A Pert, *International Humanitarian Law* (Cambridge University Press: 2015) Chapter 2.

42 Convention for the Amelioration of the Condition of the Wounded and Sick in Armed Forces in the Field (GC I); Convention for the Amelioration of the Condition of Wounded, Sick and Shipwrecked Members of Armed Forces at Sea (GC II); Convention Relative to the Treatment of Prisoners of War (GC III); and the Convention Relative to the Protection of Civilian Persons in Time of War (GC IV).

of international human rights law.[43] Conceivably where a trade war does result in violations of human rights international human rights law could come into play. A trade war can result in violations of human rights although the circumstances wherein this can happen may not be obvious and extreme. Circumstances that could raise questions relating to human rights violations may be consequential upon the application of sanctions, for example where these involve freezing assets of innocent individuals; arresting individuals for violations of illegally imposed tariffs; applying retrospective tariffs that have an effect equivalent to expropriation in character; suspending or raising very high tariffs on vital medicinal supplies that constituted lifelines for patients. Some measures used in a trade war also may have a bearing in affecting a country's ability to achieve the 2030 Sustainable Development goals.

In sum, there are cogent reasons for drawing on the lessons from IHL in a focus on the manner of the conduct of a trade war. Conceivably in some limited circumstances State responsibility may be implicated under international law although it may be difficult to clearly substantiate. The fact that States have a freedom to trade or not and to some extent freedom to discriminate in trade under general international law, is not exhaustive of the legal consequences that could flow upon the exercise of that freedom.

But certainly, there is scope for codifying a set of basic principles setting out the responsibilities of the State. In time these could develop into norms of State Responsibility in international law, particularly if the case for State responsibility at present is considered controversial. Such a code would need proper dissemination to relevant decision-makers. Currently, the machinery for enforcement of IHL is somewhat weak in relation to the more powerful world actors prone to embarking on trade wars. Thus, neither the US or China have accepted the jurisdiction of the International Criminal Court, an appropriate forum for the enforcement of IHL.

The ethical dimension of a trade war is concerned with the welfare costs/social justice and human rights aspects of a trade war. The theatre of a trade war as well as its weapons are not decoupled from humanity, human rights, and questions of distributive justice. Trade policy instruments impact on livelihoods and lifesaving supplies without any cushions. They shift and distort supply chains in a reckless manner without adequate warning for adjustment measures. The weaponization of trade measures such as tariffs shifts the focus on numbers, percentages, targeted goods, and equivalence in tariffs. The economic analysis should, however, focus on the costs to humanity, the environment, and the vulnerable sections of society. An impact analysis is needed of the weaponization of trade policy instruments before they are triggered. This is necessary for the ethical discourse that should follow it.

43 ICJ, Legality of the Threat or Use of Nuclear Weapons, Advisory opinion, 8 July 1996, ICJ Reports 1996.

Currency Wars

'Currency wars' are not new in international economic relations although not defined in IEL as such. A principal aspect of a currency war is currency rate manipulation which is an aspect of a trade war. It can be considered in that context as a weapon of a trade war and/or discreetly in its own right as a weapon of monetary policy. It is a weapon of stealth and can be devastating in its effect. The slightest hint of it can trigger a response. Currency rate manipulation is defined in the IMF and is prohibited.[44] It is, however, difficult to prove currency rate manipulation under the IMF in the face of a denial of an intention to manipulate, which is a requirement; alternative explanations proffered; and the benefit of reasonable doubt in favour of the member accused.[45] Moreover, it is also worth mentioning the difficulties of enforcement of a violation, if found, as against a major economic power.[46]

Be that as it may, the US independently has set up an apparatus to determine currency manipulation and engage within the IMF and/or bilaterally with the currency manipulator State to bring change in its policies.[47] Under US law whilst the US is expected to consult with the IMF, the US nevertheless can make its own unilateral determination of a currency manipulator of a State which has a significant bilateral trade surplus with the US; or a State that has material global current account surplus. The determination of currency manipulation is done by the executive branch of the US with fewer constraints in establishing proof of manipulation than in the IMF. In sum, the process of determination allows for judgement by the executive, with no oversight of this process within the constitutional setting of the US. The US process is more flexible than that of the IMF in terms of evidentiary requirements and criteria, as is evidenced by the discrepancy between a recent US determination of China as a currency manipulator without a similar determination by the IMF.[48] That said, although the US legislation does not appear to be mirrored in the practice of other States expressly as such, this does not mean that other States are not responding to threats of currency manipulation by other States. Indeed, they may well be responding to it in less than a transparent manner than the US. In sum, currency rate manipulation and responses to it are set in an opaque location wherein economic power can magnify the lethal effects of its engagement, with consequences beyond two States and their respective relations.

44 See Article IV of the IMF Articles of Agreement and IMF EB Decision No.15203-(12/72), 18 July 2012.

45 Ibid.

46 See for example R W Staiger & A Sykes, '"Currency manipulation" and World Trade,' *World T.R.* Vol. 9 No. 4 (2010) 583–627.

47 The Omnibus Trade and Competitiveness Act of 1988. See further Chapter 3 herein.

48 See US Department of Treasury August 2019, available at https://home.treasury.gov/news/press-releases/sm751 (last visited February 2022).

Currency War and State Responsibility

Is State responsibility implicated in the conduct of currency manipulation beyond the multilateral IMF framework and the US-led unilateral initiative?[49] Currency manipulation can be a possible weapon of 'mass destruction' in a trade war. Competitive devaluation involves State responsibility towards its residents, as much as inter-state responsibility. The State manipulates conditions which give a competitive advantage to its export sector. However, for certain other sectors within its economy reliant on imports, there is a negative impact. Similarly, there are negative consequences for the consumers reliant upon imported consumer goods and services, and foreign remittances, made for example by migrant workers to their home countries, become costlier. However, the value of foreign assets held by residents on the other hand appreciates. Cost benefit analysis could to some extent reflect an overall benefit to the economy, at some time trickling down positive effects generally. However, be that as it may, there is here a circumstance that reflects arbitrary distribution of benefits and burdens amongst residents of the State, not to mention welfare costs on some; for example, the sick dependent on vital lifesaving imported medicine. Herein is a circumstance where Rawls's distributive justice[156] analysis has a bearing. Thus, to borrow one of Rawls's analytical tools, a 'behind the veil of ignorance' analysis, would call for, in terms of substantive justice, an egalitarian distribution of the costs and benefits, consequent upon an engineered revaluation of the domestic currency exchange rate; and, in accordance with Rawls' differential principle, some positive discrimination in favour of the most disadvantaged from the currency devaluation. Competitive devaluation also involves an unfair advantage vis--vis another State and its residents and therefore raises questions of unjust enrichment.

In terms of procedural justice, the decision-making process of the valuation of the currency needs to be procedurally fair conforming to due process, and to the extent possible, transparent. This means the decision to intervene in the market and/or devalue needs to be justified, lend itself to accountability, and be transparent albeit *post facto*—as for example intervention reports *ex post facto* in Japan. In this context, decisions about intervening in the currency market where these are the business of the Finance Ministry and not that of the Central Bank imply that such decisions are more politicised than otherwise. Of course, the nature of the intervention and decision-making prior to its being carried out needs to be confidential. But within the framework of such a constraint, it is still possible that there is a process of decision with a paper trail, such that the decision can be scrutinised *post facto*; and that the decision and interventions in the currency markets are rendered transparent *post facto*, barring exceptional national security considerations.

49 The following two paragraphs are based on Asif H Qureshi, *Contextualising International Law in Northeast Asia* (Hart: 2018) 148–149.

Weaponisation of the Dollar

In a trade war involving an issuing State of an international reserve currency such as the dollar the temptation to 'arm the dollar' in the heat of the war cannot be ignored. Indeed, there is already a discourse around the idea of the weaponisation of the dollar.[50] The dollar is a major international reserve currency and has become central to the international financial system. Its weaponisation can take different forms, including the manipulation of the value of the dollar through monetary policy (interest rate/exchange rates and money supply in the domestic economy) and placing restrictions on its use for international payments, for example for international payments through SWIFT (an international payments system owned by a group of US banks).[51] In this circumstance, there has been some focus in reducing dependency on the dollar through mainly domestic and regional efforts.[52]

Here the focus is normative, directed at the responsibility of the dollar-issuing State. Are there ethical standards that could establish some level of state responsibility herein? Such standards could include distributive justice concerns to the extent that the international currency status is attributable to arbitrary distribution of the international resources, as Frank Garcia has suggested.[53] In this respect the following is to be noted.[54] International reserve currencies are necessary for the functioning of the international economic system, in the absence of the existence of an international currency. The conditions for acquiring international reserve currency status are in some measure informed by the criteria set for these by the IMF;[167]and include for instance such considerations as the country's level of exports and the extent to which it is freely usable. These conditions, however, are economic in nature and command legitimacy as such for this reason. They are not informed by justice considerations.

The costs and benefits to the issuer of the currency have been variously described.[55] At the non-State level, the national banking sector has a built-in comparative advantage given the ready access to the national currency;[56] and

50 See for example Julius Sen, 'The Weaponisation of the Dollar; Policy Options for Small Countries,' LSE IDEAS Strategic Update 2019. Available at <http://www.lse.ac.uk/ideas/Assets/Documents/updates/LSE-IDEAS-Weaponisation-Dollar.pdf> (last visited October 2019).

51 Ibid.

52 Ibid.

53 See F Garcia, 'Evaluating IMF Crisis Prevention as a Matter of Global Justice,' *ILSA Journal of International and Comparative Law* Vol. 14 (2008) 467–476.

54 The following paragraphs are based on Asif H Qureshi, *Contextualising International Law in Northeast Asia*, op. cit., 151.

55 See for example Benjamin J Cohen, *Currency Power: Understanding Monetary Rivalry* (Princeton University Press: 2015). The author adumbrates the benefits under the following categories: transaction costs; seigniorage; macroeconomic flexibility; leverage and reputation. The costs are categorised as reputation; appreciation; external constraints; and policy responsibility.

56 Ibid., 20.

generally national foreign business enjoys lower exchange risks, as do nationals when abroad.[57] At the level of the State, there is the benefit of seigniorage accruing to the national economy; greater autonomy in national policy-making given fewer constraints arising from balance of payments pressures with the ready access to the national/international currency; and finally the State has enhanced international reputation and capacity to influence other States.[58] On the downside, one cost of particular note is that the demand for the currency puts pressure on the currency to appreciate and be overvalued.[59] Moreover, with the internationalisation of the currency comes also pressure to engage responsibly in monetary relations.[60] Overall it seems there are considerable advantages for the issuing State[61]—the international reserve currency country acquires a 'built-in advantage in the supply' of this sought-after currency.[62]

Both fair competition and State responsibility concerns are in some measure inter alia grounded in distributive justice. First, fair access considerations operate in terms of the equal/unequal opportunity of access to a fair value of national currency. Exchange rate manipulation disrupts this equality of opportunity of a fair exchange rate. Every State is equally entitled to a means of exchange that reflects its relative value that is not unfairly distorted. This is distinct from contending that every State is entitled to a certain share of hard currency. In the absence of a universal means of exchange, behind Rawls's 'veil of ignorance' this is the second best that all States would agree to. Depriving a State deliberately of the fair relative value of its currency is unjust. Moreover, if the States are competitors and the exchange rate manipulation gives the residents of one State (including the State itself and its economy) a competitive advantage over the residents and economy of another State, questions of rectificatory justice,[63] as between the two States also arise, on the premise that every State enjoys equal opportunity of access to a fair value of its currency. To realise this, for example, an affected State could legislate to enable its residents to seek compensation from the responsible State the erosion of their asset values arising from a deliberately distorted relative exchange rate value—leaving aside questions of proof. Although the point here has been framed in terms of the opportunity for realising a fair value of a national currency, the same considerations are equally in point in the context of a quest for acquiring an international reserve currency status.

Second, generally, as Frank Garcia aptly points out, the fact that 'certain currencies are considered hard, and others are not necessarily creates inequality in the distribution of trade currencies.'[64] This inequality, where it is a consequence

57 Ibid.
58 Ibid
59 Ibid.
60 Ibid.
61 Ibid.
62 Garcia, op. cit., 469.
63 See for example G Collste, *Global Rectificatory Justice* (Palgrave Macmillan: 2015).
64 Garcia, op. cit., 469.

of and attributable to the arbitrary distribution of resources, is the subject of distributive justice. Moreover, given that there are indeed benefits to an issuing State of an international reserve currency, there is a case that those benefits should be accompanied by some measure of responsibility, in ensuring stability of the international monetary system. At first blush this suggestion may seem naïve but given that acquiring an international reserve currency status is also about perceptions of a currency, and the issuing State's behaviour, users of the currency already engage in the currency with a set of expectations. Articulating those expectations in a code for reserve currencies is not a quantum leap and is in fact conducive to an orderly international monetary framework. Indeed, it is recognised that the Fund has a mandate to 'discuss with the member the manner in which their policies are directed towards the achievement of better international liquidity, and changes in policy that may be necessary for this purpose.'[65] Would not a sudden massive depreciation of the currency call for concern?

Leaving aside legality, however, what of the response that the issuing country's currency has an international currency status merely because of a spillover of sound economic policies and consequential growth, and therefore should not be accompanied by any responsibilities over and above those currently found in IMF law?[66] This is indeed a persuasive argument that deserves careful consideration. However, can the acquisition of the status of an international reserve currency be exclusively attributable to a country's own sound economic policies and growth? Should the availability of an export market by third countries not command some stake in the calculation of the export performance? Exports are informed by the competitive nature of a country's exports. But they are also informed by the availability of a market provided externally.[67] Finally, however the currency status has been acquired, is it a morally defensible argument to proclaim complete non-responsibility? After all, what is being proposed is not the redistribution of resources if that is not justified on grounds of distributive justice, but rather merely some measure of responsibility in the way the currency is subsequently managed once it acquires its international status. Even in the distributive justice world of Rawls, the equality of opportunity conceded does not extend to using realised assets through that opportunity in a manner destructive of the community at large.

65 See IMF Legal Department, 'The Fund's Mandate: The Legal Framework' (2010), para 26.

66 I am grateful to Mr Rhee Chang Young of the IMF for drawing this argument to my attention.

67 In the sphere of international taxation, in the discourse on attributing different taxation rights, as between a residence and source State, the argument has been put forward that the right to tax in the case of profits from the international sale of goods and services needs to be apportioned as between the source and residence States, on grounds of equity, to the source country also where the sales have taken place, for its provision of the market for the exports. See Klaus Vogel, 'Worldwide vs Source Taxation of Income—A Review and Re-Evaluation of Arguments,' *Intertax* Vol. 16 No. 8/9 (1988) 2016–2029.

In sum, reserve currency status is determined in the 'law of the jungle,' and once acquired it seems the 'crowned lion' is not accountable for the manner of its behaviour, self-aggrandisement, or hegemonic tendencies. There is a case, therefore, to articulate a special code of conduct for international reserve currencies that takes the responsibility of questions on board. Indeed, an obligation to have due regard may be read in Article IV of the IMF Articles of Agreement. The latter question could focus at the manner of any future fundamental changes in the arrangements of currency rates; interventions in the market; and the manner of the applications of the 'national security exception' with respect to the currency.

State Responsibility for Negative Spillovers?

Both in the trade and the monetary spheres, economically successful States whose economies have an important impact on the world economy should have certain responsibilities in an interdependent globalised world economy. The basis of this expectation derives from the fact that the success of these economies in some measure derives from the existence of the globalised interdependent market. It follows that it is reasonable to expect some discipline in State action that restraints State conduct in not damaging the delicate fabric of the very system which has contributed to their success. In other words, the exercise of State autonomy in international economic relations should not exhibit characteristics of unjust enrichment. Indeed, there are grounds for suggesting that in such circumstances reliance on State autonomy of action in international economic relations should be estopped. In addition, such States have a responsibility at the least to reflect on the negative spillovers of their monetary and trade policies on other States where these have adverse consequences which are foreseeable, intended, and unfair in terms of level playing fields; or the undermining of a universally agreed communal objective under Customary International Law, for example genocide of a people through deprivation of vital food/medicine resources.

The proposition that there is no prohibition under customary international law on States to refrain from engaging in foreseeable and intended actions that result in negative spillovers on the economy of others cannot if articulated stand uncontested.[68] First, the membership of the IMF (near universal membership), has agreed to the principle of non-harm under the IMF mandate. Thus, Article IV of the IMF Articles of Agreement sets out a duty owed not only to the Fund but also to other members to collaborate in preventing negative spillovers. This edict to collaborate is on the assumption that there is an obligation to prevent negative spillovers.[69] Moreover, the Articles of Agreement of the IMF, are underpinned by the management of negative spillovers, for example the prohibition

68 The arguments here build upon the points made in Asif H Qureshi, *Contextualising International Law in Northeast Asia*, op. cit.

69 This point was pointed out to by Sean Hagan in 2016 by the then general Counsel of the IMF.

on manipulation of currency rates and measures destructive of the international economy in addressing balance of payments problems. Further, under customary international law the counterfeiting of the currency of another State is prohibited. Second, in the field of trade, the underlying thrust of the WTO agreements focuses on negative spillovers of domestic and regional trade policy measures that impact market access and level playing fields. In sum, whilst both these State practices in monetary and trade spheres are set mainly in multilateral agreements, nevertheless their impact on the building blocks of a norm of customary international law must be addressed. If such a general wide sweeping proposition cannot be extrapolated from this evidence of State practice, at least there are grounds for suggesting that States have an obligation to reflect on whether their actions in the exercise of their State autonomy will result in negative spillovers where there is such a likelihood.

Third, there is State practice in other spheres wherein negative spillovers are regulated. Thus, there is the State obligation to prevent transboundary harm in environmental law;[70] the notion of harmful tax competition which erodes the tax base of other countries, in international taxation;[71] and anti-trust law where anti-competitive behaviour from another country affects the level playing fields within. Moreover, it is common for States to have legislation which authorises responses to negative economic effects from outside the territory. Whilst this sheds light on its authority, nevertheless the nature of that authority is informed by a sense of what is/should be prohibited. Equally, the fact that States have not legislated to act in a negative manner towards other countries in the economic sphere to deliberately/foreseeably impact on others, is indicative of a belief of the existence of a prohibition to act in this manner. In the circumstances, do not these multilateral regimes including domestic State practice cumulatively evidence a norm of customary international law that at the least calls for prior reflection in engaging in actions which result in harm inflicted intentionally and that is foreseeable? Large economies in this interdependent global economy have a greater likelihood of impacting through their actions on other economies and therefore may be reluctant to acknowledge the suggestion being made here. However, where action is deliberate/foreseeable and of a level that far outweighs any overall benefit is surely conduct that should be placed in the realms of the prohibited.

In sum, success in the economic sphere is in part a result of arbitrary endowments of nature and the result of the globalised access to capital, labour, and markets. As such there is a case in justice for responsible behaviour. There are also grounds for suggesting the existence of restraining norms in customary

70 Trail Smelter Arbitration, U.S.-Canada, Decision, 11 March 1941, RIAA, Vol. 3, 1938–1982.

71 See developments in OECD under the Harmful Taxation and Base Erosion and profit shifting (BEPs). See also Reuven S Avi-Yonah, *International Tax as International Law* (Cambridge University Press: 2007) (although this author elsewhere has disagreed with Avi-Yonah's analysis on international law).

international law with respect to certain intended and foreseeable negative spill overs arising from State measures in the monetary and trade spheres. At the least, there is a basis for an invitation for reflection before action is taken in such circumstances. The principle of sovereign equality of States calls for such an understanding of the autonomy of States in international economic relations.

To some extent multilateral institutional surveillance through the IMF and trade policy review exercises of the WTO already work towards inculcating reflection with respect to negative spillover effects of monetary and trade policies. In some measure where international law is constitutionally embedded in domestic law international constraints could have a bearing. And whereas it may be difficult to enforce such a restraint on powerful economies, its articulation is not in vain. Norm setting is a preliminary to its enforcement.

Conclusions

The phenomenon of the Americanisation of the IEO has been for the purposes of the analysis here mainly a reference to the problem of a superpower wherein that entity could exude a propensity to arrogate communal decision-making; impose intentionally or consequentially its world view on the world; and expect a preferential treatment in dispute settlement and decision-making. In this chapter the need for specific scrutiny of this phenomenon has been explained. There must be upfront discourse about it in any organisation of a normative framework. It is simply nonsense to muffle discourse on it by the mere assertion that 'law is constituted by both power and reason, exercising its authority both through coercion and a normativity that is grounded in legal reasoning and process.'[72] Moreover, that discourse should lead to a normative framework within which the phenomenon of the Americanisation of the IEO is addressed. The basis for such normativity is to be found in International Law and policy analysis of what constitutes responsible State behaviour and the need for the design of innovative reforms. Certainly, there are cogent reasons for a normative discourse on the phenomenon of the Americanisation of the IEO.

The exercise of sustainable power can only coexist with power per se, if it defers to the rule of law in dispute resolution and decision-making. There is no logic in the exercise of State power which calls for a preferential treatment in the adherence to agreed upon norms. In the same vein, agreed processes of decision-making in international organisations do have set parameters for their exercise. Where the agreed decision-making reflects the political or economic power structures, proper safeguards should be put in place so that the decision-making is not the subject of abuse. With privilege in decision-making must come transparency and accountability in its making.

The theory of comparative advantage is not premised on absolute economic capacity. Moreover, the modern state of international trade and investment is to

72 Halliday & Shaffer, op. cit., Chapter 1.

a fair degree not just about functional transmissions of goods services and investment it is also laden with non-functional values. Given this, there is not only the need for caution in their importation as there is to some extent currently but also some measure of responsibility on those who engage in their transmission (this is not the case currently, although there are now developments in export controls[73]). Moreover, economic warfare conducted through trade and currency wars can raise questions of a State's responsibility and engage State responsibility in ethical/justice discourse—both in the instigation of such warfare, as much as during it. There is scope here for the development of codes of conduct that rein in the manner of the conduct of such warfare.

73 See this author herein Chapter 6.

2 United States Special 301 Reviews of Foreign Intellectual Property Protection[1]

'The ownership of the world's resources rests with mankind. International allocative decisions therefore ultimately need to be informed by this paradigm—whether made multilaterally, nationally or in terms of individuals.'

Introduction

The United States (US) has several legislative mechanisms through which it scrutinises, with a view to bringing about changes in the regulation by foreign States of aspects of their respective domestic economies, when that conduct affects US economic concerns. The scholarly analysis of these ranges from being defensive of the mechanisms from the perspective of the US[2] to being strongly critical.[3] There is empirical analysis in terms of the efficacy of the measures, case studies of individual countries, and legal analysis mainly from the perspective of World Trade Organization (WTO) law. Moreover, there has also been a chorus of concerns expressed in the WTO dispute settlement framework, especially of late.[4]

In this chapter Special 301 is the principal mechanism identified for elucidation. It focuses on intellectual property rights (IPRs) protection in third countries.

1 This chapter is based on 'United States Special 301—A Deeply Flawed Tool for IPR Regulation?' *Journal of World Trade* Vol. 55 No. 3 (2021).

2 Greg Mastel, *American Trade Laws: After the Uruguay Round* (M.E. Sharpe: 1996).

3 Aileen Kwa & Peter Lunenborg, 'US' Section 301 Actions: Why They Are Illegitimate and Misguided,' South Centre 2018; and J Bhagwati & H T Patrick (eds), *Aggressive Unilateralism* (University of Michigan Press: 1990).

4 United States – Section 337 of the Tariff Act of 1930, Report by the GATT Panel adopted 7 November 1989 (L/6439 – 36S/345); United States – Section 337 of the Tariff Act of 1930 and Amendments thereto (DS 186: 2000); United States – Sections 301–310 of the Trade Act of 1974 (WTO DS 152: (2000)); United States – Section 306 of the Trade Act 1974 and Amendments thereto (DS2200 (2000); United States – Tariff Measures on Certain Goods from China II (DS WT/DS565/1 (2018 ongoing)); United States – Tariff Measures on Certain Goods from China III (WT/DS587/ (2019 ongoing)); United States – Tariff Measures on Certain Goods from China (DS543 (2019 ongoing)); United States – Certain Measures on Steel and Aluminum Products (DS548/564/556/554/552/548/547/544 (2019–ongoing)).

DOI: 10.4324/9781003047575-3

This chapter will describe the main features of this unilateral mechanism and its normative impact on foreign States. The criteria for evaluating Special 301 can draw from several sources. First, US law itself can potentially be of relevance, from a procedural perspective—to echo a widely held sentiment albeit concerning Section 301—in such an engagement the US acts as 'judge, jury, and executioner.'[5] Special 301 does not exist in isolation from the rest of US law—constitutional, substantive, and procedural. Thus, the preamble of the US constitution refers to the establishment of justice and the promotion of the general welfare of the people of the United States (contra interests of rent-seekers). Justice embraces both substantive justice and by definition precludes blindness to the justice impacting foreigners and also procedural justice.[6] US enactments that raise revenue directly or indirectly for certain US concerns must be the subject of discourse, scrutiny, and representative consensus. Thus, the raising of revenue through the opening up of markets for certain US concerns and the imposition of tariffs fall within this requirement of due process.[7] Congress has to ensure that taxes are to be collected for the common welfare of the United States. Moreover, Congress is to regulate commerce with foreign nations. The rule of law has a bearing on foreign commerce,[8] and there is recognition of this in the US.[9] Congress is prohibited from legislating laws that curtail the free exercise of religion. This would include a belief system that emphasises community and common ownership.[10] No person is to be deprived of property without due process of law.[11] Private property can only be taken for public purpose with just compensation.[12] An accused is entitled to an impartial hearing, due process, and assistance of counsel.[13] Rules of common law apply to civil/administrative proceedings including principles of natural justice.[14]

Second, there is economic analysis. This is relevant variously—in verifying the economic criteria set in the mechanism, in evaluating overall economic outcomes from the user of Special 301 to secure fair market access, and in considering the US economic impact claim of the other State's legislative practices. Thus, the Reagan administrations' use of Section 301 to prize open Japan's semi-conductor market through the imposition of tariffs has been documented as resulting in the carving out of a cartel for the US semi-conductor industry in the Japanese

5 Japanese Ambassador Hatano in the 1990s: Quote cited in Kwa & Lunenborg, op. cit.
6 US Declaration of Independence.
7 Article 1 Section 7 of US Constitution.
8 Article 1 Section 8 of US Constitution.
9 Letter of the President of the Federal Convention, Dated 17 September 1787, to the President of Congress, Transmitting the Constitution.
10 Article [I] (Amendment 1 – Freedom of Expression and Religion) 13.
11 Article [XIV] (Amendment 14 – Rights Guaranteed: Privileges and Immunities of Citizenship, Due Process, and Equal Protection).
12 Article [V] (Amendment 5 – Rights of Persons).
13 Article [VI] (Amendment 6 – Rights of Accused in Criminal Prosecutions).
14 Article [VII] (Amendment 7 – Civil Trials).

market.[15] Third, the application of the measures under Special 301 have to be contextualised with the foreign nation's constitution, laws, and practices as these are the subject of interpretation and scrutiny.

Fourth, the Special 301 and its outcomes are the subject of international law—both general international law and international agreements. Special 301 process exudes the characteristics of an administrative enquiry having consequences for foreign entities/individuals albeit extraterritorially. Therefore, the same famous US arbitration against Mexico that spawned the concept of the minimum standard for the treatment of aliens (including fair and equitable treatment in investment law) has relevance here. It is the case that the enquiry focuses on State conduct but whether the alien is a foreign State or a foreign individual/artificial entity is not relevant to its application. In any event the enquiry ultimately impacts on non-State actors. Thus, Special 301 processes have to conform at the least to the Neer articulation of the minimum standard (1926) as it has now developed. This international minimum standard is recognised by the US as a rule of customary international law. It has been recognised as an evolving customary standard in investment tribunal decisions.[16] In the same vein, State immunity under international law has a bearing here. The doctrine of State immunity involves another State not being the subject of judicial/ administrative process in another State. Of course, this immunity can be waived but if it is being waived under duress the integrity of a fundamental rule of international law is being undermined. Similarly, Special 301 involves extraterritorial engagement in prescriptive and/or enforcement jurisdiction and thus has to be considered under international law.

Finally, Special 301 must command legitimacy and/or be set in some notion of justice if it is not to be pictured as a naked instrument of power.

This chapter is set against this general background drawing from the Special 301 Reports between 2018 and 2020. It focuses on the pharmaceutical and transfer of technology sectors against the background of the recent China–US trade war. The chapter sets out to take a critical stance on Special 301 given the relative paucity of such treatment amongst scholars generally, and in particular US scholars. In sum, this evaluation is intended to be an input from an international perspective aimed mainly at those who are at its receiving end.

The Special 301 Process

The Special 301 process was established in 1988 and is set alongside the internationally infamous Section 301.[17] The governing provisions are to be found in two different locations establishing a principal US surveillance mechanism of IPR practices of countries of interest to US trade and investment. In this manner the

15 Tom Meinderts, 'The Power of Section 301: The Reagan Tariffs in an Age of Economic Globalization,' *Globalizations* Vol. 17 No. 4 (2019) 746–758.

16 *ADF v US* (2003) & *Merril & Ring* (2010)

17 Mastel, op. cit.

US advances its particular agenda on IPR—which it also promotes through the Trade-Related Aspects of Intellectual Property Rights (TRIPS) Council[18] and bilateral channels, e.g., the US Trade and Investment Framework Agreements (TFAs); regional channels, e.g., APEC Intellectual Property Experts Group; and finally through conditions imposed under unilateral systems, e.g., the US Generalized System of Preferences (GSP), including US technical assistance in the IPR sphere.[19]

First, a direction is made to the United States Trade Representative (USTR) in consultation with other US governmental agencies to (1) identify certain countries including certain US investors concerned with barriers to US trade and investment;[20] and (2) estimate the distorting impact to the US. Following this analysis, the USTR is to present an annual report on or before every March to the President, the Senate, and the House of Representatives.[21] The report is also to contain any action taken in response to the findings with respect to the 'act, policy, or practice identified' of the foreign country.[22] Guidance is provided for estimating the distorting impact on US trade.

The following observations are proffered in relation to the identification process within the framework of the legislation. First, the identification involves exports of goods and services from the US alone. The focus is on 'barriers' to trade to the US involving a subjective formulation of such barriers. Second, it involves the protection of specific IPRs viz., 'trademarks, patents, and copyrights' of goods and services exported or licenced by US persons. It is not concerned generally with IP in foreign countries. There is no reference to 'traditional knowledge, traditional cultural expressions, and genetic resources.'[23] Third, it is concerned with outward foreign direct investment by US persons—trade-related investment. Again, there is an articulation of a subjective formulation of 'barriers' to investment flows. A plea for special consideration. Fourth, the focus is on the 'acts, policies, or practices' of the foreign State. Thus, acts, policies, or practices of non-State entities, unless attributable to the foreign State, are presumably not covered. Moreover, this is a very wide remit given that acts and practices have actual impact, whereas a policy may be in the realm of a State's 'consciousness' or for that matter its ideology. Fifth, the legislation is concerned with significant barriers or distortions which have an impact on US trade and foreign investment.

18 US submission to the TRIPS Council in 2018 titled 'The Societal Value of Intellectual Property in the New Economy' and US-initiated sessions in the TRIPS Council 2019 entitled 'Public-Private Collaboration in Innovation.'

19 Special 301 Report 2019.

20 Under Section 2241(b) of Title 19. Customs Duties, Chapter 12. Trade Act of 1974.

21 Title 19. Customs Duties Chapter 12. Trade Act of 1974, § 2241 (b). This report is known as the National Trade Estimate Report (NTE).

22 Title 19. Customs Duties Chapter 12. Trade Act of 1974, § 2241.

23 Ambassador Amina C Mohamed of the Republic of Kenya, at the International Conference on Intellectual Property and Development 20 May 2019, at WIPO, <https://www.wipo.int/wipo_magazine/en/2019/03/article_0002.html> (last visited June 2020).

There is the need here to establish in principle a causal link between the significant barrier/distortion and US trade from an independent perspective. Sixth, there is reference to taking *into account* international agreements that the US is a party to. This does not square well with the US constitution on the status of international agreements in the US.[24] International agreements under the constitution are not a matter of 'taking into account.' There is no discretion or judgement involved in terms of the role the international agreement is to be given. Seventh, agreements to which the US is not a party need not be considered. This not only places the foreign State in double jeopardy but is inconsistent with the constraints that the US itself subscribes to in the exercise of extraterritorial jurisdiction under Articles 402 and 403 of the US Restatement (Third) of Foreign Relations Law of the United States.

Does the reference to international agreements preclude the application of general international law viz., customary international law and general principles of law? First, Special 301 must be considered against the background of the status of general international law in the US. In this respect granted there is some controversy on the status of general international law in the US legal system, nevertheless there are also standpoints affirming its status or attributing it some weight.[25] At the least US courts will strive to interpret legislation so that it does not contravene general international law.[26] The section herein does not prohibit the invocation of general international law. Finally, the enquiry focuses on the impact of US commerce. There is no reference to the impact on consumer choices, US quality of life, and indeed even such considerations as the impact on the US environment.

Second, within 30 days after the submission of the annual report (NTE), the USTR is enjoined to (1) identify countries that have certain shortcomings in their IPR regimes, including amongst those Priority Foreign Countries (PFCs); (2) take into account the guidance provided for the identification of PFCs; (3) formulate an Action Plan for countries placed on the Priority Watch List (PWL) in accordance with guidance provided; (4) assist the President with respect to necessary action to be taken where there has been non-compliance with the Action Plan; and (5) finally publish a list of PFCs and report on actions taken to the House of Representatives and the Senate.[27] This 'analysis' is contained in a report known as the Special 301 Report. In this Report countries can be placed on a Watch List (WL), a PWL, or a PFC list. This is a graduated list with the PFC being the category of country considered to have the most egregious IPR barriers. This three-tiered category is not set out as such in the legislation but

24 Article VI clause 2 of the US constitution.

25 Curtis A Bradley, *Customary International Law's Uncertain Status in the US Legal System* (Oxford University Press: 2015); Michael D Ramse, 'The Constitution's Text and Customary International Law,' *The Georgetown Law Journal* Vol. 106 (2018) 1747.

26 Known as the 'Charming Betsy Canon' in US jurisprudence. See Curtis A Bradley (2015).

27 Title 19. Customs Duties Chapter 12. Trade Act of 1974 § 2242.

created under an administrative initiative—the legislation alluding essentially to two categories.[28]

The following observations are proffered with respect to the process set out above in the identification of foreign countries determined to have flawed IPR practices. There are mainly two classes of foreign countries in this respect identified viz., the non-priority foreign countries and the priority foreign countries. Both are placed on a WL compiled by the USTR. First, the criteria of identifying foreign countries of IPR concern (both NPFC and PFC) refers to denials of either adequate and effective IPR protection, or fair and equitable market share for US concerns relying on IPR. Moreover, 'adequate and effective' IPR protection has an element of subjectivity about it and can go beyond obligations under the WTO TRIPs agreement. In the same vein, a fair and equitable market share is not as such an obligation under the WTO agreements. It is also discriminatory given that it calls for a certain treatment not similarly accorded to other US or foreign concerns.

The criteria for PFCs are further qualified for the purposes of identifying 'fair and equitable market access' and adequate and effective IPRs. First, they are restricted to the 'most onerous or egregious acts, policies, or practices' of the foreign State. Second, the concerned actions must have the 'greatest adverse impact (actual or potential) on the relevant United States products.' Third, insofar 'as the denial of fair and equitable market access' for US concerns that rely upon intellectual property protection—this condition is qualified by the requirement that its existence must have a factual basis, and is in violation of international law or agreement. This qualification does place the condition under international law. With respect to fair and equitable market access denied because of inadequate IPR protection these are material only if they violate international law or an international agreement to which the US and foreign country are parties to; or are discriminatory non-tariff barriers. However, where there is no violation of the TRIPS agreement the IPRs can still be considered inadequate and ineffective if in violation of international law or a mutual agreement. Thus, with respect to inadequate IPRs the qualifications are also all within the remit of international law. In short, these qualifications bring ***at any rate in form*** the characterisation of PFCs within the legitimate bounds of WTO obligations and international law. It will be noted though that these qualifications do not apply to the NPFCs and therefore issues with respect to WTO obligations remain. Moreover, the requirement that the factual basis in all the determinations must be to the satisfaction of the USTR is contrary to the WTO stipulation that such determinations can only be made through recourse to the WTO dispute settlement process.[29]

In addition, a PFC must enter with the US in negotiations in good faith or be making progress in bilateral or multilateral negotiations for the protection of

28 Raj Bhala, *International Trade Law: Volume One*, 4th ed. (Carolina Academic Press: 2015) at 1448.

29 Article 23 of WTO DSU.

IPR. This is clearly a coercive edict given the context it is set in—not only forcing countries to negotiate with the US under threat of sanctions but also enjoining them to negotiate in 'good faith' (to add insult to injury). By the same token the injunction to make progress in bilateral or multilateral negotiations for IPR protection partakes of undue pressure. These expectations are counter to the principle of sovereignty and sovereign equality of States as found in international law and enshrined in the UN Charter. Indeed, they are an affront to the dignity of other nations. There is a strong case for having it expunged from the US legislation.

Once a foreign country has been designated a PFC it is subject to an Action Plan with specific benchmarks for performance unilaterally set by the USTR according to what it determines as being the appropriate action to be taken to solve the IPR and related market access issues. If after one year there has been a failure of compliance with the Action Plan, the President may take appropriate action. The actions the President may take are not spelt out and are not expressly set under international law.

Finally, the USTR is to produce an Annual Report (known as the Special 301 Report) setting out the list of PFCs and the Action Plan that they are to comply with. The Special 301 review process resulting in the Annual Report involves consultations with various US governmental agencies, stakeholders, and foreign governments including written submissions and a public hearing. The submissions are made public, and the hearing can be viewed on video by the public. According to the 2018 Special 301 Report the

> assessment is necessarily conducted on a case-by-case basis, taking into account diverse factors such as a trading partner's level of development, its international obligations and commitments, the concerns of right holders and other interested parties, and the trade and investment policies of the United States.

As part of the review process countries are placed on a PWL and WL—the former list of countries being the subject of an Action Plan.

This review process, which can have a far-reaching impact on the domestic legislation of a foreign country, does not manifest itself as an impartial judicious process even in its unilateral nature. First, the objectives of the review are clearly set out variously in the Reports to 'aggressively' further US interests and American jobs (not objectively, impartially in a measured manner to ensure IPR, and level playing fields).[30] Such pronouncements repeated verbatim in various reports do not sit well with the also repeated observation that the USTR conducts a broad and balanced assessment of US trading partners' IPR protection.[31] Second, and following from the above, there is a due process aspect to the Special

30 Special 301 Report (2018).
31 Special 301 Annual Report (2019).

301 that calls for scrutiny. Thus, the parameters within which the USTR may make determinations to give the USTR a wide measure of discretion in the range of factors that can be taken into account, including the kind of framework available for representation. Thus, Special 301 involves making a policy judgement about the optimum balance between the rights of an IP holder on the one hand and fair competition and a society's public interests on the other. Such a judgement must be set against the background of a full accounting of that foreign public interest not to mention that the US is not the domain for such a consideration. The assertion that the evaluation is set against the background of the level of development of the particular country in question in the reports is not convincing in the light of the conclusions arrived at. In any event level of development on its own if indeed taken into account does not factor in the socio/political/cultural background that is material to a State's policy on IPR. Special 301 reviews and outcomes are mainly driven by interested US commercial concerns and US drive against this backdrop on the development of international IPR protection. Discourse on IPRs cannot be conducted purely from the viewpoint of the intellectual property holders. Nor can the US public interest be transplanted into another society. Moreover, there are factual determinations made not just about foreign legislative practices but also about a directly competitive foreign domestic industry that does not seem to have a direct input in the Special 301 process. Granted that as part of the process of review the USTR requests for written submissions through the Federal Register along with open hearings for interested parties who can afford to attend at their expense to give testimony all the way in the US—the fact remains that such a process is procedurally more advantageous to US stakeholders. There is no system of appeal and/or review of the Special 301 process. The Reports do not put forward the arguments made during the hearing and in the written representations of the non-US parties. The Reports do not give a reasoned account of how the conclusions are arrived at or why the contra-arguments made by the country representatives and others have not been accepted. It should be noted also that the Special 301 Reports are prepared through soliciting 'substantial information' from U.S. embassies around the world.[32] If this information involved investigative and/or policing operations without the consent of the States in question it would raise questions with respect to the legality of the exercise of such extraterritorial jurisdiction under international law. In the same vein, information from the US Office of the National Counterintelligence and Security Centre is availed in informing various conclusions e.g., 'misuse of trade secret owners to government institutions for compliance with regulatory obligations.'[33] For this information to have any weight more details need to be provided as to the methods used for obtaining it; precisely what information was obtained including whether the same source facilitated the

32 Special 301 Report (2020) Acknowledgements.
33 Reported in the 2018, 2019, and 2020 Special 301 Reports in the Trade Secrets sections.

eliciting of trade secrets of non-US origins of trade secrets; and how compliant with international law were these methods of obtaining information.

Finally, the Special 301 process relies on several factors for its enforcement. First, it involves a softly approach through the creation of the WL including a graduated category of countries on the WL depending on how they are perceived to respond to the US Special 301 criteria/conditions at any given time. The review process includes a so-called Out-Of-Cycle Reviews where this is called for. Second, it is enforced through imposition of an Action Plan with specific benchmarks for those countries on the PWL for at least one year. Third, it is enforced through action under Section 301 of the Trade Act, WTO dispute settlement, and other bilateral and international dispute resolution mechanisms.

The WTO Analysis

The Special 301 is problematic from the perspective of WTO in several respects. First, it entails unilateral determinations outside the framework of the WTO leading to unilateral application of economic sanctions.[34] Second, the US provides market opening services for certain US persons and products in trade and investment dependent on a certain level of intellectual property protection. Under the WTO Agreement on Subsidies and Countervailing Measures a subsidy is deemed to exist when the government provides 'services other than general infrastructure, or purchases goods' and a benefit is thereby conferred.[35] As this subsidy is contingent on export performance or the fact or potential of export it is specific and is a prohibited subsidy.[36] Moreover, the US securing an equitable share of the market in another country could impact on the competitiveness of foreign exports from third countries placing them at a disadvantage. Third, there is a possible breach of the national treatment under GATT 1994. This is because whereas certain US exporters enjoy the advantage of the Special 301 process to facilitate changes in the policies practices and laws of third countries, exporters to the US of products that need adequate and effective IPRs not available in the US do not have the advantage of a Special 301 process to change similarly US policies, practices, and legislation in their favour. Fourth, the Special 301 process involves opening up markets specifically for the US exports. It is a process that carves out a preferential arrangement for certain US exports specifically. As such this is a category of preferential arrangements that are not allowed under Article XXIV of GATT 1994 as they are not preferential arrangements that comprise of customs unions, free trade agreements, or such interim arrangements. Moreover, Special 301 does not facilitate generalised systems of preferences for developing countries.[37] Additionally,

34 Article 23 (2) (a) of DSU.
35 Article 1 of the Agreement on Subsidies and Countervailing Measures.
36 Article 3 of the Agreement on Subsidies and Countervailing Measures.
37 Decision on Differential and More Favourable Treatment, Reciprocity and Fuller Participation of Developing Countries adopted under GATT in 1979.

is this an advantage under Article 1 of GATT 1994 (most-favoured-nation treatment)? Article 1 applies to exports and Special 301 is an advantage facilitated with another country attributable to the US and its Special 301 process. The outcome of this advantage—namely better access to a particular market in a foreign country—is integral to the advantage. This improved market access corridor between the US and a PFC country may not be available to a third country wanting a similar access. Finally, the USTR is authorised to monitor compliance with measures under Section 301 investigation with the authority to impose sanctions in case of non-compliance under Section 306 of the Trade Act 1974.[38] Section 306 itself has been the subject of a challenge[39] in the WTO and is infamously referred to as the carrousel legislation. According to an EU complaint it 'provides for a mandatory and unilateral revision of the list of products subject to suspension of GATT 1994 concessions or other Section 301 (a) action 120 days after the application of the first suspension and then every 180 days thereafter, in order to affect imports from Members which have been determined by the United States not to have implemented recommendations made pursuant to a WTO dispute settlement proceeding.'

Theory

IPRs are grounded in the domestic cultural/social/political/economic/historical setting of States. In this sense IPRs are territorial and do not have an extra-territorial basis. A minimum level of IPR protection has now developed but it is not based on displacing these considerations. Rather, it integrates certain notions of fair play, the exigencies of globalisation, the underpinnings of trade liberalisation. Both the domestic and international dimensions need to consider the civilisational contributions of different peoples and civilisations to the development of the world order. The premise that there is complete ownership *ab initio* of an invention by a certain people is nonsensical. It is tantamount to theft of the historical contributions of mankind to include particular civilisations to inventions. Most inventions are incremental, and this axiom can get lost in the rush to protect IPRs. In the same vein distributive justice including the idea of differential treatment imbedded in it calls for a stake by non-creators in the inventions. Similarly, in a globalised world, foreign labour movements have contributed to the growth and development of other nations. Such foreign labour directly or indirectly has contributed to inventive developments—and herein the mother countries of such migrant workers have a degree of claim on foreign inventions.

The imposition of higher and different IPRs unilaterally formulated cannot be the sole basis for opening market access into another country. Whilst their

38 United States – Sections 301–310 of the Trade Act 1974 (WTO:DS 152 -1999). Section 306 of the Trade Act of 1974, as amended by Section 407 of the Trade and Development Act of 2000 (Public Law 106–200).

39 United States – Section 306 of the Trade Act 1974 and Amendments thereto.

regulation features in the WTO and free trade agreements, they have not been an instrument for liberalisation of trade in isolation from other considerations which form the basis for reciprocal negotiations in international trade. If imposed in isolation outside the context of the establishment of a reciprocal framework for greater market access for trade and investment, they encroach on the right of a State not to open its market in trade and allow entry of foreign investment including the right to discriminate in these spheres under general international law. Moreover, could such a foreign extraterritorial regulatory instrument be considered as partaking of indirect expropriation of the property of foreigners through regulatory processes of the profits and assets of the domestic competing industry in another State? Could it be argued that given the 'taking' can be attributed to a foreign State through attribution of its foreign regulatory measure the 'profits and assets' in question acquire a foreign character because of the origin of the measure?

The development needs of every country are different. Developing countries have a basis for setting their general levels of IPR protection according to their development targets. These countries have public policy objectives that can be specific to their socio-political-cultural setting. Sustainable development has a direct bearing on the discourse on IPRs in the international context. Thus, amongst the principles associated with it are the right to development, 'common but differentiated responsibility,' 'inter-nation equity,' and the achievement of the 2030 Agenda for Sustainable Development to which all nations are committed to. The latter is relevant in informing the public policy that is set in response to IPR protection.

Much of the US IPR drive is underpinned by the notion that they are necessary for innovation—to incentivise innovation. Moreover, this approach is undifferentiating in terms of the subject matter of the invention. However, such a justification is not an absolute truism. There are other drivers for innovation. There are differing views on what constitutes just reward. The discourse on IPRs must be set against the background of the fact that innovation takes place in different sectors and that all the sectors cannot be painted with the same brush. Moreover, the business of IPRs competes in terms of resources and time with another State's legislative priorities and resources. In some developing countries for example it currently takes on average some 20 years for property disputes to be settled. The draconian sanctions that the US is prepared to impose on countries for the satisfaction of its IPR holders alone is a serious digression from addressing the more pressing internal issues currently faced by developing countries.

In the circumstances against what criteria are the foreign practices identified in the Special 301 Reports to be evaluated? These can be categorised as follows: legitimate concerns; non-legitimate concerns; and concerns the basis of which is lacking in due process. US concerns that command legitimacy can be those which reiterate and enforce internationally agreed IPRs in accordance with internationally agreed norms. Non-legitimate concerns are those which seek to impose US specific expectations of IPRs under the coercive Special 301 framework. These include concerns which displace the legitimate balance of a country's IPR system with its domestic public policy. The lack of due process category is a basket to place conclusions that are informed through untested and/or unlawful sources. This analysis will be applied to the 2018, 2019, and 2020 Special 301 Reports. The focus on the Reports will be confined in this chapter to the pharmaceutical sector and transfer of technology. Both of these have multilateral civilisational dimensions.

Insights from Special 301 Reports Between 2018 and 2020

In the 2018 Special 301 Report some 11 countries were placed on the PWL and some 24 others were placed on the WL. In 2019 there were similarly 11 countries on the PWL and an increase in the number of countries on the WL to 26. In 2020 there were 10 countries placed in the PWL and 24 in the WL. During this time span some countries were removed from the PWL and others put on the WL and still others removed from the WL. A significant number of countries however have remained on the 'watch' either in the PWL or WL throughout this period. The Reports follow broadly a similar template with much of the market-oriented mantra to serve US interests repeated verbatim in particular in relation to the pharmaceutical sector and technology transfer.

Market Access for US Pharmaceuticals

On pharmaceuticals the US is concerned with IP protection as observed variously in the Special 301 Reports 'in order to promote affordable healthcare for American patients today...so that trading partners contribute their fair share to research and development of new treatments and cures.' There are a number of questions here. Are there other ways of ensuring affordable healthcare for American patients apart from the extraterritorial imposition of American IPR protections? Should the burden of facilitating affordable healthcare for American patients (including wealthy American patients) be placed on trading partners (developing and less developing countries) through market access for US pharmaceuticals? Is there a proven correlation between IP protection in a third country and greater innovation in the US?

Leaving aside the question of the propriety of US motivations the international trading system is intended to facilitate market access to goods generally regardless of its nature. In this context a State is entitled to highlight impediments to market access that are recognised under the WTO rules. A State, however, is not entitled to insist on an increase in its market share in another country, over and above the WTO rules facilitate, however commendable the domestic cause may be. Thus, it may be legitimate to insist on fair, transparent, and non-discriminatory treatment in medical pricing and reimbursement policies (Korea and Japan). It may be legitimate to highlight the 'unauthorized disclosure, of test or other data generated to obtain marketing approval for pharmaceutical products' (China/India/Argentina/Saudi Arabia); the slow 'implementation of an effective mechanism for the early resolution of potential patent disputes' (China); and 'unreasonable regulatory approval delays.' But is it legitimate to ask for reform on 'patentability criteria, criteria for compulsory licensing' (India/Indonesia/Argentina); 'local manufacturing and use requirements' (Indonesia); a ban on imported pharmaceutical products and medical devices (Algeria); the pricing of patented pharmaceuticals (Canada/Japan/Korea/New Zealand)?

With respect to compulsory licencing the following is observed. First, the US alleges concern over the threat of the use of compulsory licences. It is not clear what the US means by 'threat.' Some 156 countries as of 2019 are reported to have compulsory licencing legislation in place.[40] Is having such a legislation per se a threat? Moreover, it is understandable for a State faced with a mighty multinational company as a negotiating strategy to engage against the backdrop of its legislation. It is the same approach that underpins the Special 301 process—ultimately the 'threat' of sanctions under Section 301 of the US Trade Act. Several countries have reported successful negotiations against the backdrop of their legislation on compulsory licencing resulting in substantial reduction of the prices of medicine.[41] Second, the contention that compulsory licencing will

> reduce incentives to invest in research and development for new treatments and cures, unfairly shift the burden for funding such research and development to American patients and those in other markets that properly respect IP, and discourage the introduction of important new medicines into affected markets

is a conclusion not backed at least in the Special 301 Report by evidence that demonstrates causal links. In fact, economic studies on this relationship are limited[42] to substantiate the claim. At best the evidence such as it is, is equivocal, at worst the causal connection depends on the specific circumstances involved. It is not possible to generalise.[43] Moreover, the amount of profits and/or the proportionality of the profits made by pharmaceutical companies generally is not factored into this discourse. Nor is there any indication that US pharmaceuticals will indeed invest in research that is relevant to that overseas market.

Third, the advice that 'governments should use compulsory licenses only in extremely limited circumstances';[44] and that the 'implementation of that exception, like any other exception, should strike a delicate balance, as an unrestrained application of that exception had potential to undermine patentee's rights, reduce incentives to invest in research and development for new inventions, unfairly shift

40 WIPO Standing Committee on the Law of Patents Draft Reference Document on the exception regarding compulsory licensing WIPO SCP/30/3 21 May 2019 para 72.

41 WIPO Standing Committee on the Law of Patents Draft Reference Document 21 May 2019 Part 7.

42 WIPO Standing Committee on the Law of Patents Draft Reference Document 21 May 2019 paras 223 and 229.

43 Ibid.

44 Special 301 Reports 2018/19/20.

the burden for funding such research and development to foreign markets and discourage the introduction of new important inventions'[45]—is advice that seeks to further reduce the mandated circumstances under the international legal system. In fact, States are entitled to implement fully and maximally their authority to introduce compulsory licencing. A much-commended study by WIPO on the international legal framework for compulsory licencing of patents documents the substantial State practice in the field of States having compulsory licencing legislation. This legislation is set against the backdrop of a State's right to have such legislation under general international law as informed by international agreements viz., the Article 5A (2) of the Paris Convention for the Protection of Industrial Property, and Articles 2.1, 31, and 31 bis of TRIPS.[46] Moreover, generally the international agreements do not restrict a State's freedom to 'determine the grounds upon which compulsory licences are granted under their respective laws.'[47] In State practice generally the grounds for compulsory licencing have been identified as follows: public interest; prevention of abuse of patent rights; public health; national security and emergencies.[48] Indeed, given the extent of this practice there is now a question as to whether this practice has crystallised under customary international law. In addition, the problem is not so much the restrictive use of this exception; rather it is the case that generally in State practice it is not being used enough.[49] In the light of this, the US may be more constructive by assisting countries in overcoming some of the practical obstacles that countries face in realising the potential of compulsory licencing to achieve their national development goals.

With respect to the unauthorised disclosure of data the Special 301 Reports do not provide evidence for the basis of the claims that a number of countries have been privy to the unauthorised disclosure of data obtained during the process of obtaining marketing approval. In the case of Argentina there is a bilateral investment agreement between the USA and Argentina yet there is not a single investment dispute brought against Argentina by any US pharmaceutical company based on this ground. If the local remedies were inadequate for this surely the much-extolled investor-State arbitration route would have been a fruitful venue for profit-driven US pharmaceuticals. In short, are the perceived market access impediments to American pharmaceuticals based on proper verifiable information obtained transparently with the consent of the foreign country and established under the legal system of the foreign State?

45 Statement made by US delegation at the WIPO Standing Committee on the Law of Patents Thirtieth Session, Geneva, 24–27 June 2019 SCP/30/11 PROV. 2.

46 WIPO Standing Committee on the Law of Patents Draft Reference Document on the exception regarding compulsory licensing WIPO SCP/30/3 21 May 2019 Part 3.

47 WIPO Standing Committee on the Law of Patents Draft Reference Document on the exception regarding compulsory licensing WIPO SCP/30/3 21 May 2019 para 9.

48 Ibid Part 1.

49 Ibid Part 6.

With respect to bans of certain pharmaceuticals and medical devices (Algeria) there can be justifications based on national security and human welfare, indeed even on moral grounds. In the case of Algeria, it was not a member of the WTO at the relevant time. In the same vein, with respect to the management of the pricing of pharmaceuticals, in particular patented ones (Japan/Korea/Canada/New Zealand), there can be sound public policy arguments for the management of the pricing of such items.

Transfer of Technology

With respect to transfer of technology the allegation is that pressure is brought on US companies to transfer technologies which act as market access barriers in trade and investment. Several examples of such measures are proffered in the Reports. This allegation seems to focus on China amongst other countries—coined as 'coercive technology transfer and local content policies' (China/Indonesia/Nigeria/Turkey).

In the Special 301 2020 Report reference is made to China's 'enforceable commitments to address forced technology transfer' in the China Economic and Trade Agreement (Phase One Agreement).[50] This agreement appears in important parts to be WTO incompatible insofar as the agreement is specific to both countries alone in the sphere of international trade that is covered in the WTO and that displaces the function of the WTO in matters concerned with the WTO. This includes provisions in Chapter 1 on Intellectual Property; Chapter 2 on Transfer of Technology; Chapter 6 on Expanding Trade; and Chapter 7 Bilateral Evaluation and Dispute Settlement. Of note is Article 7.6 in which both parties 'affirm their existing rights and obligations with respect to each other under the WTO Agreement and other agreements to which the Parties are party.' Can this provision give China the right not to honour any of the special concessions granted to the US that are specific to it and that contravene provisions in the WTO and therefore do not conform to the most favoured nation (MFN) in the WTO? Moreover, insofar as the enforcement of this agreement is concerned, this is only possible by the parties to this agreement within the framework of its dispute settlement system. This advantage is not available to third countries.

But the idea of the universalisation of this agreement as a general code on transfer of technology must be resisted. First, the circumstances of the conclusion of this agreement including the agreement itself is the result of undue pressure brought upon China. Ironically, this is an agreement that purports to ensure voluntary agreements in the sphere of transfer of technology without undue pressure. The agreement is unbalanced. For example, the agreement is replete with

50 Economic and Trade Agreement Between the Government of the United States of America and the Government of the People's Republic of China January 2020, <https://ustr.gov/sites/default/files/files/agreements/phase%20one%20agreement/Economic_And_Trade_Agreement_Between_The_United_States_And_China_Text.pdf> (last visited July 2020).

the assertion that 'The United States affirms that existing U.S. measures afford treatment equivalent to that provided' in the Articles/Chapters of the agreement. This is not necessarily an undertaking by the US to have identical obligations. There is no obligation contained herein to rectify that. What if the US obligations were not in fact 'equivalent'? Moreover, the affirmation is only with respect to existing US measures. Second, the agreement is unclear with respect to several issues in relation to technology transfer. It is not clear if it covers industrial espionage conducted by both parties. The agreement leaves it to both parties to choose 'appropriate methods of implementation';[51] and with respect to prosecution of relevant individuals the obligation is not stated in mandatory terms. In the same vein, it is not clear if China has been divested of its rights to compulsory licensing in the pharmaceutical sector given on the one hand Article 2.2 on the one hand, and Article 7.6 on the other.

Third, the agreement purports to divest/limit the capacity of a country to receive transfer of technology with adequate safeguards for the domestic industry concerned including the State itself. This could include its fiscal policy designed to attract transfer of technology through tax incentives; and the introduction of screening mechanisms of transfer of technology inflows to examine restrictive practices, e.g., in relation to imports of competing technologies, restrictions on adapting the technology to suit local conditions; to ensure the technology transfer is to the advantage of the acquiring State; and the use of local inputs to maximise the transfer.[52] A State is entitled to impose conditions for the entry of foreign investment. Moreover, a State is entitled to offer a price for the technology transfer, including directing its State-owned enterprises the terms upon which it should acquire technology. However, such conditions for market access for goods/services could contravene WTO obligations. The US has a record of using the WTO dispute settlement to ensure US IPRs are protected where there are market access issues generally. For this the WTO is the relevant form.

The discourse on transfer of technology in relation to China in the framework of the US–China trade war is set out in the Special 301 Reports; the subsequent US–China agreement 2020; in the WTO in a case brought by the European Union;[53] and in academe.[54] Herein the focus will be on academe and a recent thought-provoking article on the subject. In academe there is scholarship and there is also advocacy. Julia Ya Qin's recent work on 'forced technology' transfer in the context of the US–China trade war is a work that is strongly orientated in the latter, taking its cue from the recent US Section 301 retaliation against China. There are several difficulties with her paper. First and foremost, it relies on and gives

51 Article 1.34 of the US/China Agreement 2020.

52 These were concerns set out in the UNCTAD, 'Draft International Code of Conduct on the Transfer of Technology,' UN Doc. E/ 1990/ 94 (1990).

53 China – Certain Measures on the Transfer of Technology (DS549-2018).

54 Julia Ya Qin, 'Forced Technology Transfer and the US-China-Trade War: Implications for International Economic Law,' *Journal of International Economic Law* Vol. 22 No. 4 (2019) 743–762.

weight without reflection to information set out in the US Section 301 Report. Section 301 Reports and their basis are political in nature. There is therefore the need for caution in how they are to be understood. Moreover, it is puzzling that despite the literature on the legality of Section 301 and the consensus on the US Section 301 tariffs imposed by the US on China in the ongoing trade war, the author is prepared to characterise the legitimacy of the Section 301 tariffs imposed on China as comprising a mere 'apparent WTO-illegality.' All this in an article that seeks to introduce the rule of law and international regulations in the field of technology transfer. To further buttress the case the author points to the support of US concerns with respect to technology transfer from the European Union and Japan including the documentation of some FTAs wherein restrictive provisions in relation to technology transfer feature. This does not necessarily give legitimacy to the US arguments. The EU and Japan have a strong interest in restricting technology transfer and moreover FTAs are negotiated in an environment of give and take—indeed push. Much more significantly there is little accounting for the opinions of developing countries—surely an important stakeholder in this dear topic of concern to them! Second, the author characterises the issue as one involving the 'regulation' of transfer of technology. This is very much a West-centric approach and is premised on the assumption that transfer of technology needs restrictive regulation. In fact, transfer of technology is essentially a discourse that is and should and has always been set in the realms of a facilitative normative framework. It is principally concerned with the facilitation of the transfer of technology. This is the first premise. The secondary issue relates to the environment/conditions within which that transfer takes place—this is where concern for the legitimate safeguards for the holders/givers of transfer of technology are set. The issue of systemic importance is not the regulation of transfer of technology it is and continues to be the quest to formulate an effective normative framework to facilitate the transfer of technology. Third, the author contributes to the characterisation of the problem as one of 'forced technology transfer.' If there is a problem the problem is of unauthorised disclosure. This is not a 'new issue of systemic importance'. It was recognised as long ago as the TRIPS agreement, given the prohibition in TRIPS on unauthorised disclosure,[55] as well as in the work of UNCTAD as long ago as 1985.[56] But there are also here two evidential points that need to be highlighted. The existence of the unauthorised passing of information including the intent for the purposes of creating an unfair advantage has to be proven. If this information has been unlawfully obtained by a foreign power through e.g., intelligence sources, then perhaps the systemic problem is that of industrial espionage and the normative international challenge is its regulation. In the same vein the author relies on US claims of oral instructions to coerce technology transfer. But this has to be substantiated. Moreover, the coerciveness of these instructions (contra suggestions)

55 Article 39 of TRIPS.

56 UNCTAD, 'Draft International Code of Conduct on the Transfer of Technology' (1990).

has to be evaluated against the background of the parties involved and the degree of hierarchical relations between the parties. Fourth, the claim is that information is asked that is 'unnecessary for any legitimate regulatory purposes.' This is coincidently also set out in the US–China 2020 agreement.[57] But who decides what is necessary? And sometimes it may be necessary to have all the information in order to decide what is necessary. There may also be national security/health and public interest considerations that call for a full disclosure beyond the scope of the immediate regulation in question. Fifth, there is much ado about the Chinese commitments under its Protocol of Accession in particular Article 7 (3). This provision is very clear insofar as its reference to investment and technology transfer is concerned. A condition of technology transfer cannot be imposed *if there is a right of investment.* Article 7 (3) is relevant and operative only insofar as investment is concerned *if* there is a right of investment implicated, for instance, through a bilateral investment agreement or in the limited circumstances in which GATS has a bearing on investment issues. In general international law there is, as is repeatedly stated by West-centric writers on investment, no right of entry for foreign investment.

Sixth, the author constructs the disclosure through administrative practices as constituting 'disguised government expropriation' of foreign IPRs 'in violation of generally accepted international principles.' To this the following is to be noted. First, the protection afforded to foreign investment in general international law extends only to foreign direct investment and not to indirect/portfolio/intangible investment.[58] IPR protection in the investment sphere was initiated through its incorporation in investment agreements in the definition of investment. Moreover, if expropriation is to have been found to have taken place, would it be a regulatory expropriation not attracting any compensation? Second, the taking has to be attributable to the State. Merely eliciting information in administrative processing on its own is not sufficient; nor can joint venture requirements per se be characterised as acts of taking by the State. There has to be proven unauthorised disclosure. Not based on the mere assumption that because it is China this is a fair assumption. Seventh, the author asserts technology transfer requirements are 'in essence a policy of market for technology.' There is no market be it for trade or investment that is free and open in international law. Subject to WTO and investment agreements the level of market opening is negotiated in these agreements. Be that as it may, the purpose of transfer of technology is multi-fold viz., the development of a State; the redistribution of the world's resources in a more equitable manner; the sharing of a common heritage of mankind; the intrinsic merit of knowledge dissemination. To caricature the transfer of technology essentially in a transactional manner as a price for market access is to deflect from the responsibility of technology holders in sharing their knowledge includ-

57 Article 1 (9)(2).

58 M Sornarajah, *The International Law on Foreign Direct Investment*, 4th ed. (Cambridge University Press: 2017) at 11.

ing the more nuanced domestic reasons for technology transfer. Besides, if this is reduced to a matter of barter then difficult questions of calibration arise not to mention the fact that a country with a limited market capacity would become a poor purchaser in such a situation. In fact, the market perspective is that of the IPR exporter imputed on to the State technology receiver. This is the mindset of the private entrepreneur driven by cost benefit analysis. States have a wider, more long term, and nuanced a perspective. Moreover, only by constructing this economic analysis to transfer of technology can the monopsony characterisation of the State, which the author makes, is enabled. The State, however (unless it is directly involved), is not the purchaser in the so-called forced technology transfer circumstances—it is simply mediating in the transfer of technology. Therefore, this attribution of monopsony power is misplaced. In fact, whether or not the State exercises monopsony power or is simply negotiating a set of appropriate conditions for the investment— in economic analysis the actions of the State on potential investors is certainly amenable to a cost-benefit calculus in terms of the amount of investment or foregone investment. But economic analysis also has a function in measuring the profits foregone by the investor. However, the amount of investment foregone by the State is not the final measure of a transfer of technology policy. It is the value of the technology transferred to the State that is significant—not merely in terms of its economic benefits immediate or future but also the wider benefits to the country and its people. In other words, the economic calculation that focuses on potential forgone investment arising from such a policy is an argument intended to focus on the disadvantages of such a development policy. A focus on the benefits of transfer of technology as a policy tool to the State in question is about buttressing the case for transfer of technology. Eighth, the author argues that the US–China trade war is challenging the often used joint-venture approach to transfer of technology. This remains to be seen. Joint ventures as such have not been prohibited in the US–China agreement 2020. Moreover, it is not appropriate to extrapolate from the US–China trade war general principles for the use of joint ventures as a policy tool for development—let alone frankly suggesting a code from this distorted prism of 'forced technology transfer'. Finally, the author concludes that the level of development of a State has a bearing on the degree of competitive disadvantage for the foreign entrepreneur consequent upon the so-called 'forced transfer of technology' and therefore this should be reflected in the nature of the regulation of 'forced transfer of technology.' The economic analysis here is not convincing. Regardless of the level of development of the country, if there is a competitive disadvantage precipitated by 'forced transfer' for a foreign firm that disadvantage will be the same to the foreign firm regardless of the degree of the development of the State. It may be different if the level of development of the domestic competing industry reflects the level of development of the receiving country in question. The unfairness according to the author is located in the level of development of the State. In other words, it seems the author is arguing that the intrinsic merits of the justifications for transfer of technology are directly informed by the level of development of a State. But has the author not herein engaged in an intellectual leap from her arguments and concerns with respect to the fairness towards the foreign enterprise to fairness with respect to the State concerned in the receiving of the transfer of technology? This latter discourse is about international competition for economic superiority as between States. Objectively the arguments for transfer of technology are set not merely in a development discourse but also outside that context. To sum up—the author has only identified two examples of the so-called forced transfer of technology viz. information disclosure through administrative process and requirements of joint venture—omitting to mention industrial espionage presumably practiced by several States as well as non-State actors. The real problem here is about unauthorised disclosure not about transfer of technology. A serious discourse on a code for transfer of technology must take as its starting point the facilitative spirit of the challenge of transfer of technology as attempted in the work of UNCTAD.[59] It is not appropriate to relegate that valuable work as a passing footnote in a work that aspires to be the basis for a universal code on transfer of technology. Such a code cannot be informed/inspired by the disgraceful trade war that has unfolded in the history of multilateral trade relations between the US and China. Thus, discourse on transfer of technology is about development including sustainable development, about the nature of property rights, about redressing historic unjust enrichment, about the role of market forces in the availing of technology transfer, about distributive justice as it relates to technology transfer, and about the common heritage of mankind. To focus alone on certain concerns in the process of technology transfer is to engage in an incomplete discussion.

Conclusion

Generally Special 301 is a poorly drafted legislation. It seeks to introduce transparency but is itself questionably transparent. Crucially it is lacking in informed, expert, and empirically based inputs in economics, international law, and good governance. Above all it lends itself to being hijacked by the agenda of an executive—the subject of rent-seekers without the constitutional safeguards for those it is targeted at. Regrettably, its foundations are set in US might rather than international law and the rule of international law. The arrangements that come out of it in the end reflect the caricature of a US policeman kneeling on an innocent victim who is screaming ‘I cannot breathe but since you have your knee there I cannot but consent to your request.’

59 UNCTAD, ‘Draft International Code of Conduct on the Transfer of Technology’ (1990).

3 US Surveillance of Foreign Currency Exchange and Macroeconomic Practices[1]

'A State's foreign exchange policy cannot be solely informed by the concerns of another State.'

Introduction

The phenomenon of currency exchange manipulation has been of concern both in political and academic discourse as far back as the competitive devaluations during the Great Depression of the 1930s, and the subsequent establishment of the International Monetary Fund (IMF)[2] in 1945 to regulate the exchange rate practices of members of the IMF. In the same vein, in the regulation of the relationship between exchange rates and fair competition in international trade, GATT 1994 has provisions that focus on the impact of the level playing fields in international trade, including mutually reinforcing provisions in relation to the IMF mandate.[3] The IMF now focuses on exchange rates through the normative prisms of a discretionary exchange rate system, implemented mainly through regular annual country-specific surveillance exercises.[4] This focus forms an important mandate of the IMF. Of late, exchange manipulation has been the subject of the United States' (US) concern through a preoccupation with its trade deficit in relation to China.[5] To this end, the US has been operating a surveillance

1 This chapter is based on 'US Surveillance of Foreign Currency Exchange & Macroeconomic Practices,' *World Trade Review* Vol. 20 No. 5 (2021) 690–706. I am grateful to Nadia Rendak of the IMF Legal Department for her observations on an earlier draft of this chapter. The analysis, opinion, and errors, however, are those of this author.

2 Article 1 and IV of the Articles of Agreement of the IMF 1945 and its subsequent amendment in 1978 as it concerns the regulation of exchange rates.

3 Article XV of GATT 1994 and the Agreement on Subsidies and Countervailing Measures.

4 Article IV of IMF Articles of Agreement and IMF EB Decision No.15203-(12/72), 18 July 2012.

5 In August 2019 China was declared a currency manipulator under Section 3004 of the US Omnibus Trade and Competitiveness Act of 1988. This designation lasted until January 2020. Previously, China had been similarly declared in 1994. See Ana Swanson, 'The US Labeled China a Currency Manipulator: Here's What it Means,' *The New York Times* August 6 2019.

DOI: 10.4324/9781003047575-4

apparatus since 1988 in parallel with that of the IMF, involving the monitoring of exchange and macroeconomic practices of other States of concern to US trade. Clearly international trade and exchange rates have a causal relationship, which is addressed in varying degrees both in the IMF and the World Trade Organization (WTO). Moreover, the international monetary system is reliant on the US dollar. The US legislation is a symptom of the disaffection with the IMF and WTO order as it concerns exchange rates, in particular the soft nature of the IMF exchange rate regime, and the IMF's inability to enforce it effectively against advanced economies. The IMF has never found any member in violation of its exchange rate obligations under Article IV of its Articles of Agreement.[6]

Herein a critical legal focus is set out of the US surveillance apparatus. To this end, the relevant US legislation is examined along with the US monitoring and enforcement actions. This examination is set mainly against the backdrop of US obligations, generally under the IMF and the WTO. The focus in this chapter is not on the nature of the IMF or the WTO apparatus as these pertain to currency manipulation. There is ample focus on this as it is.[7] The nature and the efficacy of the disciplines in the IMF and WTO with respect to currency manipulation are of course relevant in shedding light on the US motivation for setting up its own unilateral machinery for managing currency manipulation.[8] Briefly, IMF disciplines with respect to currency manipulation, including the process involved in their enforcement, are considered inadequate. Moreover, the reference in GATT 1994 to the authority of the IMF in this sphere is considered to be a hindrance in the capacity of the WTO to respond to currency manipulation. However, this criticism of the Bretton Woods institutions whether or not warranted does not displace the need to focus on the US legislation in its own right against the backdrop of the general disciplines of the IMF and WTO. If *arguendo* the disciplines in the IMF and WTO with respect to the management of currency evaluation are considered to be flawed this does not render the other disciplines in these institutions including their overall architecture irrelevant. Indeed, in a legal appraisal of the US legislation the WTO and IMF disciplines on currency manipulation themselves are in a sense not relevant other than for the purposes of comparison and shedding light on the motivation for the US legislation. This chapter inevitably draws more on the IMF than the WTO, given the primacy of the IMF in

6 I am grateful to Nadia Rendak for pointing this out.

7 See for example Vera Thorstensen et al., 'Exchange Rate Measures: Who Judges The Issue—IMF or WTO?' *Journal of International Economic Law* Vol. 0 (2015) 1–20; C. Fred Bergsten and Joseph E. Gagnon, 'Currency Manipulation, the US Economy, and the Global Economic Order,' *Policy Brief*, Peterson Institute for International Economics (December 2012); and Aluisio de Lima-Campos et al., 'A Case for Misaligned Currencies as Countervailable,' UNCTAD XIII Pre-Conference Event Policy Dialogue: Redefining the Role of the Government in Tomorrow's International Trade (2012).

8 I am grateful to an anonymous referee for prompting me to include in this article this background to the US legislation on currency manipulation including writings that critique the IMF and the WTO in this respect.

this field, and the fact that the US legislation does not merely focus on currency manipulation *stricto sensu* but also that phenomenon in the context of foreign macroeconomic policy and practices. To reiterate it is not intended here to focus on what the scope and possibilities of IMF and WTO disciplines are, with respect to the management of currency manipulation practices.

The US Legislation on Currency Manipulation & Macroeconomic Practices

There are two sets of US legislation mandating a focus on foreign country currency practices including relevant macroeconomic policies. The Omnibus Trade and Competitiveness Act of 1988 (the 1988 Act) is a piece of legislation focusing on currency manipulation from a narrow standpoint, whereas the later legislation the Trade Facilitation and Trade Enforcement Act of 2015 (the 2015 Act), has a wider focus on currency practices so as include currency manipulation amongst other currency practices (sections 701–702).

The 1988 Act

The 1988 Act sets out three provisions dealing with the obligations of the US President multilaterally and bilaterally, including the setting up of reporting requirements to assist the President in the discharge of his obligations.

The President's Mandate under the 1988 Act

With respect to multilateral negotiations under Section 3004 (a), the US President:

> shall seek to confer and negotiate with other countries—(1) to achieve—(A) better coordination of macroeconomic policies of the major industrialized nations; and (B) more appropriate and sustainable levels of trade and current account balances, and exchange rates of the dollar and other currencies consistent with such balances; and (2) to develop a program for improving existing mechanisms for coordination and improving the functioning of the exchange rate system to provide for long-term exchange rate stability consistent with more appropriate and sustainable current account balances.[9]

This endeavour on the face of it seems fine. But it bypasses the IMF as a forum for raising such initiatives although it was specifically set up for this purpose. Even if it is accepted that the IMF has failed in its calling with respect to managing currency manipulation practices of its members, it is incumbent on its members, in particular the US, given its command of its share of the weighted voting in the

9 Section 3004 (a) of the 1988 Act.

IMF to work harder within the IMF and even harder to understand with humility the alternative standpoints of other members, in particular to see the extent to which they can be accommodated in achieving the common goals of the IMF. If the US can decide to take a unilateral path it can also decide to take a multilateral path. It is easy for the US to take a unilateral approach and justify that from its own utilitarian perspective, but the bigger question is whether this is a rational approach that considers the concerns of all its members and the long-term development of the international economic order. A coordinated macroeconomic policy amongst major industrialised groups can have an impact on the economies of non-major industrialised nations. In an interconnected world, it is questionable if it is appropriate to exclude a large group of nations in multilateral macroeconomic policy coordination. For example, a coordinated negative approach to quantitative easing can have an undesirable impact on investment flows in developing countries. However, the major industrialised nations are important in the impact they make on the international economy; and such an opportunity can indeed be availed with the US to discuss its macroeconomic policies, including any suggestion of the 'weaponisation' of the dollar and the replacement of the dollar by some other reserve 'currency' not subject to any form of potential or actual US politicisation as a medium of exchange. Moreover, of note here, insofar as exchange rate policy is concerned, States have agreed to follow exchange policies compatible with the undertakings set out under Article IV Section 1 of the Articles of Agreement of the IMF. Under this section, apart from the reference to manipulation of exchange rates in the context of effective balance of payments adjustment, there is no reference to 'appropriate and sustainable levels of trade and current account balances, and exchange rates of the dollar and other currencies consistent with such balances'.[10] Incidentally here 'sustainable levels' is not a reference to 'sustainable development'—in fact such a desideratum is consistent with the unsustainable use of the world's resources. The IMF[11] and the WTO[12] have both embraced the 2030 Sustainable Development goals.

The Mandate for Bilateral Negotiations for the US Secretary of Treasury under the 1988 Act

With respect to bilateral negotiations under Section 3004 (b), the US Secretary of the Treasury:

> shall analyze on an annual basis the exchange rate policies of foreign countries, in consultation with the International Monetary Fund, and consider

10 Section 3004 (a) (1) (B) of 1988 Act.

11 See <https://www.imf.org/en/Topics/SDG> (last visited August 2020).

12 See WTO, *Mainstreaming Trade to Attain the Sustainable Development Goals* (2018), <www.wto.org/english/res_e/publications_e/sdg_e.htm#:~:text=%22Mainstreaming%20trade%20to%20attain%20the,SDGs%2C%20just%20as%20it%20did> (last visited March 2021).

> whether countries manipulate the rate of exchange between their currency and the United States dollar for purposes of preventing effective balance of payments adjustments or gaining unfair competitive advantage in international trade. If the Secretary considers that such manipulation is occurring with respect to countries that (1) have material global current account surpluses; and (2) have significant bilateral trade surpluses with the United States, the Secretary of the Treasury shall take action to initiate negotiations with such foreign countries on an expedited basis, in the International Monetary Fund or bilaterally, for the purpose of ensuring that such countries regularly and promptly adjust the rate of exchange between their currencies and the United States dollar to permit effective balance of payments adjustments and to eliminate the unfair advantage. The Secretary shall not be required to initiate negotiations in cases where such negotiations would have a serious detrimental impact on vital national economic and security interests; in such cases, the Secretary shall inform the chairman and the ranking minority member of the Committee on Banking, Housing, and Urban Affairs of the Senate and of the Committee on Banking, Finance and Urban Affairs of the House of Representatives of his determination.[13]

It will be noted here, first, that the annual analysis of exchange rate policies focuses on all foreign countries. Second, the analysis involves establishing a *mens rea* for the manipulation for the purposes of preventing effective balance of payments adjustments or gaining unfair competitive advantage in international trade.

Third, whilst there is a requirement for consultation with the IMF, the analysis and consideration is ultimately the function of the US Secretary of Treasury. There is no obligation set to take on board the IMF perspective. This is reinforced by the mandate given to the Secretary of the Treasury to initiate negotiations with foreign countries found to be wanting independently of the IMF, if necessary. Thus, the US perspective on the Chinese exchange rate has been at variance with that of the IMF. However, the Fund has been powerless in the face of the weight of the US. Be that as it may, the determination under the legislation, as much as the legislation itself, raises questions of consistency with obligations of the US under the IMF. The US has, as have other members of the IMF, given the role of oversight of the international monetary system to the IMF as per Article IV. 3 (a) of the IMF Articles of Agreement as follows:

> The Fund shall oversee the international monetary system in order to ensure its effective operation, and shall oversee the compliance of each member with its obligations under Section 1 of this Article.[14]

13 Section 3004 (b) of the 1988 Act.
14 Article IV 3 (a) of the IMF Articles of Agreement.

Where a member engages in oversight activity unilaterally, this undermines the role of the IMF—indeed, it may even result in a conflict with IMF oversight operations and insights. In the same vein, if the US engages unilaterally with a member contrary to the IMF prescriptions, it would be non-compliant with its obligations to collaborate with the IMF under Article IV Section 1. Under this provision, there is a requirement that 'each member ***undertakes to collaborate*** with the Fund and other members to assure orderly exchange arrangements and to promote a stable system of exchange rates' (emphasis added).[15] Furthermore, the authority to determine currency manipulation rests solely with the Fund.[16] The significance of this 'authority' is twofold. First, the US has accepted this authority as part of its obligations as a member of the IMF. Second, the location of this authority as such is indispensable to an objective determination of a currency manipulation. The obligation to cooperate with the Fund is also reinforced under Article XV Sections 1 and 2 of GATT 1994. Were this determination to be at the behest of individual members of the IMF concurrently the very integrity of the policy underpinning the prohibition on currency manipulation would be undermined with any country levelling a claim against another of currency manipulation informed by subjective and varied criteria to that of the IMF.

Fourth, the US has in its sights not only a country that is engaging in currency manipulation but in particular it is interested in ensuring currency rate adjustments where 'manipulation is occurring with respect to countries that (1) have material global current account surpluses; and (2) have significant bilateral trade surpluses with the United States.' Neither of these conditions partake of the IMF definition of currency manipulation;[17] nor are they symptomatic of currency manipulation in themselves. The discourse amongst economists as to the relationship between these two conditions and currency intervention is not clear and divided.[18] The US use of a monetary technique to induce a trade restrictive objec-

15 Article IV Section 1 of the Articles of Agreement of the IMF.

16 See IMF Executive Board Decision No. 15203-(12/720, 18 July 2012, Annex paragraphs 1–2: 1. Article IV, Section 1(iii) of the Fund's Articles provides that members shall 'avoid manipulating exchange rates or the international monetary system in order to prevent effective balance of payments adjustment or to gain an unfair competitive advantage over other members.' The language of this provision is repeated in Principle A contained in Part II of this Decision. The text set forth below is designed to provide further guidance regarding the meaning of this provision. 2. A member would only be acting inconsistently with Article IV, Section 1(iii) if the Fund determined both that: (a) the member was manipulating its exchange rate or the international monetary system and (b) such manipulation was being carried out for one of the two purposes specifically identified in Article IV, Section 1(iii).

17 Article IV Section 1 (3) and Executive Board Decision No. 15203-(12/720), 18 July 2012.

18 See for example Anwar Sheikh & Isabella Weber, 'The U.S.-China Trade Balance and the Theory of Free Trade: Debunking the Currency Manipulation Argument,' March 2020, Working Paper Series No. 505, Political Economy Research Institute, University of Massachusetts, Amhurst, USA; Rebecca M Nelson, 'Debates over Exchange Rates: Overview and Issues for Congress,' US Congressional Research Service, June 22 2018; Romesh Vaitilingam, 'Does Currency Manipulation Explain US Trade Deficits?' *Chicago Booth Review* 29

tive brings its legislation in the domain of a disguised restriction in international trade. Moreover, where these two conditions coincide with currency manipulation as the sole basis for US-instigated adjustment, an asymmetrical and discriminatory approach to the enforcement of currency manipulation would result—not to mention that the US approach assumes it is appropriate to analyse a bilateral relationship of currencies in clinical isolation with other currencies (including reserve currencies) and trading relationships.

Fifth, there are no clear criteria to discern the exchange rate that would 'permit effective balance of payments adjustments and to eliminate the unfair advantage.'[19] There are no clear criteria to determine the precise degree of currency misalignment with actual market exchange rate. Such ambiguity may or may not also exist within the IMF. However, if this is the case it is no justification to replicate here.

Sixth, there is discretion afforded to the US Secretary of the Treasury to treat countries differently if to the US 'a serious detrimental impact on vital national economic and security interests would ensue.' This is a curious provision that allows for a wide measure of political discretion to come into play. The logic including the causal relationship between manipulation of exchange rates, balance of trade surpluses/current account surpluses, and the restraint on counter measures to correct these perceived maladies informed by national economic/ security interests is not very apparent.

Reporting Requirements under the 1988 Act

With respect to the reporting requirements, the Secretary of the US Treasury is to prepare a written report annually 'on international economic policy, including exchange rate policy' as per Section 3005 of the 1988 Act. The initial report is to be followed by an update six months later. The report is to reflect the following content:[20]

> Each report submitted under subsection (a) shall contain—(1) an analysis of currency market developments and the relationship between the United States dollar and the currencies of our major trade competitors; (2) an evaluation of the factors in the United States and other economies that underline conditions in the currency markets, including developments in bilateral trade and capital flows; (3) a description of currency intervention or other actions undertaken to adjust the actual exchange rate of the dollar; (4) an assessment of the impact of the exchange rate of the United States dollar on—(A) the ability of the United States to maintain a more appropriate and sustainable

June 2019, <https://review.chicagobooth.edu/economics/2019/article/does-currency-manipulation-explain-us-trade-deficits> (last visited August 2020).

19 See for example Anwar Sheikh & Isabella Weber, ibid.

20 Section 3005 of the Omnibus Trade and Competitiveness Act of 1988.

> balance in its current account and merchandise trade account; (B) production, employment, and noninflationary growth in the United States; (C) the international competitive performance of United States industries and the external indebtedness of the United States; (5) recommendations for any changes necessary in United States economic policy to attain a more appropriate and sustainable balance in the current account; (6) the results of negotiations conducted pursuant to section 3004; (7) key issues in United States policies arising from the most recent consultation requested by the International Monetary Fund under article IV of the Fund's Articles of Agreement; and (8) a report on the size and composition of international capital flows, and the factors contributing to such flows, including, where possible, an assessment of the impact of such flows on exchange rates and trade flows.

The range of considerations to be focused upon here are an appropriate basis of analysis for a country. However, the focus on the

> impact of the exchange rate of the United States dollar on— (A) the ability of the United States to maintain a more appropriate and sustainable balance in its current account and merchandise trade account; (B) production, employment, and noninflationary growth in the United States; (C) the international competitive performance of United States industries and the external indebtedness of the United States

is itself a focus on the US dollar exchange rate, and the degree to which it can be adjusted/manipulated to achieve US targets as per A, B, and C above. The concern here is that in an analysis of a foreign currency exchange rate manipulation the degree to which the US dollar could be manipulated to achieve desirable US macroeconomic targets is factored in.

Conclusion—1988 Act

In sum, there is no transparent focus here on the meaning of currency manipulation, leaving the US a wide measure of discretion to bring to bear pressure on third countries to serve its political and economic interests. If, as a consequence of the US actions under this legislation currency adjustments are inflicted upon third countries that have no basis in sound economic analysis and that result in fact in a form of 'currency exchange manipulation' by the US, there is a call for an examination of the US actions under the WTO Agreement on Subsidies.[21] In the same vein, Article XV Section 3 of GATT 1994 prohibits a WTO member through 'exchange action,' to 'frustrate the intent of the provisions of'

21 See for an explanation as to whether currency undervaluation can constitute a prohibited subsidy Aluisio de Lima-Campos et al., op. cit.

GATT 1994 or 'by trade action, the intent of the provisions of the Articles of Agreement of the International Monetary Fund.' The exchange adjustment required by the US of a third country can be construed as 'exchange action' attributable to the US.[22]

The 2015 Act—Enhanced Engagement with Major Trading Partners

The 2015 Act Title VII is entitled 'Engagement on Currency Exchange Rate and Economic Policies.' In particular, Section 701 focuses on the 'Enhancement of engagement on currency exchange rate and economic policies with certain major trading partners of the United States.' The enhancement involves the following. First, the Secretary of the US Treasury is to compile a report on a regular basis with respect to the currency exchange rate and economic policies of certain major trading partners of the United States. Each report is to contain information of (i) US major trading partners as follows:[23]

(I) that country's bilateral trade balance with the United States;
(II) that country's current account balance as a percentage of its gross domestic product;
(III) the change in that country's current account balance as a percentage of its gross domestic product during the 3-year period preceding the submission of the report;
that country's foreign exchange reserves as a percentage of its short-term debt; and
(IV) that country's foreign exchange reserves as a percentage of its gross domestic product; and

(ii) an enhanced analysis of macroeconomic and exchange rate policies for each country that is a major trading partner of the United States that has—(I) a significant bilateral trade surplus with the United States; (II) a material current account surplus; and (III) engaged in persistent one-sided intervention in the foreign exchange market.

This is a more elaborate list of elements to be focused on than those set out in the 1988 Act. In particular, those major trading partners who satisfy the three conditions in Section 701 (ii) (I) to (III) above are the subject of enhanced analysis of their macroeconomic and exchange rate policies. In the 1988 Act only the first two conditions trigger more interest. These have already been commented upon. The 2015 Act adds 'persistent one-sided interventions' assuming

22 See for an interpretation of Article XV of GATT 1994 Thorstensen et al., op. cit. See also on the difficulties of interpretation of 'exchange action' including the scope for its interpretation GATT L/332/Rev.1 and Addenda, adopted on 2, 4 and 5 March 1955, 3S/170, 196, para. 2. 0.

23 Section 701 (a) 2 (A) of the Trade Facilitation and Trade Enforcement Act of 2015.

there is evidence of this. There are no thresholds set out in the legislation itself for these three conditions. However, the US Treasury has added its elaboration which it revised recently in 2019 as follows.[24] First, the US will 'assess all U.S. trading partners whose bilateral goods trade with the United States exceeds $40 billion annually.' Second, the three thresholds in the criteria have been increased as follows:

> (1) A significant bilateral trade surplus with the United States is one that is at least $20 billion. (2) A material current account surplus is one that is at least 2 percent of gross domestic product (GDP). (3) Persistent, one-sided intervention occurs when net purchases of foreign currency are conducted repeatedly, in at least 6 out of 12 months, and these net purchases total at least 2 percent of an economy's GDP over a 12-month period.[25]

In relation to the third condition the following further elaboration is proffered:[26]

> Other patterns of intervention, with lesser amounts or less frequent interventions, might also meet the criterion depending on the circumstances of the intervention.

There is no apparent clear explanation for these particular thresholds in terms of their relevance specifically to currency manipulation and unfair competitive advantages. It is clear, however, that these thresholds have been identified to ensure the capture of a maximum number of US trading partner of US interest. Thus, it is stated:[27]

> In 2016, the $20 billion bilateral trade surplus threshold captured almost 80 percent of the value of all trade surpluses with the United States, while the 3 percent current account threshold captured more than three fourths of the nominal value of global current account surpluses.

The trade surplus only pertains to trade in goods not services. The explanation given by the US Treasury, set out in a footnote of the various reports, for this speaks for itself! It is as follows:[28]

> Given data limitations, Treasury focuses in this Report on trade in goods, not including services. The United States has a surplus in services trade with

24 US Treasury Department's Semi-Annual Report to Congress: Macroeconomic and Foreign Exchange Policies of Major Trading Partners of the United States, October 2017. Hereinafter referred to as 'Reports'.
25 May 2019 Report.
26 October 2017 Report.
27 Ibid.
28 See for example ibid.

many economies in this report, including Canada, China, Japan, Korea, Mexico, Switzerland, and the United Kingdom. Taking into account services trade would reduce the bilateral trade surplus of these economies with the United States.

It is not clear how difficult the data limitations are to overcome. Certainly, omitting services could be said to be like the US practice of zeroing facilitating the desired trade effect. Moreover, such evidential concerns have not prevented the US from proceeding certainly when it is to its advantage. Thus, not all countries are transparent for various reasons about their frequency and degree of currency interventions yet this has not prevented the US from including it as a criterion for evaluating its trading partners for enhanced evaluation.

Second, the enhanced analysis for each country should include:[29]

(i) a description of developments in the currency markets of that country, including, to the greatest extent feasible, developments with respect to currency interventions;
(ii) a description of trends in the real effective exchange rate of the currency of that country and in the degree of undervaluation of that currency;
(iii) an analysis of changes in the capital controls and trade restrictions of that country; and
(iv) patterns in the reserve accumulation of that country.

It will be noted (i) and (ii) need to be descriptive only whereas (iii) and (iv) involve analysis. Moreover, here there is no reference to 'currency manipulation' for the purposes of 'preventing effective balance of payments adjustments or gaining unfair competitive advantage in international trade.' And the 'real effective exchange rate' is not informed by economic fundamentals of the country but in accordance with a statutory definition determined with reference to 'a weighted average of bilateral exchange rates, expressed in price-adjusted terms.' In sum, the 2015 Act simply sets out a set of macroeconomic variables which if found to exist draw on the US interest.

Third, it is a requirement of both the 1988 and 2015 legislation that the US Treasury make available semi-annual Reports on the foreign exchange policies of the major trading partners of the United States. Under the 2015 Act this involves compiling a Monitoring List. A country meeting at least two of the three criteria is placed on the Monitoring List. Once on the list it will remain on it for two consecutive reports. Furthermore, under the Trump administration a trading partner would be placed on the Monitoring List 'that accounts for a large and disproportionate share of the overall U.S. trade deficit even if that economy has not met two of the three criteria from the 2015 Act.'[30] Under

29 Section 701 (a) 2 (B) of the Trade Facilitation and Trade Enforcement Act of 2015.
30 October 2017 Report.

the 2015 Act in April 2017 the list comprised China, Japan, Korea, Taiwan, Germany, and Switzerland; and in October 2017 the list comprised China, Japan, Korea, Germany, and Switzerland. No major partner was found wanting under the 1988 Act in 2017. In 2018 China, Japan, Korea, Germany, Switzerland, and India were on the list under the 2015 Act. No major trading partner was found wanting in 2018 under the 1988 Act. Following the revised thresholds by the Treasury of the criteria under the 2015 Act in May 2019 the following countries were on the list: China, Japan, Korea, Germany, Italy, Ireland, Singapore, Malaysia, and Vietnam, although no major partner of the US was found wanting in terms of the 1988 Act. However, in August 2019 China was found wanting under the 1988 Act. The 2020 list comprised of China, Japan, Korea, Germany, Italy, Ireland, Switzerland, Singapore, Malaysia, and Vietnam with no country found wanting under the 1988 Act, China having been removed under the 1988 Act as a manipulator in 2020 following a US–China agreement. In sum, the list of countries on the Monitoring List under the 2015 Act has been growing: from six in 2017 to ten in January 2020.

Fourth, based on the report prepared, the President, through the US Secretary of Treasury, is to engage in bilateral negotiations with the trading partner for whom an 'enhanced analysis of macroeconomic and currency exchange rate policies' has been prepared.[31] Remedial measures can follow the negotiations. The negotiations involve impressing upon the trading partner the following:[32]

(A) urge implementation of policies to address the causes of the undervaluation of its currency, its significant bilateral trade surplus with the United States, and its material current account surplus, including undervaluation and surpluses relating to exchange rate management;
(B) express the concern of the United States with respect to the adverse trade and economic effects of that undervaluation and those surpluses;
(C) advise that country of the ability of the President to take action under subsection (c); and/or
(D) develop a plan with specific actions to address that undervaluation and those surpluses.

It will be noted here too the narrative of a bilateral trade surplus is conflated with undervaluation. Moreover, given that both exchange rates and a bilateral trade surplus are expressions of a relationship between two economies there is no reference to the actions that could be taken on the US side of this relationship. The negotiations are about what the trading partner should do—there is no scope with respect to the propriety and correctness of the determinations made through the enhanced analysis. The full cost of the reorientation of the relationship is to be borne by the trading partner under the ever-presence of US threats.

31 Section 701 (b) 1 of the Trade Facilitation and Trade Enforcement Act of 2015.
32 Ibid.

Remedial Actions under 2015 Act

Section 701 subsection (c) is titled Remedial Actions. It sets out the range of options available at the disposal of the President, if there is a determination that the country in question has 'failed to adopt appropriate policies to correct the undervaluation and surpluses' as follows:

(A) Prohibit the Overseas Private Investment Corporation from approving any new financing (including any insurance, reinsurance, or guarantee) with respect to a project located in that country on and after such date.
(B) ...prohibit the Federal Government from procuring, or entering into any contract for the procurement of, goods or services from that country on and after such date.
(C) Instruct the United States Executive Director of the International Monetary Fund to call for additional rigorous surveillance of the macroeconomic and exchange rate policies of that country and, as appropriate, formal consultations on findings of currency manipulation.
(D) Instruct the United States Trade Representative to take into account, in consultation with the Secretary, in assessing whether to enter into a bilateral or regional trade agreement with that country or to initiate or participate in negotiations with respect to a bilateral or regional trade agreement with that country, the extent to which that country has failed to adopt appropriate policies to correct the undervaluation and surpluses described in subsection (b)(1)(A).

This is an assorted list of possible remedial actions of varying degree of effectiveness. Paragraph A could involve the hindering of foreign investment given that it includes insurance and guarantees. This could affect investment agreements or chapters in free trade agreements between the US and other countries depending on the provisions of those agreements. Paragraph B would need to be considered against the background of the WTO Government Procurement Agreement including in particular (Article IV non-discrimination, and Article XVIII), to which the US is a party. This prohibition is, however, qualified by two specific provisions. First, the prohibition may not be applied 'in a manner that is inconsistent with United States obligations under international agreements.' And second, the prohibition may not apply where 'such prohibition would subject the taxpayers of the United States to unreasonable cost.' Paragraph C assumes that the US has ownership of the IMF and can through its Executive Director force any decision on the membership of the IMF. This is not the case despite the weighted voting system in the IMF and the US command of the veto with respect to certain important decisions. The US can only exhort the Fund to act in a certain manner. Moreover, in any event the conceptions of IMF and US 'currency manipulation' are at variance. Paragraph D involves either inflicting trade agreements on third countries or undoing binding existing international commitments undertaken by the US under pressure.

Fifth, generally the requirement to take remedial actions can be waived at the behest of the President if 'the President determines that taking remedial action under paragraph (1) would— (i) have an adverse impact on the United States economy greater than the benefits of taking remedial action; or (ii) would cause serious harm to the national security of the United States.

Advisory Committee on International Exchange Rate Policy under the 2015 Act

Finally, to assist the US Secretary of Treasury an Advisory Committee on International Exchange Rate Policy has been set up.[33] The US President has an important say in the composition of this committee. This, prominence of the executive branch in the organisation of the US monetary policy in the sphere of foreign exchange rates—underlined as it is with the involvement of the President and US Treasury Secretary in both the 1988 and 2015 legislation—is to be contrasted with the received wisdom in the IMF and the practice of many Central Banks, to accord autonomy and independence to such organs, in the making of monetary policy decisions, thus insulating them from the vicissitudes of domestic politics—at any rate when this is focused exclusively internally.[34] There are surely sound reasons why this paradigm of Central Bank operations should have relevance to US monetary policy (including exchange rate) functions as it relates to the domain of foreign monetary/exchange rate policy making. Moreover, the US Reports themselves are littered with the mantra that foreign exchange interventions should be exceptional; and *a fortiori*, that the foreign exchange system should essentially be market driven. The market prescription is about the insulation of foreign exchange management from external considerations.

The Reports of the US Treasury Macroeconomic and Foreign Exchange Policies of Major Trading Partners of the United States

The US Treasury started issuing the Macroeconomic and Foreign Exchange Reports when the 1988 Act came into effect.[35] Over the years, however, the reports seem to have grown in length and information. In this focus the reports since October 2017 to January 2020 set out on the US Treasury website are used as the basis of some observations on the US practice of monitoring the exchange

33 Section 702 of the Trade Facilitation and Trade Enforcement Act of 2015.

34 See for instance 'Central Bank Accountability, Independence, and Transparency,' November 25 2019 IMFBLOG at <https://blogs.imf.org/2019/11/25/central-bank-accountability-independence-and-transparency/> (last visited August 2019).

35 Not all the reports, however, seem to be available in electronic form on the US Treasury website. Thus, in the April 1989 Report there is a reference to Korea and Taiwan having been found to have manipulated their currencies as set out in the October 1988 Report. This report is not available electronically.

rate practices of foreign countries. The reports contain analysis and conclusions under both the relevant US Acts.

International Agreements

US concern with respect to the manipulation of currency exchange finds expression not only in the 1988 and 2015 Acts but also in international agreements. By way of example, first is the USMCA[36] which has a Chapter 33 titled 'Macroeconomic Policies and Exchange Rate Matters' concerned with the regulation of exchange rates in the framework of a free trade agreement. It mainly sets out in hortatory terms an affirmation/reiteration on the one hand of obligations set out in Article IV of the IMF Articles of Agreement. On the other hand, it could be seen to be departing from the IMF system in that it calls for a market-determined exchange rate, whereas the exchange rate system advanced in the IMF for members is a discretionary system of exchange rates, giving the members the choice as to whether for example they want to have a fixed or a floating exchange rate system. However, noting a market exchange rate could in the long run necessitate a readjustment to a fixed exchange rate system. Equally, Chapter 33 preserves the autonomy of the States in the regulation/supervision of the parties to the USMCA in the monetary/fiscal and related fields as it affects exchange rates. The chapter has binding obligations relating to transparency and reporting with respect to interventions in the exchange rates, and exchange reserves. Finally, it sets up a Macroeconomic Committee with a mandate for the coordination of macroeconomic policies of the parties to USMCA to meet on a regular basis; provides a basis for bilateral consultations; and with respect alone to transparency obligations avails of the dispute settlement system under USMCA.

In sum, Chapter 33 has been set up as a template for inclusion in other free trade agreements (FTAs). As such it calls for some scrutiny. First, the normative framework involves a collective appreciation of macroeconomic and exchange rate policies unlike the approach adopted in the 1988 and 2015 Acts. This is a commendable approach although somewhat diminished by the inclusion of bilateral consultations. Second, the inclusion of Chapter 33 genre of clauses in FTAs generally could cause pockets of bilateral/regional macroeconomic and exchange rate regimes that depart from the multilaterally agreed IMF framework. They could also raise questions under Article XV (4) of GATT 1994, in particular if they frustrate the intent of any of its provisions. Third, a bilateral/regional approach to macroeconomic and exchange rates could impact on third parties. Does such an approach displace IMF oversight of such cooperation? Elsewhere this author has written at length on this.[37] First, of note is that IMF law applies

36 Agreement between the United States of America, the United Mexican States, and Canada (2019).

37 See 'International Legal Aspects of "Monetary" Relations in North East Asia,' Chapter 5 in Asif H Qureshi, *Contextualising International Law in Northeast Asia* (Hart: 2018).

to these arrangements independently of the reference to it in them. Second, the IMF is obligated to cooperate 'within the terms' of its agreement with other international organisations such as the WTO. This is reinforced by the obligation under Article XV of GATT 1994 that GATT Contracting Parties 'shall not, by exchange action, frustrate' the intentions of the provisions of GATT 1994. Moreover, the guidelines approved under an IMF Executive Board decision state:[38]

> The Fund, given its responsibilities in the rates, can contribute to assessing issues of coherence between macroeconomic and trade policies. The Fund can also contribute to greater policy coherence by taking into account in its work the concerns of the WTO in the trade area.

Third, the Fund has a wide mandate 'to oversee' the international monetary system in order to ensure its effective operation including compliance with Article IV Section 1 obligations (which include the obligation to avoid manipulating exchange rates).

The second normative US innovation is to be found in the US/China Economic Trade Agreement 2020.[39] Chapter 5 of this is titled 'Macroeconomic Policies and Exchange Rate Matters and Transparency,' and mirrors somewhat Chapter 33 of USMCA. The parties reaffirm obligations set out in the IMF and G20 Communiqués; and emphasise a market-determined exchange rate. The chapter also has a transparency provision set out in obligatory terms. The substantive provisions are accompanied by an enforcement mechanism under the agreement's general Bilateral Evaluation and Dispute Resolution Arrangement. Of note Chapter 5's focus on transparency does not refer specifically to the reporting of currency exchange interventions although Chapter 33 of USMCA does.

In sum, both Chapter 33 USMCA and Chapter 5 US/China are mainly reaffirmation of existing IMF obligations on exchange rates with transparency-related obligations. The UMCA, however, has a more developed coordinating mechanism for macroeconomic and exchange rate policy coordination. Both these instruments are not at the moment the subject of the kind of criteria set out in the US 1988 and 2015 legislation. The agreements, however, as discussed above undermine the role of the IMF as the principal multilateral organisation charged with the oversight of exchange rates and macroeconomic coordination.

Substantive Issues

Generally, US focus on exchange rates and macroeconomic coordination raises two important substantive questions. First, the criteria under the 2015 Act focus

38 IMF EB Decision No. A-9786-(93/20) as amended.

39 Economic and Trade Agreement Between the Government of the United States of America and the Government of the People's Republic of China 2020.

on certain countries for enhanced analysis only, if their trade exceeded certain thresholds.[40] These thresholds mainly calibrate exports to the US for the purposes of triggering US monitoring, leading potentially to the imposition of certain sanctions. Such a calibration can amount to a quantitative restriction under the WTO and as such trigger its jurisdiction. Article XI of GATT 1994 reads in relevant part as follows:

> 1. No prohibitions or restrictions other than duties, taxes or other charges, whether made effective through quotas, import or export licences or other measures, shall be instituted or maintained by any contracting party on the importation of any product of the territory of any other contracting party or on the exportation or sale for export of any product destined for the territory of any other contracting party.

The criteria triggering US interest is a restriction under Article XI of GATT 1994 for the following reasons. First, it is a clear enunciation of a US policy that considers a certain level of exports to the US as being objectionable on grounds that are not justifiable under the WTO. Second, it has a chilling effect[41] on those countries caught under this calibration. Third, it results in the countries involved having to engage with the US, in the provision of certain information with respect to their exchange rates and discussion of their macroeconomic policies. Fourth, this engagement or non-engagement can involve the country being castigated as a 'currency manipulator,' or being placed under what is essentially a 'negative' monitoring list. Finally, the countries are the subject of macroeconomic policy advise proffered by the US under a cloud of potential sanctions.

Moreover, such a targeting of certain countries alone is discriminatory contrary to GATT 1994 most-favoured-nation principle. Article I of GATT specifically refers to 'any advantage, favour, privilege or immunity granted by any contracting party to any product originating in or destined for any other country shall be accorded immediately and unconditionally to the like product originating in or destined for the territories of all other contracting parties.' There is here an advantage that countries trading with the US whose trade is not above a certain threshold are receiving, an advantage which is not being accorded unconditionally to the countries under the monitoring list.

Second, there is much ado by the US about publication of foreign-exchange interventions by its major trading partners in the reports. Some countries on the US Monitoring List have acceded to the US pressure and agreed to publish their foreign exchange interventions e.g., Korea from 2019. Notable examples of countries that do not are China and Switzerland, although China has agreed in

40 See May 2019 Report.

41 United States – Sections 301–310 of the Trade Act of 1974, Report of the Panel, paras 7.88–7.90; and Thailand – Customs and Fiscal Measures on Cigarettes from the Philippines Second Recourse to Article 21.5 of the DSU by the Philippines, Report of the Panel T/DS/371/RW2 para 7.164.

the US/China 2020 Phase One agreement to publish 'relevant data' that could shed light on interventions—but not specifically foreign exchange interventions. The question of a priori transparency in foreign-exchange interventions of course has a prudential aspect set in confidentiality informed by its impact on the market. Leaving that aside there is here a question as to whether there could conceivably be sound justifications for being opaque on grounds of national security. In the WTO there is a national security exception under Article XXI of GATT 1994 that permits non-disclosure by a 'contracting party to furnish any information the disclosure of which it considers contrary to its essential security interests.' In the IMF a member is obligated to provide certain information necessary for the Fund's activities under Article VIII Section 5 of the IMF Articles. This does not mean that a member needs to publish the information. Moreover, Article VIII Section 5 does not expressly authorise the withholding of information that it requires on national security grounds. However, the Fund has interpreted with respect to exchange restrictions Articles VIII and XIV to permit a Member to impose exchange restrictions for the preservation of national and international security.[42] There is no general security exception as such spelt out in the IMF Articles of Agreement, and the Executive Board Decision that refers to national security is focused on exchange restrictions, and not with reference to disclosure of information in relation to interventions in the foreign exchange market. Is it possible then to interpret Fund law to allow for data on currency intervention even if post-facto to be withheld on national security grounds?[43] There are sound reasons for suggesting that the Fund law allows for non-disclosure of currency interventions on security grounds. First, the Fund's Executive Decision on currency restrictions on national security grounds is a generous interpretation of the Articles, in contrast to the stricter WTO national security exception, in particular as it has now been interpreted.[44] A member merely has to notify the Fund if it considers in its judgement that there is a national security reason for the imposition of the restriction. The reasons for the national security exception as stated in the EB Decision are not intrinsic to currency restrictions rather the Fund set out the following reasons for its decision:

> The Fund does not, however, provide a suitable forum for discussion of the political and military considerations leading to actions of this kind. In view of the fact that it is not possible to draw a precise line between cases involving only considerations of this nature and cases involving, in whole or in part, economic motivations and effects for which the Fund does provide the appropriate forum for discussion.

42 See IMF Executive Decision No. 144-(52/51), August 14, 1952.

43 Needless to say disclosure that would hamper the objective of the intervention in the first place (leaving aside national security concerns) would not be forthcoming nor expected.

44 Russia – Measures Concerning Traffic in Transit – Panel Report WTO DS/512 (2019).

Given this rationale it can be argued that this decision or its underlying direction extends and/or can be extended to data on foreign currency exchange interventions in particular given that foreign currency interventions can deliver the same impact as a currency restriction. The same reasoning is embedded in the Fund's EB Decision on Surveillance,[45] wherein with respect to currency manipulation, a member is given the benefit of reasonable doubt with respect to representations made by the member about its exchange rate policies. Second, the furnishing of data on currency interventions is conspicuously absent in the albeit non-exhaustive list of information required under Article VIII Section 5. Third, the defence of necessity under Customary International Law (CIL)[46] which is available for national security is not displaced by any of the Articles of Agreement of the IMF. Moreover, the Fund law is to be interpreted as per Article 31 (3) (c) of the Vienna Convention such as to take into account the defence of necessity under CIL.

There may be a case for withholding information on currency interventions especially in extreme circumstances. First, a country with large reserves in a reserve currency such as the dollar may have an interest in preserving the value of those reserves in relation to its own currency given the amounts at stake. Second, economic and political rivalry—indeed trade wars—may create a circumstance of distrust, particularly when there are no codes governing the manner in which a leading reserve currency that the rest of the world avails of is managed.[47] This is underlined by the fact that there is international concern that a leading reserve currency has been understood to have been weaponised and/or having the capacity to be weaponised.[48] In those circumstances States may well feel inclined to have the capacity to respond in kind to a weaponisation of a reserve currency through covert currency interventions. Third, transparency in foreign exchange interventions could result in a country self-incriminating itself on a number of fronts.

Against this background the US insistence on transparency in foreign exchange interventions undermines the basic right of a State not to disclose information on grounds of national security as per IMF and WTO regimes, not to mention customary international law. In sum, the US unilateral insistence on such disclosure does not comfortably sit with international norms.

Due Process Aspects

A number of observations may be made with respect to the process involved in the US surveillance of foreign currency exchange and macroeconomic practices. First, the threshold criteria set by the USTR under the 2015 legislation is the subject

45 EB Decision No. 15203-(12/72), July 18, 2012.

46 Article 25 of the ILC Draft Articles on State Responsibility.

47 See this author, 'International Legal Aspects of "Monetary" Relations in Northeast Asia', Chapter 5 in *Contextualizing International Law in Northeast Asia*, op. cit., 147–155.

48 See Julius Sen, 'The Weaponization of the Dollar: Policy Options for Small Countries,' *LSE Ideas!* August 2019, <https://www.lse.ac.uk/ideas/Assets/Documents/updates/LSE-IDEAS-Weaponisation-Dollar.pdf> (last visited August 2020).

of change without advance notice. Thus, the goalposts seemed to be moved suddenly in May 2019. Second, where data on foreign currency interventions are not available to the US the determinations are made based on estimates. It would be reasonable to assume that these are generally overestimates even though the reports state they may be under or over. Estimates can be the basis for placing the burden of proof on the other side in the sphere of taxation when the State has an incomplete account of a taxpayer. However, the use of such a mechanism in international relations amongst sovereign States, in particular when the consequences can be serious for individuals in an economy, is unfortunate. Third, the process of evaluation lacks a structure for independent and objective evaluation of economic data based on the possibility of a fair input by all the parties concerned.

Fourth, the criteria set under the 2015 Act is fundamentally flawed, leaving aside questions of compatibility with international law. The objective of the Act is to identify a relevant pool of countries of 'significance' to the US—whose currency exchange rate and macroeconomic policies could have an unfair advantage for US competitors and US balance of payments. Nevertheless, any trading partner regardless of the criteria set, can be the subject of US interest as stated variously in the reports:[49]

> As a further measure, this Administration will add and retain on the Monitoring List any major trading partner that accounts for a large and disproportionate share of the overall U.S. trade deficit even if that economy has not met two of the three criteria from the 2015 Act.

This gloss on the criteria not only raises questions about compatibility with the 2015 legislation itself but partakes of arbitrariness. It begs the question as to the purpose of the criteria set in the Act and the thresholds grafted upon it by the US Treasury.

Moreover, the criteria enunciated in the legislation with respect to exchange rates and macroeconomic policies of third countries is fundamentally flawed given that the whole analysis to the extent that it is not arbitrary, derives from the prisms of trade and exclusively from the US balance of trade. An important premise of the legislation is so flawed that it calls into question the very validity of the Act in terms of the due process involved in its enactment.

Fifth, and related, the criteria focus on interventions in the foreign exchange market in terms of frequency and amounts. However, what is significant is not the frequency or amounts as the actual impact on the foreign exchange rates of the interventions. Sixth, a balance of payments is a relationship between a country and the rest of the world or in this case with certain countries. It is a relationship that has two dimensions—the US and the other trading partner. The analysis requires as thorough a look at the US policies on exchange rates and its macroeconomic policies as that of the trading partner. This also involves a consideration of the

49 May 2019 Report.

US dollar as a leading reserve currency and the advantages that this entails for the US economy and the management of its macroeconomic policies. Alas the reports are short in their analysis of the US in this respect. Seventh, reliance on IMF in the reports is eclectic—resorted to suit the US analysis, and absent or short when it is not convenient, for example in the case of China. Seventh, the US focus is on the balance of trade as it relates to trade in goods alone. In a footnote alone is this acknowledged including the fact that in some cases the overall balance may well be different if services were factored in. The absence of a more thorough analysis of the services sector in a discourse on balance of payments has the effect of skewing the conclusions. Eight, the focus is on a country's foreign exchange reserve in relation to GDP and as a percentage of short-term debts. These are certainly the elements that feature in the discourse on the adequacy of currency reserves. However, in passing it is to be noted that the size of a population can be a factor in informing the demand for reserves.[50] Finally, the reports contain repeated references to historic practices, for example that China and Korea have a long history of undervaluation. Yet the historical antecedents are not important to an objective analysis of what is taking place currently. Moreover, this copy past approach from past reports casts a negative light on the quality of the analysis in the reports generally.

US Policy Advice to Countries on its Monitoring List

The US policy advice is focused on reducing the trading partners' trading surplus with the US in goods. To this end the US presumes to give advice to the countries on its Monitoring List as to how (1) the country might generate internal demand to capture the 'exports' within the country; (2) reduce its foreign currency reserves; (3) increase market access for US goods for instance by eliminating restrictive practices and subsidies. Thus, the US advises countries to implement fiscal reforms in particular reducing taxes, having broad tax bases, and increasing public sector spending, for example by expanding the social safety net in health care/unemployment and pension. Similarly, there is focus on monetary policy, in particular limiting interventions in the currency market to 'truly exceptional circumstances of disorderly market conditions.'[51]

In fact, the US Treasury has interpreted Section 3004 of the 1988 Act as to give authority to analyse[52]

> a broad range of factors, including not only trade and current account imbalances and foreign exchange intervention (criteria under the second piece

50 See for example Bank for International Settlements, 'The Size of Foreign Exchange Reserves,' BIS Papers chapters, in Bank for International Settlements (ed.), *Reserve Management and FX Intervention* Vol. 104 (2019) 1–23.

51 See for example advice to Korea in all the reports between 2017 and 2020.

52 See for example January 2020 Report.

> of legislation…), but also currency developments, the design of exchange rate regimes and exchange rate practices, foreign exchange reserve coverage, capital controls, monetary policy, and trade policy actions, as well as foreign exchange activities by quasi-official entities that may be undertaken on behalf of official entities, among other factors.

This is a very broad range of considerations that touch upon the mandate of the IMF and the WTO (including consistency with those regimes) and also that raise questions as to the conformity of this interpretation with the 1988 Act itself.

In this advice there is no critical self-evaluation. The macroeconomic focus on others is essentially from the US trade deficit perspective. There is no reference to the IMF advice to these countries, that would be set in IMF surveillance exercises of these countries. The advice touches on important State macroeconomic reins from a standpoint of US self-interest.

Conclusion

In conclusion the level of US focus on certain vital macroeconomic variables of a third country is significant, and the potential call for adjustments to be made by the third country can be wide-ranging and intrusive. The focus of the two pieces of relevant legislation on other countries' exchange rate regimes is essentially US trade interest centred, lacking a sound economic basis whilst challenging and undermining existing multilateral institutions, the rule of international economic law and due process at the level of the management of foreign economic relations as it affects third countries and the residents of those countries. It is far from clear if this is a process that is about ensuring a level playing field in international competition. The entire enterprise reeks of politics!

Finally, does such a legal perspective serve any purpose? After all the Trump administration has now been widely understood as not caring about deferring to the rule of international economic law. However, the two Acts considered herein predate the Trump administration. And therefore, the critique here is not of a passing phenomenon. Moreover, scholarship calls for a rigorous analysis and legal exposition for the annals of history. Legal analysis serves not only to account, to challenge but also to shame and condemn.

Elements of the US legislation raise questions both under the IMF and the WTO. Indeed, they even raise questions about the adequacy of these institutions in managing such issues. And in this latter context, it should be acknowledged here that the linkage with trade is also a very potent tool for the enforcement of level playing fields in the field of currency exchange, given the enforcement deficiencies in these institutions.

This chapter is not intended as a legal opinion, rather it is a modest scholarly contribution. Therefore, the question of whether a claim should be made, given the questions raised, and under which institution a claim is best brought, are questions that need not be spelt out here.

4 A Public International Law Perspective of the US National Security Approach to Foreign Trade[1]

'A State's sense of its national security is no longer its exclusive business.'

Introduction

In international economic relations, the scope of what constitutes national security is being expanded as well as challenged. This phenomenon is magnified by the power and size of some national economies and exacerbated by fierce economic competition between them. National security has both an internal and external focus, with the potential of having significant negative consequences on the international economy, in particular important trading partners. The nature and scope of this focus, whilst being dynamically contingent upon political, technological, and economic developments, is essentially rooted in State sovereignty.

The relationship between economic interests and national security concerns is not new and stretches over the historical annals of our times. National security, however, is the Achilles' heel that threatens the insulation of international economic relations from politics, and thus economic development. The national authority to intervene in international economic relations is found in disparate sources: in the inherent exercise of sovereign powers of a State at the international and domestic levels; in the discretion afforded to the executive of a State in the conduct of foreign affairs, as set forth in domestic constitutions; in ad hoc pieces of legislation responding to particular national security occasions; and now, increasingly institutionalised in legislation specifically concerning international trade in goods and services and foreign investment.[2] Historically, the building blocks of national security have been deliberately formulated in an open-ended manner, and reinforced by a general lack of accountability and transparency in the manner in which they are availed.[3] Moreover, the historical backdrop

1 This chapter is based on 'A Public International Law Perspective of Section 232 of the U.S. Trade Expansion Act,' *Kansas Journal of Law and Public Policy* Vol. 3 No. 3 (2021).

2 See for example Trade Expansion Act of 1962 § 232, 19 USCA § 1862 (West).

3 National security is a part of a State's foreign policy, which hitherto has been the preserve of the sovereign/executive.

DOI: 10.4324/9781003047575-5

of national security was set with reference to conventional warfare of a different era. Generally, modern wars, whether in the form of a conventional or nuclear war, tend to be relatively more short-lived than conflicts in the past. In the same vein, foreign policy has historically been concentrated in the hands of the sovereign or executive.[4]

In the contemporary, democratic era—whilst this trend has been restrained of late through some legislative oversight of the executive in some constitutional practices—the integration of national economic concerns into the national security phenomenon is alarming. An absence of economic protection in the context of national security has been likened to 'economic disarmament.'[5] The normative ambiguity in the legislation and the concentration in the location of national security power with the executive is exacerbated by the duality in the functional nature of goods, services, and technology. It is similarly affected by flexible interpretations of relevant timescales, which are precipitated by the inclusion of national economic concerns.

Despite the domestic practice, in the United States (US) and globally of using this sovereignty-based prism, an international perspective must bring to bear a normative focus that reduces its scope. This focus cannot take its cue from either a domestic or international legal system. Rather, this focus must incorporate considerations that facilitate a fair and efficient relationship between both systems. National security can operate at the interface between the national and international. Discourse therefore must be both at the *lex lata* and *lex feranda* levels—in particular, the latter given that the authority to manage national security has historically had few parameters.

Like all domestic laws, the authority to manage national security must conform to certain basic constitutional safeguards and expectations of good governance. Constitutional safeguards require adherence to the separation of powers doctrine, including the checks and balances of legislative or judicial oversight of the executive.[6] Unnecessary domestic obstacles to such oversight, for example, absolute judicial deference to executive determinations of national security must be removed such that legislative and judicial bodies can scrutinise executive decisions. This is now the case in the sphere of trade and investment in the international setting.[7] If a national security decision could be scrutinised

4 See for example Ernst-Ulrich Petersmann, 'How to Constitutionalize International Law and Foreign Policy for the Benefit of Civil Society?' *The Michigan Journal of International Law* Vol. 20 No. 1 (1998) 25.

5 Mona Pinchis-Paulsen, 'Trade Multilateralism and U.S. National Security: The Making of the GATT Security Exceptions,' *The Michigan Journal of International Law* Vol. 41 (2020) 109–135 (looking at US internal deliberations on the scope of national security).

6 See Ernst-Ulrich Petersmann, 'National Constitutions and International Economic Law,' in *National Constitutions and International Economic Law* Vol 8. No. 3 (1993) 8–34.

7 See Panel Report, *Russia–Measures Concerning Traffic in Transit*, WTO Doc. WT/DS512/R (adopted April 5, 2019) [hereinafter *Traffic in Transit*]; *LG&E Energy Corp. v. Arg. Republic*, ICSID Case No. ARB/02/1, Decision on Liability, (Oct. 3, 2006), 11 ICSID Rep. 411

at the international level, domestic legislative and judicial bodies would be in dereliction of their oversight responsibilities if they did not avert a justifiable international disapprobation. In addition, good governance[8] requires an up-to-date, consensus-based, clearly articulated national security mandate. However, this may not be in the national legislative priorities at the relevant time. Many national security mandates may be set in constitutions or legislation of a different era and are not appropriate for modern systems of governance and armed conflicts.

Moreover, not only must there be transparency with respect to the mandate, but also in its operation—such that there is a paper trail of accountable, justifiable decision-making. In the case of goods, services, and technology it must be evident to foreign entrepreneurs in advance of their international trade and investment decisions as to what falls within and outside a State's national security. The operation of the national security mandate must conform to certain qualitative standards such as the rule of law, efficiency, equity, and proportionality. This means, for instance, that there must be an objective rationale that is non-discriminatory in its operation and impact. Market integrity and fair play must not be displaced without strong justification based squarely on the exigencies of national security.

Against this background, the following discussion is focused on US national security legislation viz., Section 232 of the Trade Expansion Act of 1962, as it concerns international trade in goods and services (excluding petroleum imports). This legislation is the subject of the current trade war between the US and China as it has unfolded in the World Trade Organization (WTO).[9] The legislation

(2007); *Cont'l Cas. Co. v. Arg. Republic*, ICSID Case No. ARB/03/9, Award, (Sept. 5, 2008), 18 ICSID Rep. 155 (2020).

8 Good governance 'is participatory, consensus oriented, accountable, transparent, responsive, effective and efficient, equitable and inclusive and follows the rule of law.' 'What is Good Governance?' *U.N. Econ. & Soc. Comm. for Asia & the Pac.* (July 10, 2009), <https:// www .unescap.org/sites/default/files/good-governance.pdf> [https://perma.cc/3UQM-8TAC] (last visited February 2022).

9 See Dispute Settlement, *United States–Certain Measures on Steel and Aluminum Products*, WTO Doc. WT/DS544/11 (Feb. 8, 2021); Dispute Settlement, *United States–Certain Measures on Steel and Aluminum products*, WTO Doc. WT/DS550/R (July 11, 2019); Dispute Settlement, *United States–Certain Measures on Steel and Aluminum Products*, WTO Doc. WT/DS548/17 (Feb. 8, 2021); Dispute Settlement, *United States–Certain Measures on Steel and Aluminum Products*, WTO Doc. WT/DS547/11 (Feb. 8, 2021); Dispute Settlement, *United States–Certain Measures on Steel and Aluminum Products*, WTO Doc. WT/DS551/R (July 11, 2019); Dispute Settlement, *United States–Certain Measures on Steel and Aluminum Products*, WTO Doc. WT/DS552/13 (Feb. 8, 2021); Dispute Settlement, *United States–Certain Measures on Steel and Aluminum Products*, WTO Doc. WT/DS554/20 (Feb. 8, 2021); Dispute Settlement, *United States–Certain Measures on Steel and Aluminum Products*, WTO Doc. WT/DS556/18 (Feb. 8, 2021); Dispute Settlement, *United States–Certain Measures on Steel and Aluminum Products*, WTO Doc. WT/DS564/18 (Feb. 8, 2021).

has also sparked scholarly discourse recently; consisting essentially of American 'navel-gazing.'[10]

Literature Review

This recent discourse entails a number of strands herein briefly summarised. First, the rationale and the historical antecedents of the legislation as described by scholars.[11] That legislation and its amendments were set mainly in the Cold War era, and thus somewhat outdated. Second, Section 232 has been analysed in terms of the ambiguous definition of 'national security,' thus highlighting the possibilities of differing political interpretations.[12] Third, there has been a focus on the procedures involved in the invocation and implementation of Section 232, including the methodology to establish how a particular good is estimated to be in short supply, in times of war, with reference to specific investigations.[13]

Fourth, US Constitutional doctrines—such as the separation of powers and the constitutional balance between the executive and legislative branches, the non-delegation doctrine and the protections against the executive exceeding its authority—have been brought to bear on the operation of Section 232.[14] In the US, the power to make national security decisions under Section 232 is primarily in the hands of the executive.[15] This power has historically been justified by the understanding that the executive branch can make decisions quicker and has a better understanding of international affairs than the legislature.[16] Moreover, it is contended that the executive needs authority over the application of tariffs to be more credible in discourse with adversaries.[17] On the other hand, it has been

10 See David D Knoll, 'Section 232 of the Trade Expansion Act of 1962: Industrial Fasteners, Machine Tools and Beyond,' *The Maryland Journal of International Law* Vol. 10 (1986) 55–59 (1986); Kathleen Claussen, 'Trade's Security Exceptionalism,' *The Stanford Law Review* Vol. 72 (2020) 1097–1164; Kayla Scott, 'Steel Standing: What's Next for Section 232?' *Duke Journal of Comparative & International Law* Vol. 30 (2020) 379, 439–440; Pinchis-Paulsen, op. cit., 190–192; David Scott Nance & Jessica Wasserman, 'Regulation of Imports and Foreign Investment in the United States on National Security Grounds,' *The Michigan Journal of International Law* Vol. 11 (1990) 926, 985–986; Richard Levine, 'Trade vs. National Security: Section 232 Cases,' *A Compensation Strategy* Vol. 7 (1998) 133, 141.

11 See Levine, op. cit., 134–136; Nance & Wasserman, op. cit., 930–931.

12 Nance & Wasserman, ibid, 935.

13 Levine, op. cit., 135–136.

14 See Scott, op. cit., 392–410; Claussen, op. cit., 1162.

15 See Arim Jenny Kim, 'The Untouchable Executive Authority: Trump and the Section 232 Tariffs on Steel and Aluminum,' *University of Miami Business Law Review*. Vol. 28 (2019) 176, 185–188. See for example Jonathan Masters, *US Foreign Policy Powers: Congress and the President*, Council On Foreign Rel.: *Backgrounder* (March 2, 2017), <https://www.cfr.org/backgrounder/us-foreign-policy-powers-congress-and-president> [https://perma.cc/DSV2-UW8B] (last visited February 2022).

16 Ibid.

17 Claussen, op. cit., 1133–1134.

suggested that because tariffs have an impact on the domestic economy the legislature is the better place for such discourse.[18] Equally, it has been pointed out that in practice the US legislature has more scrutiny over trade liberalisation policy than over the exercise of the national security exception.[19] The scholarship, however, does not delve into the need for foreigners to have similar constitutional safeguards extended to them.

Fifth, there has been some theoretical justification of Section 232 with reference to how it supports, rather than undermines, the ethos of liberal trade that the international trading system is based on.[20] International trade and national security are complementary, it is contended, rather than contradictory as assumed in received wisdom.[21] National security is a necessary condition for liberal trade. Economic sanctions forestall the use of armed conflict that could be more dangerous to the international trading system. Moreover, the national security exception serves to facilitate entering into international agreements as it embodies the assurance that if anything goes wrong the country is protected with this exception.[22]

Finally, of late there has been a growing focus on Section 232 from a WTO perspective given the recent challenges in the WTO with reference to steel and aluminium imports to the US.[23]

Explanations for the Lack of Public International Law Analysis of Section 232

There has been little, if any, analysis of Section 232 within the context of public international law by which the US is bound. Such an analysis brings to bear the wider set of principles and concepts that exist in public international law. There are many explanations for the lack of this analysis. One explanation is the belief, as asserted by one US analyst, that 'in classical international law…states have an unfettered discretion to determine their national security needs and to act in accordance with that determination.'[24] This understanding, as it informs contemporary international law, is highly controversial. First, it is not consistent with State practice and *opinio juris* necessary for its normative claim.

Second, the assertion that there is 'unfettered discretion' empowering the State to act in accordance with its determination, does not coincide with the well-established international law principle of State sovereign equality. One State does not have unfettered discretion to shape the 'equality' of another State, let alone

18 Scott, op. cit., 404–405.
19 See Claussen, op. cit., 1142–1143.
20 See ibid.; Knoll, op. cit., 58.
21 See for example Raj Bhala, 'National Security and International Trade Law: What the GATT Says, and What the US Does', *University of Pennsylvania Journal of International Economic Law* Vol. 19 (1998) 263, 264–265.
22 Claussen, op. cit., 1134–1135.
23 Scott, op. cit., 381–382, 436; Pinchis-Paulsen, op. cit., 112–113.
24 Knoll, op. cit., 83.

the international community of States, through its own national security legislation. Finally, the history of the national security exception, as applied to international agreements, does not support this belief.[25] For example, interpretations of the national security exception in the WTO have not reinforced the belief that States have unfettered power.[26] Indeed, the influence of the US in the negotiations of the national security exception in the General Agreement on Tariffs and Trade (GATT) of 1947 did not have such an understanding of national security under Customary International Law.[27]

Third, some scholars suggest that economic independence is included in any conception of national security.[28] This line of reasoning is supported by the international law principles of self-determination and State sovereignty. However, such a conception, couched in absolute terms, is somewhat flawed. Economic independence can certainly involve a sense of national security, but economic independence can also be secured and achieved by delegating national security concerns to external entities or engagements,[29] or for example, stockpiling on essential commodities.

Such cursory allusions to general international law principles without further consideration could be attributed to the US' parochial approach to US standing in international relations. To be more generous, this approach could also be a consequence of the fact that the national security phenomenon is often considered solely from the very narrow perspective of international trade law.

Unexplored Dimensions of the National Security Exception

From an international law and policy perspective, there are four dimensions of the national security exception that are generally relatively unexplored. One dimension is the impact of the protective actions taken under the national security exception on foreign non-State actors. Such restrictions obviously have economic consequences for trading, including consumer concerns in other States. However, this point does need emphasising since national security is often analysed from an internal perspective alone. Thus, a cost-benefit analysis of economic sanctions on national security grounds is typically considered, if at all, in terms

25 See for example General Agreement on Tariffs and Trade Article XXI, Oct. 30, 1947, 61 Stat. A-11, 55 U.N.T.S. 194, as amended by Marrakesh Agreement Establishing the World Trade Organization, Apr. 15, 1994, Annex 1A, 1867 U.N.T.S. 190, 33 I.L.M. 1125 [hereinafter GATT].

26 *Traffic in Transit*, op. cit., paras 7.102–7.104.

27 See Pinchis-Paulsen, op. cit., 116, 148; *Traffic in Transit*, op. cit., para 7.100.

28 See Claussen, op. cit., at 1140–1141 (citing John Gerard Ruggie, 'International Regimes, Transactions, and Change: Embedded Liberalism in the Postwar Economic Order,' *International Organization* Vol. 36 (1982) 379, 393–398).

29 Curtis A Bradley & Judith G Kelley, 'The Concept of International Delegation,' *Law and Contemporary Problems* Vol. 71 (2008) 1, 17 (illustrating delegation of peacekeeping duties to NATO); see also Karl Raustiala, 'Rethinking the Sovereignty Debate in International Economic Law,' *The Journal of International Economic Law* Vol. 6 (2003) 841, 845.

of the domestic impact on domestic industry and consumers, not its external economic consequences.

Yet, the impact can be directly on the exports of foreign domestic industries. In particular, the impact can be serious for long-established, export-oriented concerns having built a comparative advantage in the exports. The impact of resorting to the national security exception can be abrupt and unpredictable given that the apparatus for resorting to the national security exception within a State is often non-transparent and without adequate checks and balances. The mechanisms for an *a priori* (let alone a *post facto*) input for those foreign interests negatively affected in domestic proceedings are not foreign-friendly, to say the least. In addition, there can be indirect consequences on the exports of third-party countries in another market, which could be displaced by the diversion of exports from the sanctioned exporter. In the same vein, an exporter taking advantage of economies of scale would, with the export restrictions, need to downscale, and therefore the cost of production may increase for the supply in the domestic market of the exporter.

In sum, there are serious external consequences of economic nature for exporters on the receiving end of a national security-based import restriction. These economic consequences call for reflection on the choice of responses based on national security. They are relevant in evaluating whether the choice of response is appropriate, proportionate, and causally connected with the threat. A conception of national security that encapsulates the viability of the national economy, regardless of the external economic consequences empowering itself for 'coercive,' albeit economic responses, harken back to an era of imperialism and national self-aggrandisement. International law has, in many respects, cut the wings of such imperialistic practices but by no means all.

The second dimension is whether one nation's national security has normative consequences on the behavior of foreign concerns. A national security restriction can result in the characterisation of an entity by its foreign activity, process, or good—be it of an economic, political, or other nature—being cast in a negative light, and thus compel behavioral and locational changes or identity transformations extraterritorially. Even when the foreign activity, process, or good has an innocent connotation, its characterisation as a threat can introduce changes in economic behaviour. Moreover, given the nature of the national security justification, the presumption of association with another State, especially in a planned economy, can be difficult to rebut for the foreign enterprise. In sum, national security has an extraterritorial reach with 'chilling' consequences inducing a change in non-State behavior externally. Such extraterritorial reach may or may not be justifiable in terms of national security under international law. It may be justifiable under the protective base of extraterritorial exercise of jurisdiction. However, the protective base for the exercise of extraterritorial jurisdiction has hitherto been confined to matters that are an existential threat to a State. Thus, national security that is concerned with the welfare and development of the national economy may not be a proper basis for the exercise of jurisdiction where the temporal connection with the threat to the State is distant.

In the same vein, reliance on the effects doctrine[30] may not necessarily be that easy given that resort to it must conform to a 'reasonableness test.'[31] Under this 'reasonableness test,' a State may exercise prescriptive jurisdiction if the exercise is not unreasonable.[32] Reasonableness factors include, among others, considerations such as whether there is a substantial, direct, and foreseeable effect; the innocence of the character of the activity; whether a justifiable expectation exists that is protected under the WTO; and whether the activity could have a detrimental effect on the regulation of the international political, legal, or economic system.[33] There is some controversy in international law as to the limits of a State's legislative jurisdiction. Leaving that discourse aside for the moment, is there a conflict between the international law on the exercise of legislative jurisdiction and the defence of national security? Could the exercise of state jurisdiction, contrary to international law, in such circumstances, be justified under the defence of necessity? Perhaps, but only if it conforms to the parameters set under international law for the invocation of such a defence.[34]

A third dimension is that there is much ado in the discourse on national security that its definition and scope is essentially in the domain of the State. This may well be the case from the internal, domestic perspective. Here, it is important to note that national security has a purely domestic dimension with an international focus. Insofar as national security in the international context is concerned, it

30 See Restatement (Fourth) of Foreign Rel. L. of the US § 409 cmt. a (The American Law Institute 2018) (explaining the effects doctrine is when '[a] state may exercise prescriptive jurisdiction with respect to conduct occurring outside its territory that has an effect within its territory that creates a genuine connection between the conduct and the prescribing state').

31 Restatement (Third) of Foreign Rels. L. of the US § 403 (Am. L. Inst. 1987) ('(1) Even when one of the bases for jurisdiction under s 402 is present, a state may not exercise jurisdiction to prescribe law with respect to a person or activity having connections with another state when the exercise of such jurisdiction is unreasonable; (2) Whether exercise of jurisdiction over a person or activity is unreasonable is determined by evaluating all relevant factors, including, where appropriate: (a) the link of the activity to the territory of the regulating state, i.e., the extent to which the activity takes place within the territory, or has substantial, direct, and foreseeable effect upon or in the territory; (b) the connections, such as nationality, residence, or economic activity, between the regulating state and the person principally responsible for the activity to be regulated, or between that state and those whom the regulation is designed to protect; (c) the character of the activity to be regulated, the importance of regulation to the regulating state, the extent to which other states regulate such activities, and the degree to which the desirability of such regulation is generally accepted; (d) the existence of justified expectations that might be protected or hurt by the regulation; (e) the importance of the regulation to the international political, legal, or economic system; (f) the extent to which the regulation is consistent with the traditions of the international system; (g) the extent to which another state may have an interest in regulating the activity; and (h) the likelihood of conflict with regulation by another state.').

32 Ibid.

33 Ibid.

34 See *Report of the International Law Commission on the work of its fifty-third session*, 56 U.N. GAOR Supp. No. 10, at 193, U.N. Doc. A/56/10 (2001), reprinted in [2001] 2 Y.B. Int'l L. Comm'n 177, U.N. Doc. A/CN.4/SER.A/2001/Add.1.

touches on the very question of the continued existence of statehood. In a sense, it involves the very notion of statehood in international law—indeed, an assertion of statehood. In international law, the criteria for statehood are set out in terms of objective conditions, as well as external perceptions of the fact of statehood viz., recognition.[35] The objective conditions are fundamental but basic. The aspect of statehood that is informed by external perceptions is a feature of international law that plays a similar role in other respects as well. Thus, whilst international law leaves it to the State to determine the criteria for nationality, its external recognition is based on a genuine link.

Two inferences can be drawn from the international law criteria for statehood and diplomatic protection on behalf of nationals. First, national security is defined with reference to a state, defined as a 'permanent population'; territorial integrity of the state; governance of the state; and the capacity of the state to enter into legal relations.[36] Its scope, in fact, is informed by these criteria which focus on the existence of the state, *qua* state in an existential sense. Second, given the conceptual affinity of statehood with national security, the scope of national security is in some measure a function of the legitimacy it commands in international relations, and generally the corpus of the international legal system as a whole. In short, the national security basis for protectionist measures, if it is to command legitimacy in its extraterritorial impact, must remain within the parameters of the considerations that go into defining statehood under international law.

Recent jurisprudence in the WTO[37] and investment arbitration,[38] albeit in the context of security exceptions set out in these international agreements, affirm the justiciability of the national security exception. Also, the introduction of subjective-objective criteria informing the notion of essential national security interests of a state reinforces the point being made here, namely that the scope of the national security exception has to command legitimacy in international relations.

The fourth dimension is that there has to be some correlation between the regulation of a State's use of force under international law and a State's use of economic sanctions to respond to national security exigencies. Both are responses to national security threats, unilateral measures, and are considered legitimate under international law. Both the national rationale and the international objectives of regulation are the same. Moreover, in some circumstances, the impact of economic sanctions can arguably have the same effect as the use of force. In the same vein, economic wars can lead to armed conflicts. The underlying rationale for confining the use of force to self-defence and restricting actions to anticipatory defence is to ensure international peace and security and encourage resort to

35 See Montevideo Convention on the Rights and Duties of States Articles 1, 3, 6 (Dec. 26, 1933), 49 Stat. 3097, 165 L.N.T.S. 19.

36 Ibid. Article 1.

37 See for example *Traffic in Transit*, op. cit.

38 See for example *LG&E Energy Corp. v. Arg. Republic*, ICSID Case No. ARB/02/1, Decision on Liability (Oct. 3, 2006), 11 ICSID Rep. 411 (2007).

peaceful and proportionate methods for resolving disputes. The same considerations underpin much of the international economic order. Importantly, both the IMF and WTO regimes eschew unilateralism.

Connection Between the National Security Exception and a Nation's Use of Armed Conflict

The national security exception's association with armed conflict begs a number of questions. First, can the international regulation on the use of force be thwarted in legal analysis through economic measures? For example, international law prohibits an armed attack (unless in self-defence), let alone a pre-emptive strike on another state.[39] But, what about economic measures that effectively cripple the other State's economy and have the same impact as an armed attack? The law of armed conflict, which in some respects predates international economic law and parallels it, would not prohibit such economic measures. And in so far as the received wisdom is concerned, international economic law at a general level is underpinned by the freedom of the state to determine its foreign, economic relations, including the right to self-determine its economic system and its sovereignty over its natural resources.[40] However, as is well understood now, normative regimes in international law do not exist in 'clinical isolation from public international law.'[41] Therefore, constraints on a State's use of force under international law are relevant in informing what the nature of the disciplines is in the use of national economic measures to impact a foreign state, if any.

Second, can the principles underpinning international law on the use of force fill gaps in the regulation of economic sanctions? For example, offensive (contra defensive) economic measures to harm another state invites the question of whether the underlying principles of the prohibition on the use of force, viz., the obligation to peacefully settle disputes and not to cause unwanted harm to another State, have a bearing on the circumstances. They may also have a bearing on the interpretation of treaty-based trade and monetary disciplines.

Third, are there lessons to be drawn from international law on the use of force (including international humanitarian law) when considering international regulation of economic responses on grounds of national security? Certainly, there

39 U.N. Charter Article 2, para. 4; ibid. Article 51. Leaving aside, for the moment, any discourse on the legality of a pre-emptive strike.

40 G.A. Res. 3201 (S-VI), Declaration on the Establishment of a New International Economic Order (May 1, 1974).

41 See for example Appellate Body Report, *United States–Standards for Reformulated and Conventional Gasoline*, 17, WTO Doc. WT/DS2/AB/R (adopted Apr. 29, 1996); *Report of the International Law Commission to the General Assembly*, 61 UN GAOR Supp. No. 10, at 406, UN Doc. A/61/10 (2006), reprinted in [2006] 2 Y.B. Int'l L. Comm'n 177, UN Doc. A/CN.4/SER.A/2006/Add.1.

are.[42] International law concerning the use of force prohibits offensive use of force and prescribes a proportionate use of force in self-defence only. Also, under international humanitarian law, the use of certain types of weapons is prohibited and a distinction is made between civilians and combatants.[43]

In the same vein, economic responses to national security threats, as well as conceptions of national security, must in some measure be informed by the time and proportionality requirements set for responses similar to those required for self-defence in international law. Responses must also be set qualitatively in 'good faith,' which is already an expectation where treaty obligations are concerned.[44] National security should be conceived as being threatened or affected in the same manner as an 'armed attack.' The same conception should also exist in circumstances where 'the territorial integrity or political independence of' a 'State, or in any other manner inconsistent with the Purposes of the United Nations' is implicated.[45] In customary international law, national security is understood as involving 'an essential interest against a grave and imminent peril' and which 'does not seriously impair an essential interest of the State or States toward which the obligation exists or of the international community as a whole.'[46] The impact of economic sanctions can be circumscribed and the use of certain types of sanctions should be prohibited. In short, there are normative possibilities that set parameters for what a state can conceive of as national security and the type of economic sanctions at a State's disposal for responding to national security threats, including which individuals and entities are targeted.

Practice in International Agreements and Domestic Practice

Does the very fact that national security exceptions have to be negotiated in international agreements evidence the non-existence of unfettered discretion in defining national security under customary international law? The answer depends on the interpretation. The first interpretation is that unfettered discretion does exist but that states endeavour to preserve the integrity of the agreement by putting some limitations in place. This is to some extent borne out by the record of the negotiations of what eventually became Article XXI of GATT 1994.[47] The record

42 See generally Asif H Qureshi, 'The Americanization of the International Economic Order and Its Normative Boundaries,' *Asian Journal of WTO & International Health Law and Policy* Vol. 15 (2020) 319.

43 See generally Convention on Prohibitions or Restrictions on the Use of Certain Conventional Weapons Which May be Deemed to be Excessively Injurious or to Have Indiscriminate Effects (Protocols I, III, IV) Oct. 10, 1980, 1342 UNTS 137 (as amended Dec. 21, 2001).

44 See Vienna Convention on the Law of the Treaties pmbl., Articles 26, 31, May 23, 1969, 1155 UNTS 331 (entered into force Jan. 27, 1980).

45 UN Charter Article 2, para 4.

46 GA Res. 56/83, annex, Responsibility of States for Internationally Wrongful Acts, Article 25 (Dec. 12, 2001) [hereinafter Responsibility of States for Internationally Wrongful Acts].

47 See Pinchis-Paulsen, op. cit., at 189–190.

shows within the US, on the one hand, the desire to have an expansive or subjectively interpreted national security provision, and on the other hand the desire to preserve the integrity of the negotiated charter of the International Trade Organization.[48] Interestingly, though, according to an account of this record given by Mona Pinchis-Paulsen, there is no evidence of reliance on customary international law by those advocating a subjective interpretation of national security.[49]

The second interpretation is that discretion is limited but states are expanding their scope in international agreements. This is borne out by Article 25 of the International Law Commission's Draft Articles on Responsibility of States for Internationally Wrongful Acts, wherein the defence of 'necessity' is understood, *inter alia*, to refer to national security and does not have an open-ended meaning. Indeed, it is a defence to state responsibility available only by exception.[50]

Are the limitations on the discretion to define national security borne out by internal State practices in the field? Within a State there are several reasons why the executive's discretion to determine what a threat to a State's national security is—although granted there may be constitutional checks and balances depending on the constitution of the country in question. The internal threats are different from the ones directly emanating from abroad even if later the two have become intertwined in some respects.[51] There are more security threats internally that create a need to react more expeditiously. The threats may be purely domestic or have some external connection, but in any event, the threats are territorial and concern national security. The response apparatus for such threats essentially involves use of force. In these circumstances, the design of domestic national security should not be conflated with arrangements to respond to external security threats.

The domestic response may, at any rate, have been historically premised on the State having unlimited discretion to conceive the nature of the threat and respond

48 See generally ibid.

49 Ibid.

50 Responsibility of States for Internationally Wrongful Acts, op. cit. ('Necessity may not be invoked by a State as a ground for precluding the wrongfulness of an act not in conformity with an international obligation of that State unless the act: (a) is the only way for the State to safeguard an essential interest against a grave and imminent peril; and (b) does not seriously impair an essential interest of the State or States towards which the obligation exists, or of the international community as a whole. 2. In any case, necessity may not be invoked by a State as a ground for precluding wrongfulness if: (a) the international obligation in question excludes the possibility of invoking necessity; or (b) the State has contributed to the situation of necessity.')

51 See for example Margriet Drent, Rosa Dinnissen, Bibi van Ginkel, Hans Hogeboom & Kees Homan, *The Relationship Between External and Internal Security* (Clingendael Strategic Monitor Project: 2014), <https://www.clingendael.org/sites/default/files/pdfs/The%20relationship%20 between%20external%20and%20internal%20security.pdf> [https://perma.cc/7SBC-DT83] (last visited February 2022).

to it. Modern-day constitutional practices founded in democracy doubtless have had a part in changing this as a matter of appropriate internal governance. On the other hand, leaving aside threats arising from armed conflicts, modern-day external 'security' threats generally are more specific and accompanied by relatively more time for deliberation. However, historically, domestic and external threats may well have been intertwined in their origins. Therefore, internal constitutional and legislative practices with broad-based discretion to define a State's national security are not relevant to State practices in shedding light on normativity at the general level of international law in contemporary times. Modern-day conditions have, in a sense, brought about a decoupling of the two—domestic and external—national security threats. Unfortunately, the legacy of these historical origins is sometimes forgotten.

However, the constitutional checks and balances that protect democratic values, inculcated in the domestic apparatus of national security, do have a bearing on the establishment of a conception of national security at the international level. 'Foreign people' who are affected have a similar entitlement to the checks and balances introduced in modern constitutional practices that protect the domestic constituency from possible excesses inherent in the engagement of domestic national security concerns.

In conclusion, at the international level, conceptions of national security and responses to national security threats, as well as measures to enhance national security, fall in the province of international law. If this was not the case, the very fabric of the international community under the international legal system would be undermined. In the same manner, if there were no checks and balances at the domestic level, fundamental democratic values could be eroded. In the case of armed conflict, international law has clearly made important inroads.[52] In the economic sphere, allowing external scrutiny of the invocation of national security cannot be considered an act of 'economic disarmament.' A State's economic sphere has never—especially since the establishment of the Bretton Woods institutions—been allowed to be on a trajectory for armament, albeit economic armament.[53] Instead, the Bretton Woods' conception of the international economic system emphasises the market, levels playing fields, and open borders.[54] Competition is not to be equated with dominance. In sum, the domestic, sovereignty-based conception of national security no longer has any place in the international arena where the conception has to be based on international law.

52 See for example UN Charter Article 2, para. 4; ibid. Article 51. One example is restricting use of force to self-defence only.

53 See John W Pehle, 'The Bretton Woods Institutions,' *Yale Law Journal* Vol. 55 (1946) 1127–1128.

54 See ibid, 1128.

Section 232 of the Trade Expansion Act of 1962, as amended (19 USC. § 1862)[55]

There has been much ado lately with respect to the Trump administration's use of national security as a justification for steel and aluminum import restrictions even though the legislation existed and was relied on during previous US administrations. The current Biden administration has continued with this status-quo. As of June 2020, there were a total of eight investigations initiated under the Trump administration—five of which were acted upon.[56] Prior to this, since 1963 there had been some 26 investigations.[57] A significant number of the total investigations prior to the Trump administration, however, resulted in negative findings.[58] The last time, prior to the Trump administration, Section 232 was actually used to impose tariffs was in 1986.[59] These statistics do not imply that Section 232 is a passing phenomenon of no concern. As long as it is on the statute book, it can be availed with devastating consequences. Indeed, this is recognised in the US where the following question has been raised: 'Should Congress consider amending current delegated authorities under Section 232, such as by requiring an economic impact study, congressional consultation or approval, or by specifying further guidance?'[60]

The extent of the authority to take action under Section 232 to safeguard national security was initially limited and couched negatively. The president was prohibited from decreasing or eliminating duties or enacting other import restrictions if 'such reduction or elimination would threaten to impair the national security.'[61] In short, the safeguard action called for the maintenance of import restrictions on national security grounds. Authority to add restrictions to existing restrictions was excluded.[62] Notably, insofar as petroleum or petroleum products are concerned, the authority of the president under Section 232 is subject to congressional disapproval of presidential import adjustments by a joint resolution of either House of Congress.[63]

Currently, however, as US law stands, the actions that can be taken under Section 232 have been expanded to allow the President to 'take such other

55 Trade Expansion Act of 1962 § 232, 19 USCA § 1862 (Westlaw through Pub. L. No. 116–259).

56 See Rachel F Fefer, Cong. Rsch, Serv., IF10667, Section 232 of the Trade Expansion Act of 1962 (2020), https://fas.org/sgp/crs/misc/IF10667.pdf [https://perma.cc/TWE8-LGH4] (last visited February 2022).

57 See ibid.; but see Trade Policy Review Body, *Report by the Secretariat: Trade Policy Review*, WTO Doc. WT/TPR/S/382/Rev.1 (Mar. 27, 2019) (noting only 16 investigations have been recorded since 1980).

58 Fefer, op. cit.

59 See ibid.

60 See ibid.

61 19 USCA § 1862(a) (West).

62 See ibid.

63 See ibid. § 1862(f).

actions as the President deems necessary to adjust the imports of such article so that such imports will not threaten to impair the national security,'[64] but subject to congressional disapproval with respect to petroleum or petroleum products. Ultimately, it is the president who determines whether: an article is 'being imported into the US in such quantities or under such circumstances as to threaten or to impair the national security';[65] and 'the nature and duration of the action that, in the judgment of the President, must be taken to adjust the imports of the article and its derivatives so that such imports will not threaten to impair the national security.'[66]

Briefly, the procedure for such an action can be initiated by the 'head of any department or agency, upon application of an interested party, or upon his own motion, the Secretary of Commerce.'[67] Upon such an initiation, the Secretary of Commerce is to engage in an investigation "to determine the effects on the national security of" the imports in question.[68] The investigation is to involve consultation with the Secretary of Defense and, if appropriate, allow interested parties to provide input.[69] A report of the investigation has to be submitted to the President with the Secretary of Commerce's recommendations by a set date.[70] Upon receipt of the report, within a set timeframe, the President determines whether they concur with the report.[71] If the President does concur, the President must determine what action to take. The President is to negotiate an agreement to safeguard national security and impose such restrictions as the President deems appropriate.[72] By a set time, the President is to give a reasoned report to the US Congress of the action or inaction taken.[73]

Section 232 does not contain a definition of national security, although it contains a list of factors to be taken into account in its determination.[74] Nor is

64 Ibid. § 1862(c)(3)(A)(ii).
65 Ibid. § 1862(c)(1)(A) (noting the imports have to be of a certain 'quantity' or in 'such circumstances', neither criterion is further defined in the legislation).
66 Ibid. § 1862(c)(1)(A)(ii).
67 Ibid. § 1862(b)(1)(A).
68 Ibid.
69 Ibid. § 1862(b)(2)(A).
70 Ibid. § 1862(b)(3)(A).
71 Ibid. § 1862(c)(1)(A)(i).
72 Ibid. § 1862(c)(1)(A)(ii).
73 Ibid. § 1862(c)(2).
74 Ibid. § 1862(d) ('For the purposes of this section, the Secretary and the President shall, in the light of the requirements of national security and without excluding other relevant factors, give consideration to domestic production needed for projected national defense requirements, the capacity of domestic industries to meet such requirements, existing and anticipated availabilities of the human resources, products, raw materials, and other supplies and services essential to the national defense, the requirements of growth of such industries and such supplies and services including the investment, exploration, and development necessary to assure such growth, and the importation of goods in terms of their quantities, availabilities, character, and use as those affect such industries and the capacity of the United States to meet national security requirements. In the administration of this section,

there a definition in its implementing regulation, 15 CFR § 705.4, which reflects the Section 232 list.[75] Section 232 is also the subject of statutory interpretation—two notable ones being reports on the impact of the import of iron ore and semifinished steel on national security under Section 232.[76] It seems, however, that interpretations of Section 232 are not binding and can be diverted by subsequent administrations.[77] The list of considerations to be taken into account in Section 232 is not exhaustive.[78] The list has been interpreted as consisting of two distinct subsets of what comprise 'national security' considerations—one focusing

---

the Secretary and the President shall further recognize the close relation of the economic welfare of the Nation to our national security, and shall take into consideration the impact of foreign competition on the economic welfare of individual domestic industries; and any substantial unemployment, decrease in revenues of government, loss of skills or investment, or other serious effects resulting from the displacement of any domestic products by excessive imports shall be considered, without excluding other factors, in determining whether such weakening of our internal economy may impair the national security').

75 15 CFR § 705.4 (2020) (clarifying how the Department of Commerce should carry out its Section 232 investigations with respect to the impact of imports on national security in the Code of Federal Regulations) ('(a) To determine the effect on the national security of the imports of the article under investigation, the Department shall consider the quantity of the article in question or other circumstances related to its import. With regard for the requirements of national security, the Department shall also consider the following: (1) Domestic production needed for projected national defence requirements; (2) The capacity of domestic industries to meet projected national defence requirements; (3) The existing and anticipated availabilities of human resources, products, raw materials, production equipment and facilities, and other supplies and services essential to the national defence; (4) The growth requirements of domestic industries to meet national defence requirements and the supplies and services including the investment, exploration and development necessary to assure such growth; and (5) Any other relevant factors. (b) In recognition of the close relation between the strength of our national economy and the capacity of the US to meet national security requirements, the Department shall also, with regard for the quantity, availability, character and uses of the imported article under investigation, consider the following: (1) The impact of foreign competition on the economic welfare of any domestic industry essential to our national security; (2) The displacement of any domestic products causing substantial unemployment, decrease in the revenues of government, loss of investment or specialized skills and productive capacity, or other serious effects; and (3) Any other relevant factors that are causing or will cause a weakening of our national economy').

76 See generally Bureau of Exp. Admin., Dep't of Com., The Effect of Imports of Iron Ore and Semi-Finished Steel on the National Security: An Investigation Conducted Under Section 232 of the Trade Expansion Act of 1962, as Amended (2001) [hereinafter Iron Ore and Semi-Finished Steel]; Bureau of Exp. Admin., Dep't of Com., The Effect of Steel on the National Security (2018) [hereinafter Steel].

77 Steel, op. cit., 14 n.15 ('The 2001 Report used the phrase "fundamentally threaten to impair" when discussing how imports may threaten to impair national security. Because the term "fundamentally" is not included in the statutory text and could be perceived as establishing a higher threshold, the Secretary expressly does not use the qualifier in this report. The statutory threshold in Section 232(b)(3)(A) is unambiguously "threaten to impair" and the Secretary adopts that threshold without qualification. The statute also uses the formulation "may impair" in Section 232(d).' (citations omitted)).

78 Iron Ore and Semi-Finished Steel, op. cit., 6; see Steel, op. cit., 13, 15.

on national defence and the other on the economic welfare of the nation.[79] National defence has been interpreted not only as encompassing the defence of the US but also as 'the ability to project military capabilities globally.'[80] National defence thus includes both defensive and offensive capabilities. It includes harm to national security as well as threats to it.

The economic welfare of the nation embraces a variety of concerns viz., 'the impact of foreign competition on the economic welfare of domestic industry'[81] and the 'economic welfare of individual domestic industries,'[82] including 'any substantial unemployment, decrease in revenues of government, loss of skills or investment, or other serious effects resulting from the displacement of any domestic products by excessive imports.'[83] More specifically, economic welfare has been interpreted to include the 'general security and welfare of certain industries, beyond those necessary to satisfy national defence requirements, that are critical to the minimum operations of the economy and government,'[84] including transportation systems, the electric power grid, water systems, and energy generation systems.[85] For this purpose, a list of critical industry sectors has been compiled.[86] Finally, the Secretary of Commerce and the President are specifically directed to consider the close relationship between the nation's economic welfare and national security.[87]

From the perspective of public international law, the following conclusions can be proffered with respect to Section 232. First, it gives almost unfettered discretion to the President of the US to determine what constitutes US national security and inform its external economic response. No state, whether operating through its executive or with the approval of its legislature, can displace the role of international law in defining national security as it relates to external consequences that impact other states' rights under international law. There are certain limits here that have a bearing on the capacity of nations to determine their national security interests, including their choice of economic response.

Second, Section 232's conception of national security is open-ended. Importantly, it is not just concerned with US defence but also with its offensive capability.[88] Moreover, it is also concerned with the economic welfare of

79 Iron Ore and Semi-Finished Steel, op. cit., 5; Steel, op. cit., 75, 13–14.

80 Steel, op. cit., 13 (quoting Iron Ore and Semi-Finished Steel, op. cit., 5).

81 15 CFR § 705.4(b)(1) (2020).

82 19 USCA 1862(d) (Westlaw through Pub. L. No. 116–259).

83 Ibid.

84 Iron Ore and Semi-Finished Steel, op. cit., 5.

85 Ibid. at 14.

86 Press Release, Office of the Press Sec'y, Presidential Policy Directive—Critical Infrastructure Security and Resilience (PPD-21) (Feb. 12, 2013), <https://obamawhitehouse.archives.gov/the-press-office/2013/02/12/presidential-policy-directive-critical-infrastructure-security-and-resil> [https://perma.cc/Y4Z7-VGG8] (last visited February 2022).

87 19 USCA § 1862(d).

88 See op. cit. note 75 and accompanying text.

the nation.[89] US foreign relations, informed by strategic interests operationalised through the projection of global military capabilities, involves the imposition of a price for its exercise on foreign nations whether or not they are beneficiaries of US foreign policy. Similarly, the conflation with the nation's economic welfare considerably stretches the notion of national security. Thus, its focus includes the

> displacement of any domestic products causing substantial unemployment, decrease in the revenues of government, loss of investment or specialized skills and productive capacity, or other serious effects; and... [a]ny other relevant factors that are causing or will cause a weakening of our national economy.[90]

The wide economic character of national security is reinforced by the fact that 'an interested party' can initiate a Section 232 investigation, and in particular, that the principal investigator and interpreter or implementor of Section 232 is the Secretary of Commerce not the Secretary of Defense.[91] Moreover, both the defence and economic welfare limbs of national security are informed by a wide, temporal canvas involving projected threats without any qualifications. Both offensive military capabilities and the economic welfare of the nation, in an all-encompassing sense, do not fall within the existential character of the international conception of national security. The international conception of national security is limited to the protection of the State's very existence. In addition, this concept of national security is inconsistent with Article XXI of GATT 1994, which, in its widest form, refers to the protection of essential security interests 'taken in time of war or other emergencies in international relations.'[92] Article XXI of GATT 1994 has been interpreted as referring to 'those interests relating to the quintessential functions of the state.'[93] Moreover, these interests do not refer to 'political or economic differences' between the members of the WTO 'unless they give rise to defense and military interests, or maintenance of law and public order interests.'[94]

Third, there are due process issues that may have an impact in terms of the minimum standard under customary international law.[95] The invocation and

89 19 USCA § 1862(d).
90 15 CFR § 705.4(b)(2)–(3) (2020).
91 19 USCA § 1862(b)(1)(A).
92 GATT Article XXI(b)(iii).
93 *Traffic in Transit*, op. cit., para 7.130.
94 Ibid. para 7.75.
95 See L F H Neer (US v. Mex.), 4 R.I.A.A. 60, 61–62 (Gen. Claims Comm. 1926) ('[T]he propriety of governmental acts should be put to the test of international standards, and...the treatment of an alien, in order to constitute an international delinquency, should amount to an outrage, to bad faith, to wilful neglect of duty, or to an insufficiency of governmental action so far short of international standards that every reasonable and impartial man would readily recognize its insufficiency. Whether the insufficiency proceeds from deficient execution of an intelligent law or from the fact that the laws of the country do not empower the

application of national security legislation have a due process relevance to foreign interests and a national security apparatus that conflates defence with economic welfare. Not all relevant interested parties are accorded an assured participatory right in the investigation process. The investigation is conducted in the US and does not allow interested foreign parties to effectively participate. There is no economic impact study, nor one that takes into account the external economic impact of the chosen responses, which includes consideration of alternatives with less destructive measures of the international trading system.

Finally, the authorised responses to national security concerns do not seem to have any qualifications. Thus, exceptions to restrictions can differentiate between foreign countries, and as between US importers and foreign producer-exporters. Such discriminatory practices can be inconsistent with Articles I and III of GATT 1994.[96] Moreover, whilst the received wisdom is that under general international law there is no obligation not to discriminate between goods originating from different countries,[97] this author has elsewhere questioned this wisdom, given contemporary developments in State practice.[98] Furthermore, agreements entered into under the authority of Section 232, for example, restricting the import of goods from abroad by a US company in joint ventures with foreign companies, could implicate the foreign State in indirect expropriation with the complicity of the US government—contrary to the prohibition on expropriation without compensation. In the absence of an agreement, the US government may also be engaging in acts of expropriation of foreign property.

In sum, the national security exception would not absolve liability under international law if the rationale for the import restrictions is demonstrably based on the welfare of the US economy, albeit in a piece of legislation intended to safeguard national security. Furthermore, the national security exception would

authorities to measure up to international standards is immaterial.'); see also for example *Waste Mgmt., Inc. v. United Mexican States*, ICSID Case No. ARB(AF)/00/3, Award, para. 98 (Apr. 30, 2004), 11 ICSID Rep. 361 (2007) ('[T]he minimum standard of treatment…is infringed by conduct attributable to the State and harmful to the claimant if the conduct is arbitrary, grossly unfair, unjust or idiosyncratic, is discriminatory and exposes the claimant to sectional or racial prejudice, or involves a lack of due process leading to an outcome which offends judicial propriety—as might be the case with a manifest failure of natural justice in judicial proceedings or a complete lack of transparency and candour in an administrative process. In applying this standard it is relevant that the treatment is in breach of representations made by the host State which were reasonably relied on by the claimant.').

96 See GATT Article I, paras. (1), (4).

97 See for example Thomas Cottier & Marina Foltea, 'Constitutional Functions of the WTO and Regional Trade Agreements,' in Lorand Bartels & Federico Ortino (eds) *Regional Trade Agreements and the WTO Legal System* (Oxford University Press: 2006) 43–76; James H. Mathis, *Regional Trade Agreements in the GATT/WTO: Article XXIV and the International Trade Requirement* (TMC Asser Press: 2002) 271–285.

98 See Asif H Qureshi, *Interpreting WTO Agreements: Problems and Perspectives*, 2nd ed. (Cambridge University Press: 2015), 339–355 (discussing the question of WTO member states freedom to engage in discriminatory trade relations as a fundamental question in the relationship between the WTO and preferential trade agreements).

not absolve international responsibility if the US' measures were concerned with offensive US military operations abroad.

Conclusion

Section 232 reflects an unfortunate sense of the US' power as a nation. It does not withstand the scrutiny of international law, let alone the growing sense of civilised behaviour that infuses international economic order. Instead, it reflects the basest human instincts of opportunism, self-aggrandisement, and dominance. It is quintessentially the Achilles heel of the international economic order, which could seriously undermine it, especially given the difficulty in effectively policing Section 232's application. The conception of national security, as interpreted in Section 232, must be one that accords with international law. There is not only a need for an economic impact study but also a legal impact study.

The need for a normative framework that manages the concept of national security within an international institutional structure where it is implemented is apparent.[99] There are three distinct ways in which this can be achieved. First, through the formulation of a normative code on State national security. This is an objective that the UN International Law Commission should embark on through a more in-depth study of State practices in the economic sphere. The Commission should focus on a systematic study of State practices for defining national security and responding to national security threats from an economic perspective. But the question remains as to who will initiate such a proposal in this forum. Second, there are existing dispute settlement mechanisms, such as the WTO, investment arbitral tribunals, and the International Court of Justice that can and do serve to manage and elucidate a normative framework, albeit within the context of a dispute and against the backdrop of specialised regimes in international law. Finally, the UN Security Council may be ineffective in the introduction of disciplines in this regard. This is because the way it is organised puts decision-making authority in the hands of one member, thus inhibiting the facilitation of a uniform definition of national security on an international scale.

Overall, there is certainly a need for the UN General Assembly to engage in this field and play a more proactive role. Such an orchestrated focus on national security through an economic lens will serve to regulate the external consequences of a State's national security apparatus. The focus will also create an opportunity for the international community to bring to bear an international consensus regarding how national security concerns are to be managed domestically; thus, bringing to light some of the human rights abuses committed by States on their own people.

99 I am grateful to Professor John W Head for drawing my attention to this aspect of my paper. Professor Head is the Robert W Wagstaff Distinguished Professor at the University of Kansas School of Law.

5 US Preferential Market Access Conditions for Developing Countries

'Those who claim to have a moral high ground, have a high burden of proof of their own moral integrity.'

Introduction[1]

There has been much academic discourse, stretching over two decades, on the unilateral according by developed States of preferential market access to imports from developing countries within the normative framework of the World Trade Organization (WTO). A particular momentum to this came after the WTO Appellate Body decision involving a discriminatory preferential access to the European market, which the European Union (EU) accorded to Pakistan and India challenged.[2] There have been various themes to this discourse, post the

1 I am grateful to Professor Mark Feldman for his observations on this chapter. The errors and views remain mine.

2 European Communities – Conditions for the Granting of Tariff Preferences to Developing Countries, AB-2004-1, Report of the Appellate Body, 7 April 2004; D Anthony, 'Unilateral preferential trade programs offered by the United States, the European Union, and Canada: A Comparison,' (The Trade Partnership Publishing: 2008), https://tradepartnership.com/pdf_files/GSP_Comparison.pdf (last visited February 2022); T R Graham, 'The US Generalized System of Preferences for Developing Countries: International Innovation and the Art of the Possible,' *Am. J. Int'l L.* Vol. 72 No. 3 (1978) 513; N J Lahoud, 'Non-Discriminatory United States Generalized System of Preferences: De Facto Discrimination against the Least Developed Developing Countries,' *Harv. Int'l. LJ* Vol. 23 No. 1 (1982) 1; R I Meltzer, 'US Renewal of the GSP,' *J. World Trade L.* (1986); L Compa, 'Going Multilateral: The Evolution of US Hemispheric Labor Rights Policy Under GSP and NAFTA,' *Conn. J. Int'l L.* Vol. 10 No. 2 (1995) 337; Omar Chaudhary, 'The Propriety of Preferences: An Evaluation of EC and US GSP Schemes in the Wake of EC-Preferences,' *Asper Rev. Int'l Bus. & Trade L.* Vol. 5 (2005) 159; L Compa & J S Vogt, 'Labor Rights in the Generalized System of Preferences: A 20-Year Review,' *Comp. Lab. L. & Pol'y J.* Vol. 22 No. 2/3 (2000) 199; G M Grossman & A O Sykes, 'A Preference for Development: The Law and Economics of GSP,' *World Trade Rev.* Vol. 4 No. (2005) 41; S Shekhar & S Janardhan, 'Mercantalist Concerns in US GSP Law: Termination of GSP Benefits to India,' *Global Trade and Customs Journal* Vol. 14 No. (2019) 391; R Howse, 'Conditions in the European Community Generalized System of Preferences: A Little Known Case with Major Repercussions for

DOI: 10.4324/9781003047575-6

Indian challenge in the WTO EU-Tariff Preferences case. First, the momentum from the EU-Tariff Preferences case focused attention on its implications for the Generalised Systems of Preferences (GSP) administered by various developed countries. This discourse has to some extent been a West-centric one, with much criticism of the WTO Panel and Appellate Body decisions, but with little involvement from developing country scholars. For example, the roundtable discussion under the auspices of the World Trade Review did not include any scholars from the non-West non-developed centric spheres.[3] Second, the US scholarly narrative on the implications specifically for the US GSP system of the EU-Tariff Preferences case is mainly defensive of the US capacity to uphold 'American values'[4] through GSP conditionality. Third, there is latterly some reflection from the Indian sub-continent, given momentum by the recent termination of India's US

Political Conditionality in US Trade,' *Chi. J. Int'l L.* Vol. 4 No. 2 (2003) 385; Vivian C Jones & Liana Wong, 'Generalized System of Preferences (GSP): Overview and Issues for Congress,' US Congressional Research Service Report January 2021; Andre Sapir & Lars Lundberg, 'The US Generalized System of Preferences and Its Impacts,' in Robert E Baldwin & Anne O Krueger (eds), *The Structure and Evolution of Recent US Trade Policy* (Chicago University Press: 1984); R E Moore, 'Level of Development and GSP Treatment—An Empirical Investigation into the Differential Impacts of Export Expansion,' *J. World Trade* Vol. 26 No. 6 (1992) 19; A DiCaprio, 'Are Labor Provisions Protectionist: Evidence from Nine Labor-Augmented US Trade Arrangements,' *Comp. Lab. L. & Pol'y. J.* Vol. 26 No. 1 (2004) 1; M Saleh, 'The WTO Legality of Trade-Labour Sanctions in the US GSP Programme', *Manchester Journal of International Economic Law* Vol. 16 No. 1 (2019) 57; A Mason, 'The Degeneralization of the Generalized System of Preferences (GSP),' *Duke Law Journal* Vol. 54 No. 2 (2004) 513; K C Kennedy, 'The Generalized System of Preferences after Four Decades: Conditionality and the Shrinking Margin of Preference,' *Michigan State International Law Review* Vol. 20 No. 3 (2013) 522; R Rajesh Babu, 'On the Legality of the United States Action of Terminating India's GSP Status,' *Foreign Trade Review* Vol. 55 No. 1 (2020); Lorand Bartels, 'The WTO Enabling Clause and Positive Conditionality in the European Community's GSP Program', *J. Int'l Econ. L.* Vol. 6 No. 2 (2003) 507; Lorand Bartels, 'The Appellate Body Report in EC–Conditions for the Granting of Tariff Preferences to Developing Countries, and Its Implications for Conditionality in GSP Programs,' in E Burgi, J Pauwelyn, & T Cottier (eds), *Human Rights and International Trade* (Oxford University Press: 2005); Lorand Bartels, 'The Application of Human Rights Conditionality in the EU's Bilateral Trade Agreements and Other Trade Arrangements with Third Countries,' Directorate-General for External Policies of the Union, European Parliament, Doc EXPO-B-INTA-2008-57 PE 406.991 (2008) at 1 [Bartels, Application of Human Rights]; Pallavi Kishore, 'A Critical Analysis of Conditionalities in the Generalized System of Preferences,' *The Canadian Yearbook of International Law* Vol. 54 No. 54 (2016) 98; Gregory Shaffer & Yvonne Apea, 'Institutional Choice in the Generalized System of Preferences Case: Who Decides the Conditions for Trade Preferences? The Law and Politics of Rights,' *J World Trade* Vol. 39 No. 6 (2005) 982; Steve Charnovitz, Lorand Bartels, Robert Howse (roundtable organizer), Jane Bradley, Joost Pauwelyn, & Donald Regan, 'Internet Roundtable: The Appellate Body's GSP decision,' *World Trade Review* Vol. 3 No. 2 (2004) 239; Frank J Garcia, 'Global Justice and the Bretton Woods Institutions,' *Journal of International Economic Law* Vol. 10 No. 3 (2007) 461.

3 Charnovitz et al., op. cit.

4 See for example Howse, op. cit.

GSP status.[5] This input has been facilitated by the expanding space of academic discourse generally in international law, and the increased confidence of emerging economies in international relations. Fourth, specific aspects of US GSP conditionality have been considered, for example, in the sphere of labour standards[6] and intellectual property rights.[7] Finally, there are also empirically based works, including economic analysis of GSPs.[8] The evaluation of the economic impact of preferential schemes is generally considered to be difficult, in particular in achieving the goals of development, although where the preference margin is significant and the country is a least developed one, the contribution is understood to be positive.[9] Generally, however, the extent of the positive economic effect is a matter of some controversy, though modest and not 'trivial' gains are acknowledged.[10] Compliance costs (rules of origin and conditionality), exclusion of certain products, including distortions of investment decisions in the preference receiving country, all contribute to difficulties in estimation and the actual economic impact of the preferences. In sum, the legal analysis is mainly process-oriented—centring on the question of GSP conformity with the WTO, interspersed with some policy discourse. The full rigour of public international law and policy could be more developed.

The primary focus here is not the evaluation of the US preferential market access regimes from the perspective of consistency with WTO law. There has been much that has been written from this standpoint already that questions WTO consistency.[11] Nor is it intended to focus on the impact of the economic or non-economic conditions on the preferential market access system. The purpose

5 See for example Pallavi Kishore, op. cit.; and R Rajesh Babu, op. cit.

6 See for example Compa & Vogt, op. cit., 200.

7 See for example Jean-Frédéric Morin & Madison Cartwright, 'The US and EU's Intellectual Property Initiatives in Asia: Competition, Coordination or Replication?' *Global Policy* (2020); and H Thopacu, 'Validating South Africa's Copyright Reform through the Lens of US GSP: The Need to Abolish Reciprocal Requirements,' *Policy Insights* Vol. 84 (May 2020), <https://media.africaportal.org/documents/PI-84-EDIP-Thopacu-FINAL-WEB.pdf> (last visited February 2020).

8 See for example WTO webinar focusing on preferential rules of origin and their impact on the user of trade preferences by least developed countries. 'What Drives the Utilization of Trade Preferences?' <https://www.youtube.com/watch?v=sXAJpl08eA4> (last visited May 2021).

9 See for example André Sapir & Lars Lundberg, 'The U.S. Generalized System of Preferences and Its Impacts,' in Robert E Baldwin & Anne O Krueger (eds), *The Structure and Evolution of Recent U.S. Trade Policy* (University of Chicago Press: 1984) chapter 6, 222.

10 G M Grossman & A O Sykes, 'A Preference for Development: The Law and Economics of GSP,' *World Trade Rev.* (2005) 60. According to Jones & Wong, op. cit., in 2019 21 billion dollars of imports entered the US market duty free under the GSP. In 2020 during the pandemic and post India and Turkey out of the GSP system the total imports were 16.8 billion (see USTR 2021 Trade Policy Agenda and 2020 Annual Report).

11 See for example Bartels, 'The Appellate Body Report in EC–Conditions for the Granting of Tariff Preferences to Developing Countries, and Its Implications for Conditionality in GSP Programs,' op. cit.

of this chapter is to shed some light from the beneficiary countries' standpoint—against the background of international law and policy—on the conditionality attached in US preference schemes, the very propriety of those conditions, the extent of their normative impact, and the suitability of trade preferential schemes as vehicles for channelling conditionality. To this end the second part critically considers the very propriety of the US conditions in US unilateral preferential trade arrangements for developing and least developing countries. This is followed in the third part by a closer textual examination of the conditions in the US legislation, including their enforcement. Finally, in the fourth part some concluding observations are proffered that highlight the value orientations of the conditions transplanted into another country, and the implications for the self-determination of domestic policy-making. In sum this is a modest eclectic and textually based approach to the analysis of GSP conditionality, set against international law and policy generally.

Such a consideration is particularly relevant given current discourse and expectation in the US of increasing the conditionality to include human rights, environmental, and good governance issues in trade preferences.[12] Indeed, this model of engagement in trade relations of integrating economics with non-economic conditionality is further being expanded into a general US *modus operandi* in foreign economic relations globally, albeit fuelled by the contemporary US/China confrontational engagement in trade.[13]

The Very Propriety of Setting Conditions in 'Unilateral' Trade Preferences

The prior and fundamental question, namely the very propriety of the US imposing conditionality under preferential trade arrangements, has generally been taken as given. Based on this assumption of legitimacy,[14] the legal, ethical, and economic analyses proceed in varying degrees from it respectively.

Thus, the legal perspective of WTO law,[15] and in some measure US legislation, focuses on the scope of the mandate to accord preferential market access to developing countries. Not the mandate authority as such. The economic impact on

12 Jones & Wong, op. cit.

13 As manifest in the recent proposed US legislation titled 'Ensuring American Global Leadership and Engagement Act.' See the proposed US bill titled the EAGLE Act in particular Section 3 Statement of Policy at <https://foreignaffairs.house.gov/_cache/files/b/9/b98fd569-3e49-47c0-bb23-8fccf88d7274/4E5106A7CF429C5C518C8C6003A94AFC.eagle-act-for-introduction---signed.pdf> (last visited May 2021).

14 I am grateful to Professor Mark Feldman for asking me to elaborate on the meaning of legitimacy. Legitimacy is used here as a broader measure of validation that is not confined to legality. See for example Alexander P d'Entrèves, 'Legality and Legitimacy,' *The Review of Metaphysics* Vol. 16 No. 4 (June 1963) 687–702.

15 Bartels, 'The Appellate Body Report in EC–Conditions for the Granting of Tariff Preferences to Developing Countries, and Its Implications for Conditionality in GSP Programs,' op. cit.

the promotion of trade and development[16] of preferential market access arrangements assumes a mandate. The distributive justice stands of according preferential market access, that authors such as Frank Garcia have so commendably advanced,[17] are concerned mainly with the very fact of the imposition of the conditions, which are considered to detract from according preferential market access, as a matter of justice.

Does the US have the *locus standi* to impose conditions on the preferential market access it accords to developing countries? Does it have the *credentials* to formulate and impose any conditions? These are questions that are not directly, fully, and explicitly addressed. In sum, a focus on the very propriety of the US imposing conditions on preferential market access raises questions of capacity, credentials, fundamental principles of international law (sovereign equality, non-interference, right to self-determination, rule of law, good governance, sustainable development), and coherence in the integration of non-economic conditions with market access and development objectives. This bundle of questions is mainly set in policy and politics but can also inform legal discourse.

The widespread assumption that the US has authority to impose non-trade conditions in its preferential schemes (legitimacy premise) is based mainly on the following:

(1) That such schemes are 'voluntarily granted to developing countries to assist their economic development and not bound as legal commitments in the WTO.'[18]
(2) 'GSP benefits are 'gifts' of a sort, however, and tight limitations on their terms may put an end to them altogether.'[19]
(3) 'Congress and the President will no longer be able to grant or withdraw GSP treatment on the basis of American policy objectives and American political values'[20]

The following observations are proffered with respect to these assertions. First, there is much ado about the fact that these arrangements are 'voluntary' and therefore the suggestion that they can be withdrawn anytime. There is here a moral and political point. In so far as the US is concerned, it is a permanent member of the UN Security Council—through its historical military prowess and contribution to world peace. The developing countries with reservations have given in to the continuation of this system of political hierarchy in the

16 Kennedy, op. cit.
17 Garcia, 'Global Justice and the Bretton Woods Institutions,' op. cit.; and Frank J Garcia, *Trade, Inequality, and Justice: Towards a Liberal Theory of Just Trade* (Transnational Publishers: 2003) chapter 4.
18 See for example Howse, op. cit.
19 Grossman & Sykes, op. cit.
20 Howse, op. cit. See also Grossman & Sykes, op. cit.

international order. There is therefore surely a price that comes with it on the shoulders of the US. In addition, the US has throughout the development of the international economic order arrogated to itself the role of a leader in the sphere of liberal trade—this it has continued to do. The world trading system has been, notably, of its architectural design. The 'voluntary' chant with its implicit threat of possible withdrawal hinders market access, albeit preferential, for the goods and services of developing countries. It does not sit well with the liberal trade ethos. This analysis of 'voluntary' is reinforced by its characterisation as a 'right' to preferential market access from the perspective of distributive justice.[21]

But there is also an argument founded in law. The international consensus for the progressive liberalisation of international trade based on reciprocity, within the framework of GATT/WTO thus far achieved generally for the WTO membership, has to be set against the background of the institutionalisation of the principle of special and differential treatment (SDT) of which the GSP partakes.[22] The fact that the WTO law allows exceptionally developed countries as a group to accord albeit individually preferential market access carries with it a responsibility to interpret the 'voluntary' nature of the option, in terms of a collective responsibility intended to facilitate SDT. Members of the developed countries have a responsibility at the least as between themselves, to ensure that their collective commitment to institutionalise the facilitation of preferential market access is not undermined by all the members of the group individually declining to offer preferential access. Moreover, there is a connection between the progressive development of the general WTO regime (liberal and based on reciprocity) conceded to by the developing countries as it has now evolved, and the realisation of the SDT principle through the authorised GSP. This connection may not be direct but is certainly part of the backdrop and context of the discourse on SDT. This connection evokes legal principles of reliance/estoppel that colour the nature of the absoluteness of this perceived 'voluntariness.' It also provides the context for interpreting the Enabling Clause that contains the authority to accord preferential market access to developing countries. In addition, the authority to opt in for SDT is located not in the sovereignty of the developed State but in that sovereignty as set out in the Enabling Clause in the WTO.

In the circumstances, there is a measure of legitimacy in the positive expectation of a grant of preferential market access that developing countries are entitled to entertain and that informs the 'voluntary' nature of the GSP. The parameters of this 'positive expectation' can be described to include the following. Developing countries can request beneficiary status under a GSP and

21 Garcia, 'Global Justice and the Bretton Woods Institutions,' op. cit.

22 International consensus on the GSP dates as far back as UNCTAD II Conference in 1968. In the US it was first established in 1974. The Enabling Clause under GATT 1947 giving developed countries the mandate to establish such preferences was a decision officially called the 'Decision on Differential and More Favourable Treatment, Reciprocity and Fuller Participation of Developing Countries,' that was adopted in 1979.

are entitled to expect proper consideration of the request in fulfilment of the developed country's SDT commitments under the WTO, under a GSP system conforming to WTO law. Moreover, in the same manner as is the case with free trade and customs unions,[23] the fact of according preferential market access, albeit unilaterally, should not in principle displace the application of WTO law, unless necessary to the relationship between the donor and beneficiary country. This has a bearing on the kind of conditions that can be imposed including the circumstances of their withdrawal. With respect to the latter there is a due process question to be explored in terms of its applicability. Does the voluntary nature of market access enable a developed country without further ado at its whim to withdraw the preferential market access?

Taking all the circumstances into account, it does not behove well for the US and the scholarship within to chant this mantra of voluntary with the underlying threat that that description evokes. Whilst the precise nature of the US involvement from a narrow legal perspective could well be seen through a window 'voluntarily' opened, a more nuanced vision could well locate it more fluidly somewhere in between a spectrum with one end a 'voluntary pole,' and the other a more 'compelled to accord market access pole' which once opened has to glide back under the conditions of the window hinge. In sum, the suggestion that the US Congress and the President's ability to grant or withdraw GSP treatment should not be compromised is purely an internal US perspective. From an external standpoint, the actions of the US Congress and its President are subjects of the rule of international law, the context against which the SDT is set, the spirit of liberal trade embedded in the international trading order, including the high standards of State behaviour and responsibility expected in an interconnected world.

Second, there is much ado about the imperative of 'American policy objectives, political values, and interests.' There are essentially two aspects to this list of considerations. First, there is implicit here a claim about the existence of American values, and their value. The legitimacy and sacrosanct nature of these is taken as given and considered beyond reproach. For this reason, the capacity of the President and Congress to be armed with these to disseminate them is considered sufficiently important so as not to be jeopardised.

This idea that there is such an ethos that speaks of American values is not necessarily tenable. The unfolding of recent US internal politics has highlighted that not only are there differences within the US as to what are American values, but also that this schism is significant within the US. Moreover, even if it was possible to paint a coherent picture of American values, the nature and integrity of these as they exist and are enforced within the US would need to come under scrutiny. In the same vein, these values would come under comparison with universally held values, and those held by other civilisations. In short, this imperative is not

23 See Turkey—Restrictions on Imports of Textile and Clothing Products (WTO: DS34 (1999)).

necessarily axiomatic as a basis for GSP conditionality. Thus, whilst it is not the intention of this author here to write off the value and positive contribution that American values have played and continue to play in international relations—what is being asserted, however, is that those who claim to have a moral high ground, have a high burden of proof of their own moral integrity. Many developed countries cannot come with a clean historical slate to this high moral ground, let alone a clean one in terms of contemporary domestic and foreign practices. Moreover, the American values that are to be found in US foreign trade legislation are selective in nature and informed by US economic and national security interests.

Second, there is a noticeable utilitarian approach to GSP conditionality—as the handmaiden for the implementation of American foreign policy and interests. The US is of course entitled to have its foreign policy and interests but the conflation of this with market access—indeed the subjugation of market access to this albeit preferential access—does need some justification. The imposition of such conditionality on vulnerable developing countries can be oppressive. US self-interest can negatively impact the developing country. Non-trade concerns can be less relevant to facilitating development for the beneficiary country through market access. Moreover, a cost benefit analysis in inculcating such conditions may not result to the advantage of the developing country.

Third, the assimilation of GSP benefits as 'gifts,' albeit of a sort, is demeaning both to the exporters and the beneficiary country. It is a distortion of reality. The exported goods are bought at the market price in the US. Those who consume the goods do not consider they are imparting a gift to the exporters. Insofar as the beneficiary country is concerned, it has secured market access—a level playing field for its exports under a bundle of international trade agreements through which the developed countries secured market liberalisation and avoided a developing country veto in the consensus on those agreements. Moreover, the fact that the developed country is able to accord preferential discriminatory treatment can be indicative that the economic justifications for its restrictive access were not optimal in the first place. Indeed, this is reinforced by the fact that the US GSP system itself has a limit to the market access based on the 'impact of such action on United States producers of like or directly competitive products.'[24]

The preferential market access is an apparatus for locking in developing countries to bring about changes in their domestic market conditions as well as foreign policy, for example labour standards and intellectual property rights, along with non-trade related conditions (for example relating to terrorism and communism). In the circumstances, the US refrainment from imposing trade restrictions can hardly be reconstructed as something partaking of a gift. The beneficiary countries are reciprocating by sacrificing their own ability to regulate in the respective spheres of the conditions. Furthermore, basic international economic doctrine eschews any form of trade barriers based on foreign policy considerations—and the international trading order is based on this. From this

24 See 19 U.S.C. 2461.

economic standpoint there are no gifts being accorded in circumstances wherein barriers to trade are simply being reduced. This is analogous to a robber robbing less, and then claiming to accord a gift of the amount not robbed. In the same vein, this construction does not sit well under the WTO normative framework. The Enabling Clause authorising developed States to accord preferential market access to developing countries in no way assimilates the preferential market access as a gift. Authorising GSPs, in the same way as free trade and customs unions under Article XXIV of GATT 1994, are simply ways of facilitating further market liberalisation. In the case of developing countries, it is furthermore a ladder for them to engage with developed countries on a more reciprocal basis. The fact that arrangements under Article XXIV of GATT 1994 are accompanied by some level of reciprocity does not inform the characterisation of unilateral preferences as gifts. One-sided free trade agreements are not considered as partaking of gifts. Conversely the non-reciprocity expectation in the Enabling Clause does not in itself colour the nature of the market access as a gift. The nature of a gift is not necessarily dependent on the absence of reciprocity.

Finally, Frank Garcia's application of Rawl's theory of distributive justice, in particular his differential principle, to preferential arrangements for developing countries[25] is extremely relevant to the assumptions being considered herein—although with one small caveat. Thus, he observes as follows:

> First, as a matter of basic justice the unilateralism of existing trade preference programs must be reconsidered, since justice is not optional and unilateralism favors the more advantaged. Second, the exclusion of the goods most competitive with the manufactured goods of developed states is truly perverse: instead of structuring the trading relationship for the benefit of the least advantaged partner, the import sensitivity exclusion deliberately structures the relationship in favor of the less-competitive domestic industry of the granting state. Third, by subjecting the actual availability of the preferences to conditions clearly related to the domestic and foreign policy agendas of the granting state, GSP programs again turn the normative justification of market inequalities on its head, benefitting the granting state and not the beneficiary.

To the extent that Frank Garcia pegs his aversion to unilateralism in justice there is no disagreement given that such a stance touches on the very propriety of US conditionality. In the same vein, there is no argument with respect to the general questioning of the relevance, efficacy, and coherence of particular aspects of the US conditionality to trade and development. But the substantive criticism of the conditions presupposes the very propriety of US conditionality. Thus, to some extent the justice argument is neutral or silent on the identity and the propriety of the imposer and imposition of conditionality (aside from the fact that the donor

25 Garcia, 'Global Justice and the Bretton Woods Institutions,' op. cit.

is a developed country). This is a reference to capacity and credentials. In sum, the Rawlsian justice argument, based on Rawl's differential principle, is grounded essentially in market access as a right, regardless of these considerations.

The US GSP[26]

The US established its Generalized System of Preferences (GSP) in 1974.[27] Under this program distinction is made between developing and least developing countries, with the latter receiving a more preferential treatment. The GSP is accompanied mainly by two regional specific preference systems viz., the Caribbean Basin Initiative (CBI) set up in 1983[28] and the African Growth and Opportunity Act 2000 (AGOA).[29] The regional regimes follow the GSP model, although they are more liberal in the preferences accorded,[30] including more favourable conditions.[31]

US GSP has been attracting some 119 designated beneficiary countries/territories providing duty free access to the US market for certain designated goods considered not to be import sensitive for the US market.[32] There are some 18 beneficiary countries/territories under the CBI and around 39 under the AGOA. This makes a total of some 176 countries that are eligible for preferential

26 In this chapter, the US GSP forms the basis for analysis of US conditions for preferential trade access to its market for developing countries. The US GSP at the time of writing has expired. It has been renewed several times in the past, including with retroactive effect. There is an expectation that it will be renewed. This past is relevant in understanding US practice, and if and when renewed it will inherit the same template. In any event, the US preferential arrangements having a regional focus, have not expired, and are largely modelled in terms of it.

27 See Title V of the Trade Act of 1974 (19 U.S.C. Sections 2461–2467) as amended Title V of the Consolidated Appropriations Act, 2018 (P.L. 115–141). For GSP Regulations see 15 CFR Part 2007 and for GSP regulations of U.S. Customs and Border Protection (CBP) see 19 CFR Part 10.171–10.178. The GSP program is set for fixed periods of time. The last period expired in December 2020 and its renewal for another period is awaited. It has been renewed thus far 14 times and including retrospectively.

28 See Caribbean Basin Economic Recovery Act (CBERA)1983; the U.S.-Caribbean Basin Trade Partnership Act (CBTPA) 2000; and the Trade Act of 2002. In total there are some 18 beneficiary countries/territories covered under the CBERA eight of which are also covered by the CBTPA. Unlike the GSP and the CBTPA the CBERA has no expiry date. Unlike the GSP which is authorised under the WTO Enabling Clause the CBI operates under a WTO waiver. See <http://ctrc.sice.oas.org/prefar_e.ASP> (last visited March 2021).

29 African Growth and Opportunity Act 2000. There were some 39 eligible beneficiary countries under the AGOA in 2021 and the current expiry date of the program is 2025. See <https://ustr.gov/issue-areas/preference-programs/african-growth-and-opportunity-act-agoa/list-eligible-countries> (last visited March 2021).

30 See Kennedy, op. cit.

31 See Jones & Wong, op. cit.

32 See Office of the United States Trade Representative <https://ustr.gov/issue-areas/trade-development/preference-programs/generalized-system-preference-gsp> (last visited February 2021).

market access to the US market. In 2019 the total imports from this program, however, amounted to 21 billion dollars only, out of a total of $2.5 trillion US imports.[33] This number of imports is therefore not economically significant from the US's standpoint. However, it is of political significance, as it gives it leverage on some 176 beneficiary countries out of a total of 195 countries[34] in the world, in the furtherance of US foreign policy. The number of imports may, however, have a different significance for the beneficiary countries when compared to their overall exports, not to mention the kudos that could come from having a US GSP status. Of note, however, here is that because of the limited range of eligible goods for market access, along with the restrictive rules of origin, empirical studies have shown that the full potential of the GSP is not realised by beneficiary countries.[35]

The Conditions in the Designation of the Beneficiary Countries

The conditions set for preferential market access are formulated in different ways. First, the conditions are informed by the mandate given to the President in the establishment of preferential market access for developing countries. Under Section 501 of the Trade Act 1974, the US President can 'provide duty-free treatment for any eligible article from any beneficiary developing country.' In arriving at this decision, the US President is to have due regard to the following:

(1) the effect such action will have on furthering the economic development of developing countries through the expansion of their exports;
(2) the extent to which other major developed countries are undertaking a comparable effort to assist developing countries by granting generalized preferences with respect to imports of products of such countries;
(3) the anticipated impact of such action on United States producers of like or directly competitive products; and
(4) the extent of the beneficiary developing country's competitiveness with respect to eligible articles.[36]

This is a list of diverse considerations that the President is to consider that are not self-evidently clear; and focus on disparate parties viz. the US, the beneficiary countries, and the actions of developed States. Thus, it is not clear what the purpose of paragraph one is since it is obvious that in general greater exports will further economic development. The paragraph is superfluous unless it is

33 Jones & Wong, op. cit.
34 See <https://www.worldometers.info/geography/how-many-countries-are-there-in-the-world/> (last visited March 2021).
35 See for example D R Khanal, 'Rules of Origin in GSP Schemes and Their Impact on Nepal's Exports: A Case Study of Tea, Carpets, Pashmina and Handicrafts Products,' *Asia-Pacific Research and Training Network on Trade* Working Paper Series No. 98 (April 2011).
36 19 U.S.C. 2461.

interpreted to mean that the President should consider that the GSP furthers the economic development of the developing country. In paragraph one at any rate, the economic development of the US is excluded, as are the development of non-economic facets of the developing country. Paragraph four underlines this by identifying a circumstance wherein the economic development of the developing country is not calling out for assistance. Paragraph three highlights US concerns with respect to its directly competitive domestic industry, although this concern is already reflected in the WTO Agreements on subsidies, dumping, and safeguards. These Agreements have certain parameters for their invocation. Having paragraph three facilitates the achievement of the objectives of the WTO agreements in question, and more, but without the disciplines that accompany them in those agreements.

Second, a country cannot be designated as a beneficiary country if it falls under a designated list of developed countries.[37] This comprises a list of nine developed countries. It is not exhaustive in terms of developed States. For example, it does not include South Korea and Singapore although these countries have graduated out of the system for eligibility in terms of their level of economic development. This is a closed list and therefore could be discriminatory from the standpoint of those in the list, if their level of development changes in the long term.

Third, there is a list of negative conditions; the presence of any one of which precludes a country from being designated as a beneficiary country. The negative conditions are set out under Section 502 of the Trade Act 1974, and are considered herein, as follows.

First, there is the reference to the adherence to communism, preventing the according of preferential market access, as follows:

> (A) Such country is a Communist country, unless— (i) the products of such country receive non-discriminatory treatment, (ii) such country is a WTO Member (as such term is defined in section 2(10) of the Uruguay Round Agreements Act) (19 U.S.C. 3501(10)) and a member of the International Monetary Fund, and (iii) such country is not dominated or controlled by international communism.

Communist countries that are not members of the IMF and the WTO seem to be excluded. However, additionally such countries must not be dominated or controlled by international communism. Would a close political alliance with a communist country come within the sphere of this condition? As Kevin Kennedy points out this condition has nothing to do with a developing country's trade, finance, and development.[38] It does not sit well both with the apolitical manner in which the IMF engages with conditionality and its surveillance, nor with the

37 Section 502 (1) of Trade Act 1974.
38 Kennedy, op. cit.

Enabling Clause under the WTO[39] authorising preferential market access to developing countries. Paragraph 5 of the Enabling Clause refers to the ***developing country's*** development needs. The development needs are linked to the country's development needs, regardless of whether it is a communist or non-communist country. The ambit of sustainable development, as set out in the preamble of the Marrakesh Agreement establishing the WTO, which informs the interpretation of 'development' in the Enabling Clause—includes the ability of a people to determine their own development destiny—and certainly one that does not 'compromise the ability of future generations to meet their own needs'[40] within a communist framework of social organisation. Moreover, the condition does not sit well with international principles of sovereign equality, non-interference in the internal affairs of another State,[41] and the right of a State to its own self-determination.[42] As a matter of international human rights law, all people have individually and collectively the human right to advocate and organise their governance in accordance with communism.[43]

The advocation of communism within the US, provided it does not involve the overthrow of the 'Government of the United States, or the government of any State, Territory, District, or possession thereof, or the government of any political subdivision therein by force and violence' is not prohibited.[44] This must have a bearing in the determination of 'communism' under this condition. Moreover, given that this part of the legislation is rooted in the Cold War and the US period of McCarthyism, it is to some extent a dated background. The current geopolitical tensions may be said to have a different context. Substantively the legislation is lacking in legitimacy. It does not conform to the rule of law[45] as it applies differently between residents of the US and non-residents.[46] It is lacking in

39 See in particular paragraph 5 of The Enabling Clause—Decision of 28 November 1979 (L/4903): 'The developed countries do not expect reciprocity for commitments made by them in trade negotiations to reduce or remove tariffs and other barriers to the trade of developing countries, i.e., the developed countries do not expect the developing countries, in the course of trade negotiations, to make contributions which are inconsistent with their individual development, financial and trade needs. Developed contracting parties shall therefore not seek, neither shall less-developed contracting parties be required to make, concessions that are inconsistent with the latter's development, financial and trade needs.'

40 See Brundland Report (1987).

41 Article 2 (4) of the UN Charter: 4. 'All Members shall refrain in their international relations from the threat or use of force against the territorial integrity or political independence of any State, or in any other manner inconsistent with the Purposes of the United Nations.'

42 UN GA Res A/RES/2625 (XXV) 24 October 1970 'Declaration on Principles of International Law Concerning Friendly Relations and Co-operation among States in Accordance with the Charter of the United Nations.'

43 See for example the Universal Declaration of Human Rights 1948.

44 Communist Control Act of 1954: 50 USC Chapter 23, Subchapter IV: Communist Control Section 842.

45 Friedrich Hayek, *The Constitution of Liberty* (University of Chicago Press: 1960).

46 In other spheres of governance, the claim is made, differences between residents and non-residents is made. A prime example is taxation where there is differential tax treatment as

terms of Lon Fuller's principles of 'internal morality'[47]—in particular consistency and congruence.

Second, a country involved with others in an association that affects the international supply of vital commodity resources is ineligible. This condition is framed as follows:

> (B) Such country is a party to an arrangement of countries and participates in any action pursuant to such arrangement, the effect of which is— (i) to withhold supplies of vital commodity resources from international trade or to raise the price of such commodities to an unreasonable level, and (ii) to cause serious disruption of the world economy.

This is essentially a reference to commodity agreements, although it is not directly framed in that manner. Certainly, until the end of 1990 and therefore at the time of drafting of this legislation, the US itself was participating in six international commodity agreements viz. coffee, natural rubber, jute, sugar, tropical timber, and wheat.[48] And whilst the US non-interventionist market approach may have moved away from the era of commodity agreements,[49] the US, through the imposition of economic sanctions outside the framework of the UN, can be said to 'withhold supplies of vital commodity resources from international trade or to raise the price of such commodities to an unreasonable level.' Where those sanctions affect a major economy there can follow also serious disruptions to the world economy. The US is also party to several intellectual property rights agreements which can contribute to the raising of prices of certain vital commodity resources, contributing to serious disruption in certain sectors of the world economy.

In the same vein, this is a condition which hinders the attainment of economic objectives such as stable prices and greater revenue that is of particular interest to developing countries reliant on commodity exports. The terms of trade in commodity exports, as is well understood, are to be contrasted in the manufacturing sector where they are now given added support through an international apparatus for intellectual property protection, serving mainly the interests of developed countries. Moreover, the relationship between commodity arrangements

---

between residents and non-residents. But this is not necessarily a good example. Taxation is primarily not normative. It is essentially about the acquisition of income by the State. Moreover, even in taxation the differences are justifiable on grounds for example of fiscal efficacy, governmental benefits and the reach of a State's jurisdiction. Furthermore, the economics of taxation calls for even here neutrality and equity as between residents and non-residents. In any event, whatever may be the practice in other spheres of governance that does not undermine the criticism of discriminatory treatment being made here.

47 Lon Fuller, *The Morality of Law* (Yale University Press: 1964).

48 See Operation of the Trade Agreements Program 42nd Report, 1990 USITC Publication 2403, July 1991, Washington, USA.

49 See Table One in Christopher L Gilbert, 'International Commodity Agreements: An Obituary Notice,' *World Development* Vol. 24 No. 1 (1996) 1–19.

and development, since the advent of sustainable development, is now acknowledged.[50] Indeed, the Brundtland Report called for action as follows:

> 79. Current arrangements for commodities could be significantly improved: more compensatory financing to offset economic shocks would encourage producers to take a long-term view, and not to overproduce commodities; and more assistance could be given from diversification programmes. Commodity-specific arrangements can build on the model of the International Tropical Timber Agreement, one of the few that specifically includes ecological concerns.

A third negative condition is where a developing country 'affords preferential treatment to the products of a developed country, other than the United States, which has, or is likely to have, a significant adverse effect on United States commerce.' This is a safeguard condition that takes adverse US interests into account which on the face of it seems understandable. But it has been drafted widely to include a 'likely' significant adverse effect. It is not clear what level of probability this is to be interpreted, including the time framework covered. In theory it could potentially imply that any preferential treatment to the products of a developed country is covered, since the likelihood of a significant adverse effect could be envisioned in most circumstances in the future. Moreover, it is not clear whether 'significant adverse effect to the commerce of the US' refers to the US domestic market or domestic industry, the US competitiveness internationally, the displacement of US exports to the developing country in question, or hindering US access to vital import/supplies. If it includes all it has a very wide ambit. Furthermore, does it include preferential treatment accorded to a developed country under a WTO consistent free trade agreement? If it does then it limits the ability of a developing country to enter into a free trade agreement with other developed countries.

Fourth, there is a wide-ranging condition protecting US property interests in the developing country where the country has:

> (I) has nationalized, expropriated, or otherwise seized ownership or control of property, including patents, trademarks, or copyrights, owned by a United States citizen or by a corporation, partnership, or association which is 50 percent or more beneficially owned by United States citizens, (II) has taken steps to repudiate or nullify an existing contract or agreement with a United States citizen or a corporation, partnership, or association which is 50 percent or more beneficially owned by United States citizens, the effect of which is to nationalize, expropriate, or otherwise seize ownership or control of property, including patents, trademarks, or copyrights, so owned, or (III) has imposed or enforced taxes or other exactions, restrictive maintenance

50 See Report of the World Commission on Environment and Development: Our Common Future (known as the Brundtland Report) (Oxford University Press: 1987) Paragraph 79.

> or operational conditions, or other measures with respect to property, including patents, trademarks, or copyrights, so owned, the effect of which is to nationalize, expropriate, or otherwise seize ownership or control of such property, unless clause (ii) applies. (ii) This clause applies if the President determines that— (I) prompt, adequate, and effective compensation has been or is being made to the citizen, corporation, partnership, or association referred to in clause (i).

This provision imposes on the developing country the controversial 'prompt, adequate, and effective' compensation criteria rejected by developing countries as a basis under customary international law for measuring compensation. It refers to 'or otherwise seized ownership or control of property, including patents, trademarks, or copyrights.' This would seem to include compulsory licensing for public health purposes of pharmaceuticals authorised under TRIPS.[51]

Fifth, a developing country is to:

> act in good faith in recognizing as binding or in enforcing arbitral awards in favor of United States citizens or a corporation, partnership, or association which is 50 percent or more beneficially owned by United States citizens...to which the parties involved have submitted their dispute.

This expectation has two implications. First, that the condition could be interpreted as prioritising the enforcement of an award over other countries when it comes to US concerns. Second, the amount of investment tribunal awards can be extremely burdensome for a developing country—running into billions of dollars. A prompt compliance of such an award can create a double jeopardy for an indebted country desperately in need of export earnings for its balance of payments deficit.

Sixth, a country that facilitates terrorism cannot receive preferential access. This is stated as follows:

> (F) Such country aids or abets, by granting sanctuary from prosecution to, any individual or group which has committed an act of international terrorism or the Secretary of State makes a determination with respect to such country under section 6(j)(1)(A) of the Export Administration Act of 1979 or such country has not taken steps to support the efforts of the United States to combat terrorism.

This provision concerns 'international terrorism' in contrast to domestic terrorism. The provision covers three different circumstances. The second circumstance referring to the Export Administration Act covers the situation where a country has been found to have been supporting international terrorism and consequently

51 See Article 31bis of the TRIPS Agreement.

is subject to US export controls on goods and technology. With respect to all the circumstances the determination of the commission of acts of terrorism is by the US.[52] The final reference with respect to US efforts to combat terrorism imposes on other States a US approach to combatting terrorism. Other countries may well have a different approach or simply may not want to be seen to be involved in such an effort, without further ado. In sum, this is a provision which conflates US foreign policy with international trade.

Seventh, a condition relating to workers right is set out as follows:[53]

> (G) Such country has not taken or is not taking steps to afford internationally recognized worker rights to workers in the country (including any designated zone in that country).

Internationally recognised worker rights are defined as including the following:[54]

(A) the right of association;
(B) the right to organise and bargain collectively;
(C) a prohibition on the use of any form of forced or compulsory labor;
(D) a minimum age for the employment of children, and a prohibition on the worst forms of child labor, as defined in paragraph (6); and
(E) acceptable conditions of work with respect to minimum wages, hours of work, and occupational safety and health.

This US notion of 'international worker rights'[55] has been aptly described variously as idiosyncratic, hypocritical, oppressive, and self-serving.[56] Idiosyncratic because it does not encapsulate fully the dimension of the internationally agreed understanding of worker rights under ILO conventions. It does not

52 Does the US have due process and minimum standards with respect to aliens in the process of determining acts of terrorism?

53 This condition is repeated further as a consideration that the President may take into account in his deliberations. See Section 2462 U.S. Code Title 19—Customs Duties Chapter 12—Trade Act of 1974 Subchapter V—Generalized System of Preferences.

54 Ibid.

55 In contrast the ILO defines international worker rights as follows: 'International labour standards are legal instruments drawn up by the ILO's constituents (governments, employers and workers) setting out basic principles and rights at work. They are either Conventions (or Protocols), which are legally binding international treaties that can be ratified by member States, or Recommendations, which serve as non-binding guidelines. In many cases, a Convention lays down the basic principles to be implemented by ratifying countries, while a related Recommendation supplements the Convention by providing more detailed guidance on how it could be applied. Recommendations can also be autonomous, i.e., not linked to a Convention.' ILO, *Rules of the Game: An Introduction to the Standards-Related Work of the International Labour Organization* (ILO: 2019) 18.

56 Compa & Vogt, op. cit.; and Compa, op. cit. See also Philip Alston, 'Labor Rights Provisions in U.S. Trade Law: "Aggressive Unilateralism"?' *HuM. RTS.* Vol. 15 (1993) cited in Compa, op. cit.

cover discrimination in employment. Hypocritical because the US has only ratified 14 ILO conventions including two categorised as fundamental by the ILO.[57] Of note is the fact that the US has not ratified the following fundamental ILO conventions: Forced Labour Convention, 1930 (No. 29); Freedom of Association and Protection of the Right to Organise Convention, 1948 (No. 87); Right to Organise and Collective Bargaining Convention, 1949 (No. 98); Equal Remuneration Convention, 1951 (No. 100); Discrimination (Employment and Occupation) Convention, 1958 (No. 111); Minimum Age Convention, 1973 (No. 138). In addition, under US law a foreign investment in the US is not conditional upon the presence of a union within the investment enterprise in question. Thus, employees have a right to so organise themselves as much as a right not to.[58] In contrast, for example, Pakistan and Philippines have ratified 38 ILO Conventions including all eight fundamental conventions; Bangladesh 35 conventions excluding one fundamental convention; Cameroon 50 conventions including all the fundamental conventions. It is oppressive because it conceives of certain worker rights without reference to ILO Conventions—which conventions tailor obligations of countries according to the level of their development. For example, reference is made to measures appropriate to national conditions in Articles 3 and 4 of the Right to Organize and Collective Bargaining Convention, 1949 (No. 98), and Articles 4, 6, 8, 11, 13, 14, and 15 of the Occupational Safety and Health Convention, 1981 (No. 155), and its Protocol of 2002. Moreover, the condition allows the US to push for certain worker rights whilst denying the developing countries, who often export their labour to the US, the clear assurance of effective non-discrimination legislation as it affects foreign workers in the US—bearing in mind the manner in which black Americans fare in employment in the US. And finally, it is oppressive because it ignores the wishes of developing countries as expressed in the WTO not to link trade with labour in trade disciplines. In sum, the focus on worker rights has been labelled as a self-serving protectionist measure to avert competition from developing countries.[59]

Finally, ineligibility arises if a country 'has not implemented its commitments to eliminate the worst forms of child labor.' The concerns and considerations expressed with respect to worker rights per se apply here too.

57 See <https://www.ilo.org/dyn/normlex/en/f?p=1000:11200:0::NO:11200:P11200_COUNTRY_ID:102871> (last visited March 2021). In particular, it has not ratified two fundamental conventions: (1) Abolition of Forced Labour Convention, 1957 (No. 105); (2) Worst Forms of Child Labour Convention, 1999 (No. 182)

58 Section 7 of National Labor Relations Act (NLRA). See also documentary film directed by Steven Dognar and Julia Reichert, *American Factory* (2019). The documentary is about a Chinese investor in the US and the efforts of the US employees in the US of the Chinese investor/employer in forming a workers' union.

59 See Lance Compa & Jeffrey S Vogt citing Martin Khor, 'The World Trade Organization, Labour Standards and Trade Protectionism,' *Third World Resurgence* (May 1994) 30–34.

To conclude from a textual perspective the conditions generally are widely drafted with strong elements of US foreign policy intertwined. Moreover, some of the conditions of ineligibility involving US private investment abroad including related disputes, international terrorism abroad, the rights of workers abroad including the worst forms of child labour can be dispensed with if the President is of the view that national economic interests of the US so warrant. Note US economic interests (contra national security) can take priority over the worst forms of child labour!

Furthermore, in designating a beneficiary country the President is to consider not only an interest in access by a country and its level of development but also importantly the following. First, there is a reciprocity expectation formulated as follows:

> (4) the extent to which such country has assured the United States that it will provide equitable and reasonable access to the markets and basic commodity resources of such country and the extent to which such country has assured the United States that it will refrain from engaging in unreasonable export practices;

This condition at the outset has a blank market access reciprocity expectation which does not sit well with the Enabling Clause. Nor necessarily does an 'equitable' expectation by the US from developing/least developed countries. Second, the reference for access to basic commodity resources has an exploitative overtone tending to a dependency relationship.[60] This is endorsed in the third limb of this paragraph with respect to unreasonable export practices. It is not clear from whose perspective unreasonable is to be understood. Does it cover export restrictions on grounds of national security, food security, sustainable development, technology transfer, sanctions, efforts to keep prices stable in the international market?

Second, there is an intellectual property rights concern expressed as follows:

> (5) the extent to which such country is providing adequate and effective protection of intellectual property rights;

The condition is silent as to whether the level of protection is that set out in the WTO or is WTO plus and accompanies the special and differential provisions in TRIPs. In CBERA, however, reference is made to TRIPS or over.[61] This

60 See for example R Prebisch, 'The Economic Development of Latin America and Its Principal Problems' (UN ECLA: 1950); also published in *Economic Bulletin for Latin America* Vol. 7 (1962) 1–22.

61 See Kennedy, op. cit.

condition is self-serving and restricts developing country access to US markets on a preferential basis.[62]

Third, the President is to consider '(6) the extent to which such country has taken action to—(A) reduce trade distorting investment practices and policies (including export performance requirements); and (B) reduce or eliminate barriers to trade in services.' Trade distorting investment practices are covered under the WTO TRIMs agreement. The liberalisation of services in the WTO is essentially contingent on the concessions members of the WTO who have been willing to make in their respective schedules of concessions. This condition is an effort to push further liberalisation in this field, outside the parameters of the negotiating framework of the WTO. It results in a weakening of the developing countries' negotiating capacity in these spheres in the WTO.

Finally, the President is to take into consideration past violations of trade concessions whether within the framework of the WTO or otherwise if 'such country or instrumentality has violated trade concessions of benefit to the US and such violation has not been adequately offset by the action of the US or by such country or instrumentality.'[63] Under WTO law it is clear that disputes between members can only be resolved through the WTO dispute settlement system.

In sum, the considerations that are involved in the designation of a beneficiary country are not primarily directed at establishing a need for preferential market access or the development of the beneficiary country—they comprise in a noticeable manner conditions that reflect US economic and political interests. The conditions are formulated using wide and unclear terminology. Their formulation does not make clear the weight to be given to them respectively. For example, it is not clear whether intellectual property rights are to be considered in evaluating other conditions or is a condition in its own right. Moreover, the GSP conditions not only relate to the regulatory regimes pertaining to the list of items in the GSP scheme, but across all traded items—whether to the US or not.

62 See Ibid.
63 Section 2133 (c).

The conditions applied under the CBI and the AGOA[64] for designating ben-

64 Regarding the CBI, see 19 USC Ch. 15: Caribbean Basin Economic Recovery Section 2702 (b) and (c): In addition, the President shall not designate any country a beneficiary country under this chapter—(1) if such country is a Communist country;

(2) if such country—

(A) has nationalized, expropriated or otherwise seized ownership or control of property owned by a United States citizen or by a corporation, partnership, or association which is 50 per centum or more beneficially owned by United States citizens,

(B) has taken steps to repudiate or nullify—

(i) any existing contract or agreement with, or

(ii) any patent, trademark, or other intellectual property of, a United States citizen or a corporation, partnership, or association which is 50 per centum or more beneficially owned by United States citizens, the effect of which is to nationalize, expropriate, or otherwise seize ownership or control of property so owned, or

€ has imposed or enforced taxes or other exactions, restrictive maintenance or operational conditions, or other measures with respect to property so owned, the effect of which is to nationalize, expropriate, or otherwise seize ownership or control of such property, unless the President determines that—

(i) prompt, adequate, and effective compensation has been or is being made to such citizen, corporation, partnership, or association,

(ii) good-faith negotiations to provide prompt, adequate, and effective compensation under the applicable provisions of international law are in progress, or such country is otherwise taking steps to discharge its obligations under international law with respect to such citizen, corporation, partnership, or association, or

(iii) a dispute involving such citizen, corporation, partnership, or association, over compensation for such a seizure has been submitted to arbitration under the provisions of the Convention for the Settlement of Investment Disputes, or in another mutually agreed upon forum, and promptly furnishes a copy of such determination to the Senate and House of Representatives;

(3) if such country fails to act in good faith in recognizing as binding or in enforcing arbitral awards in favor of United States citizens or a corporation, partnership or association which is 50 per centum or more beneficially owned by United States citizens, which have been made by arbitrators appointed for each case or by permanent arbitral bodies to which the parties involved have submitted their dispute;

(4) if such country affords preferential treatment to the products of a developed country, other than the United States, which has, or is likely to have, a significant adverse effect on United States commerce, unless the President has received assurances satisfactory to him that such preferential treatment will be eliminated or that action will be taken to assure that there will be no such significant adverse effect, and he reports those assurances to the Congress;

(5) if a government-owned entity in such country engages in the broadcast of copyrighted material, including films or television material, belonging to United States copyright owners without their express consent;

(6) unless such country is a signatory to a treaty, convention, protocol, or other agreement regarding the extradition of United States citizens; and

(7) if such country has not or is not taking steps to afford internationally recognized worker rights (as defined in section 2467(4) of this title) to workers in the country (including any designated zone in that country).

Paragraphs (1), (2), (3), (5), and (7) shall not prevent the designation of any country as a beneficiary country under this Act if the President determines that such designation will be in the national economic or security interest of the United States and reports such determination to the Congress with his reasons therefor.

(c) Factors determining designation

In determining whether to designate any country a beneficiary country under this chapter, the President shall take into account—

(1) an expression by such country of its desire to be so designated;

(2) the economic conditions in such country, the living standards of its inhabitants, and any other economic factors which he deems appropriate;

(3) the extent to which such country has assured the United States it will provide equitable and reasonable access to the markets and basic commodity resources of such country;

(4) the degree to which such country follows the accepted rules of international trade provided for under the WTO Agreement and the multilateral trade agreements (as such terms are defined in paragraphs (9) and (4), respectively, of section 3501 of this title);

(5) the degree to which such country uses export subsidies or imposes export performance requirements or local content requirements which distort international trade;

(6) the degree to which the trade policies of such country as they relate to other beneficiary countries are contributing to the revitalization of the region;

(7) the degree to which such country is undertaking self-help measures to promote its own economic development;

(8) whether or not such country has taken or is taking steps to afford to workers in that country (including any designated zone in that country) internationally recognized worker rights.[1]

(9) the extent to which such country provides under its law adequate and effective means for foreign nationals to secure, exercise, and enforce exclusive rights in intellectual property, including patent, trademark, and copyright rights;

(10) the extent to which such country prohibits its nationals from engaging in the broadcast of copyrighted material, including films or television material, belonging to United States copyright owners without their express consent; and

(11) the extent to which such country is prepared to cooperate with the United States in the administration of the provisions of this chapter.

Regarding the AGOA, see 19 US Code Section 3702: Congress supports—

(1) encouraging increased trade and investment between the United States and sub-Saharan Africa;

(2) reducing tariff and nontariff barriers and other obstacles to sub-Saharan African and United States trade;

(3) expanding United States assistance to sub-Saharan Africa's regional integration efforts;

(4) negotiating reciprocal and mutually beneficial trade agreements, including the possibility of establishing free trade areas that serve the interests of both the United States and the countries of sub-Saharan Africa;

(5) focusing on countries committed to the rule of law, economic reform, and the eradication of poverty;

(6) strengthening and expanding the private sector in sub-Saharan Africa, especially enterprises owned by women and small businesses;

(7) facilitating the development of civil societies and political freedom in sub-Saharan Africa;

(8) establishing a United States-Sub-Saharan Africa Trade and Economic Cooperation Forum;

(9) the accession of the countries in sub-Saharan Africa to the Organization for Economic Cooperation and Development (OECD) Convention on Combating Bribery of Foreign Public Officials in International Business Transactions; and

(10) promoting the role of women in social, political, and economic development in sub-Saharan Africa.

eficiary countries mirror these. However, they are understood to be more liberal than the GSP.[65]

The Conditions in the Designation of the Eligible Articles for Preferential Market Access

The President, upon the advice of the International Trade Commission (ITC), is authorised to designate eligible articles from beneficiary countries for preferential market access.[66] The process in the compilation of the list is like the negotiations for a reciprocal trade agreement—with US interests at the fore. Moreover, the designation of eligible articles has normative impact on the beneficiary economy, pushing it in one export direction away from another.

---

19 U.S. Code § 3703.Eligibility requirements: The President is authorized to designate a sub-Saharan African country as an eligible sub-Saharan African country if the President determines that the country—

(1) has established, or is making continual progress toward establishing—

(A) a market-based economy that protects private property rights for men and women, incorporates an open rules-based trading system, and minimizes government interference in the economy through measures such as price controls, subsidies, and government ownership of economic assets;

(B) the rule of law, political pluralism, and the right to due process, a fair trial, and equal protection under the law;

(C) the elimination of barriers to United States trade and investment, including by—

(i) the provision of national treatment and measures to create an environment conducive to domestic and foreign investment;

(ii) the protection of intellectual property; and

(iii) the resolution of bilateral trade and investment disputes;

(D) economic policies to reduce poverty, increase the availability of health care and educational opportunities, expand physical infrastructure, promote the development of private enterprise, and encourage the formation of capital markets through micro-credit or other programs;

(E) a system to combat corruption and bribery, such as signing and implementing the Convention on Combating Bribery of Foreign Public Officials in International Business Transactions; and

(F) protection of internationally recognized worker rights, including the right of association, the right to organize and bargain collectively, a prohibition on the use of any form of forced or compulsory labor, a minimum age for the employment of children, and acceptable conditions of work with respect to minimum wages, hours of work, and occupational safety and health;

(2) does not engage in activities that undermine United States national security or foreign policy interests; and

(3) does not engage in gross violations of internationally recognized human rights or provide support for acts of international terrorism and cooperates in international efforts to eliminate human rights violations and terrorist activities.

See also Section 506 (A) of the Trade Act 1974 which also extends Section 502 eligibility criteria of the GSP to sub-Saharan African countries.

65 See Kennedy, op. cit.

66 Section 2463.

The process involves a Public Hearing with 'any interested person.'[67] Further, the ITC in preparing its advice for the President should:[68]

> (1) investigate conditions, causes, and effects relating to competition between the foreign industries producing the articles or services in question and the domestic industries producing the like or directly competitive articles or services;
>
> (2) analyze the production, trade, and consumption of each like or directly competitive article or service, taking into consideration employment, profit levels, and use of productive facilities with respect to the domestic industries concerned, and such other economic factors in such industries as it considers relevant, including prices, wages, sales, inventories, patterns of demand, capital investment, obsolescence of equipment, and diversification of production;
>
> (3) describe the probable nature and extent of any significant change in employment, profit levels, and use of productive facilities; the overall impact of such or other possible changes on the competitiveness of relevant domestic industries or sectors; and such other conditions as it deems relevant in the domestic industries or sectors concerned which it believes such modifications would cause; and
>
> (4) make special studies (including studies of real wages paid in foreign supplying countries), whenever deemed to be warranted, of particular proposed modifications affecting United States manufacturing, agriculture, mining, fishing, labor, consumers, services, intellectual property and investment, using to the fullest extent practicable United States Government facilities abroad and appropriate personnel of the United States.

The legislation also excludes certain designated import sensitive articles. The designated items on the list are of particular importance to the economies of developing countries—indeed where their comparative advantage is set. The excluded items include certain textile and apparel, watches, footwear, handbags, glass products, carpets, and agricultural goods.[69]

1 Finally, the market access of eligible goods is subject to quantitative limits referred to as 'competitive need limitation' formulated with reference to individual articles.[70] These limits can be waived if there is an adverse effect on any industry or it is in the national economic interest. In addition, the waiver is subject to:

67 Section 2153.

68 19 U.S. Code Sectoion 2151 (D).

69 Section 2463 (3) (b).

70 Section 2463 (c).

> the extent to which the beneficiary developing country has assured the United States that such country will provide equitable and reasonable access to the markets and basic commodity resources of such country, and the extent to which such country provides adequate and effective protection of intellectual property rights.[71]

Furthermore account is to be taken of any 'historical preferential trade relationship between the United States and such country…a treaty or trade agreement in force covering economic relations between such country and the United States,' and if 'such country does not discriminate against, or impose unjustifiable or unreasonable barriers to, United States commerce.'[72]

In conclusion, the selection of eligible items for preferential treatment, like the process of designating a beneficiary country, is an admixture of national economic and foreign policy concerns with a normative impact on the beneficiary country and economic actors within it.

The Discretion in the Designation of Beneficiary Countries and Eligible Articles

As is evident, the US GSP access is subject to discretionary authority vested in the President in ultimately making several decisions. Discretion is vested in the application of the criteria for designating a country as a beneficiary,[73] in the withholding of duty-free treatment for an article,[74] and in waiving some restriction on the imports from the beneficiary country.[75] Such discretion is broadly defined and generally set in the President's determination of 'national economic interests' and 'changed circumstances.' The existence of such a discretion can impact negatively on a beneficiary country. Not only can it have a chilling effect in inducing any kind of compliance with the set conditions, but it can also be a conduit for an open-ended set of non-expressly set out conditions to inflict upon vulnerable beneficiary countries.

Enforcement of the Eligibility Criteria

The enforcement of the beneficiary eligibility criteria takes place in a three-pronged manner:

> (1) assessing all GSP beneficiary countries' eligibility through an interagency process over a three-year period; (2) encouraging countries to address issues

71 Section 2463 (d).
72 Section 2463 (d).
73 See Section 2462.
74 See Section 2463 (C).
75 See Section 2463 (c) (2) (A).

> in existing GSP eligibility reviews on an expedited basis or face loss of GSP benefits; and, (3) engaging with beneficiary countries that are not currently subject to an eligibility review to emphasize the need to comply with all of the GSP eligibility criteria.[76]

The interagency three year review process is an important aspect of compliance focusing on the 15 eligibility criteria discussed above—in particular in

> enforcing arbitral awards in favour of U.S. citizens or corporations, taking steps to respect internationally recognised worker rights, providing the United States with equitable and reasonable market access, reducing trade-distorting investment practices, and providing adequate and effective protection of intellectual property (IP) rights to U.S. rights holders.[77]

The following observations are based on a reading of the transcripts[78] of the public hearings of the review of country eligibility criteria of some eight countries involving a two-day public hearing on 30 and 31 January 2020 in Washington DC, USA. This was the largest GSP hearing in decades with some 40 witnesses and over 90 written statements according to the Chairperson of that hearing.[79] The Chairperson defined the purpose of the meeting in the following terms. First, she clarified that 'Congress has established a set of 15 eligibility criteria that beneficiary countries must meet.' Second, she described the purpose of the meetings as follows:

> we are trying to answer one key question: whether or not the country is meeting the GSP eligibility criteria.

There is clearly setting out a tone here. The 15 eligibility criteria are stripped from context and purpose of the scheme. Importantly there is no reference to the fact that this Congressional indulgence is subject to WTO law—namely the disciplines, such as they are, to be found in the Enabling Clause, including the way it has been interpreted. Moreover, the purpose could be set out in a softer manner as follows:

76 See USTR, 2021 Trade Policy Agenda and 2020 Annual Report, 97.

77 Ibid. Annual and General Reviews are to be conducted under 15 CFR 2007.3. During such reviews any interested party may petition with respect to country eligibility criteria including eligibility of the articles designated for duty free treatment.

78 See <https://www.federalregister.gov/documents/2019/11/19/2019-24947/generalized-system-of-preferences-gsp-notice-regarding-a-hearing-for-country-practice-reviews-of> and <https://www.regulations.gov/document/USTR-2013-0009-0065> (last visited February 2022).

79 See Laura Buffo Chairperson's introduction in transcript of hearing on 30 January 2020, ibid.

> we are trying to answer one key question: whether or not the country should continue to receive GSP benefits given its purposes.

First, as a matter of process, the review takes place in the US. Thus, it necessitates Ministers and officials travelling from home countries all the way to the US, to respond to the questions raised in the review. The ability of developing countries to send informed high-ranking officials for this purpose varies. Also, embassy staff in the US can be at a disadvantage in the information they have immediate access to. Moreover, the fact of the hearing is announced through the US Federal Register Notice, and therefore focused on US stakeholders alone—at any rate in so far as the impact of that notice is concerned. Could a greater pool of non-State stakeholders from the beneficiary country assist in improving the review process? Could there be a greater evaluation of the development objectives of the scheme? Thus, US stakeholders can provide the cost benefit data affecting them in the event of a discontinuance of the GSP, but this opportunity is only theoretical for such an input from the beneficiary country stakeholders if the exercise does not touch on the development objectives of the exercise. Some of the questions asked in the review would also be the subject of focus in WTO trade policy reviews and US section 301 triggered reviews, and therefore may be repetitive. The review is driven by US enterprises and non-governmental organisations, and thus the focus and direction of the review is driven with a preoccupation for compliance with the conditions set for preferential access. This is not to deny that in this process other non-directly concerned stakeholders can draw attention to the consequences they may suffer if compliance with a particular eligibility criterion is pursued to its logical conclusion. Thus, the process of compliance evaluation of a criterion is informed by the wider impact of a negative finding of country eligibility on US stakeholders generally—which is as it should be. But what if that input was not there? And what of the negative impact on other stakeholders within the beneficiary country? Moreover, the review has the effect of a judicial review wherein the beneficiary country's legislative process in the enactment of its legislation is probed into. The review can also involve questions of compatibility with WTO law. For example, Indonesia's nickel export ban came under such scrutiny. Given that non-conformity with US eligibility criteria through this 'injudicious' forum on questions of WTO legality can lead to a loss of GSP status, such a process of realising WTO compatibility of a beneficiary country's trade measures is contrary to Article 23 of the WTO Dispute Settlement Understanding which makes the WTO dispute system as the exclusive forum for resolution of disputes. Finally, the review process allows for post-hearing briefs to be submitted. It is not clear whether all parties have sight of these, and whether they can respond to them.

Generally, the discourse during the review examined herein seems to have been robust—detailed and specific, with different stakeholders expressing different viewpoints for or against the beneficiary country in terms of compliance with the conditions. The review focuses both on existing and proposed changes in legislation of beneficiary countries. However, the balance and comprehensiveness of the input is informed by the stakeholders involved and present. The enforcement of 'American values' is left to market forces and not a balanced 'intelligent design.' There is no guarantee that there will be overall objectivity in such a process all the time. The stakeholders involved have a narrow focus, whereas both the US and the beneficiary State would have a wider set of concerns to consider.[80] Furthermore, the eligibility criteria are set in statutory form. This involves interpretations of US statutory language—which in turn needs to be informed by US WTO and international obligations. Yet the whole process of review has a measure of lay and loose interpretation of the eligibility criteria. The stakeholders peg their agenda on individual (indeed the entire process has this semblance to it) aspects of the eligibility criteria when in fact the review must take a holistic approach taking all the set of conditions into account—as per Section 2462 (d) wherein the President is directed to 'consider the factors set forth in section 2461 of this title and subsection (c) of this section.' In short, a bottom-up process of review does not facilitate well a holistic approach to the application of the eligibility criteria set against the background of the purposes and objectives of a preferential system. That said, some important and desirable changes are indeed brought about in beneficiary country practices.

Second, with reference to the beneficiary eligibility criteria—where this is imprecise the beneficiary country is vulnerable to high levels of interpretation of the standards involved. Thus, the standard of intellectual property rights is not spelt out; the 'equitable and reasonable access' to the beneficiary's market can potentially operate as a 'carte blanche' for any number of expectations; and the 'good faith in recognizing as binding or in enforcing arbitral awards' can be interpreted strictly or liberally in favour of the beneficiary country. Do some such vagaries in the US GSP legislation fall short of the US Due Process constitutional requirements of clarity and precision in legislation?[81] Moreover, because the stakeholders come to the review with a particular agenda and mindset, they can be blind to the fact that the eligibility criteria must be contextualised to the circumstances of the beneficiary State. The relevance of the factual context of the circumstances of the beneficiary country is reinforced by Section 2462 (c) (2) wherein the President is directed to consider 'the level of economic development of such country, including its per capita gross national product, the living standards of its inhabitants, and any other economic factors which the President deems appropriate.' Thus, South Africa with reference to its exceptions to its copyright protection rightly defended it on the basis of the long-lasting effects of apartheid, lack of bargaining powers of black artists, and the high proportion of impoverished black students in its education system.

80 See transcript, ibid.
81 See Fifth and Fourteenth Amendments to the US Constitution.

Concluding Remarks on Normative Impact of Conditions

A focus on the normative impact of the conditions cannot be undertaken with reference to the individual conditions, for example child labour, but the totality of the conditions set out in the legislation. This is because all the conditions are informed and therefore tainted with US economic interests both in terms of the beneficiary country eligibility criteria and in the designation of the articles for preferential treatment. From this perspective the following concluding observations are proffered. First, considered in this light the claim that the preferential arrangements further certain 'American values' is undermined. This is reinforced by the fact that the apparatus for the enforcement of the conditions is to a large measure left for US stakeholders through petitions for revocation of entitlements, and de facto preferential participatory rights in the review processes. Second, from the perspective of the underlying rational of facilitating development including sustainable development through trade and investment, this linkage is somewhat challenging when it comes to considering development in the broader sense of its meaning.[82] Moreover, the conditions reinforce US rights enshrined in the international investment regime. This regime itself has characteristics that hinder development objectives, insofar as its bias in favour of securing the interests of the investor over those of the development of developing countries are concerned. Third, the conditions make inroads into national economic and political priorities. This they do, for example, in the incentive provided through the selected eligible articles for preferential treatment, and the market orientation of the conditions. Fourth, the conditions are blind to realising distributive justice, sustainable development, and welfare concerns in the beneficiary country, and as between beneficiary countries. Finally, the conditions have implicit value traits. Thus, leaving aside obvious conditions that have a moral trait (for example, child labour/terrorism) seemingly purely economic conditions such as types of eligible goods, level of development in terms of graduating out of the system, levels of export thresholds linked to levels of comparative advantage, all have in one form or another a value promoting or deterring trait. Thus, the lack of preferential access in one field can result in behavioural changes and reordering of economic priorities of non-State actors as much as the State.

In conclusion, a preferential trade regime that conflates US economic interests with the pursuit of so-called American values diminishes the integrity of those values. The formulation and enforcement of these values if they have intrinsic merit need to be delinked and the leverage from the linkage needs to be attained in a more coherent and consistent manner against the background of international law and policy.

82 See Article 1 of the Declaration of the Right to Development (1986); and for example, Amartya Sen, *Development as Freedom* (Oxford University Press: 1999).

6 Exports under the US Export Control Reform Act 2018

'A State's rights to control its exports are informed as much by its sovereign rights as its responsibilities under International Law and towards mankind.'

Introduction and Current State of US System on Export Controls[1]

The US export control system is one of the most complex and far-reaching in the world. It focuses on 'exports' from the US—but with a wide definition of what constitutes 'exports.' Exports include certain intraterritorial transmissions to foreigners, 're-exports' from third countries, and exports involving controlled US technology/software or US origin plant and equipment.[2] It covers a range of exports that not only concern US national and international security—such as nuclear, chemical, and biological weapons, missiles technology and goods that would assist in the proliferation of such weapons—but also dual-use[3] items and technology and economic security[4] as an aspect of national security, including a wide-ranging set of sanctions on certain countries in the implementation of US foreign policy. And finally, the export controls are also conceived in terms of a list of individuals and end users considered to be a threat to the US national security.[5]

1 For a recent up to date account of the US Export Control System see Ian F Fergusson, C A Casey, & P K Kerr, 'The U.S. Export Control System and the Export Control Reform Act of 2018', CRS Report (R46814: June 2021). This introductory section draws from this publication. See also C Whang, 'Undermining the Consensus-Building and List-Based Standards in Export Controls: What the US Export Controls Act Means to the Global Export Control Regime,' *Journal of International Economic Law* Vol. 22 (2019) 579–599; Heejin Kim, 'Global Export Controls of Cyber Surveillance Technology and the Disrupted Triangular Dialogue,' *International & Comparative Law Quarterly* Vol. 70 No. 2 (2021) 379–415. I am grateful to Professor Mark Feldman for his observations on this chapter. The errors and views remain mine.

2 Known as the Foreign-Produced Direct Product Rule (FDPR) under ECRA 2018.

3 See ECRA (P.L. 115–232, Subtitle B, Part I) 2018. Dual-use export control is administered by the US Bureau of Industry and Security.

4 See ECRA 2018.

5 See ibid.

DOI: 10.4324/9781003047575-7

These wide-ranging policy underpinnings of US export controls impinge on the functioning of a liberal international trading system, including fair competition; have an unsolicited normative impact externally on the foreign policy of third State and non-State actors; raise fundamental questions about the very right of any State to inhibit the development of another State—indeed the rest of humanity—through controls on access to materials and technology. Moreover, export controls touch on the responsibility of all people in terms of intergenerational equity, as much as towards future generations of all people of the world. This is because export controls are about allocative/distributive decisions concerned with distributive justice and international sustainable development goals. Such sentiments are reflected in the prohibition in the US constitution on the imposition of duties on exported goods from any US state.[6] Ironically, however, the spirit of this edict in the US constitution is not reflected in the more draconian quantitative trade restriction used as an instrument of enforcement for export controls.

The US export control system is to be found in several legislative instruments;[7] and administered by a variety of agencies, including the Department of Commerce, the Department of State, and the Department of the Treasury. An important part of the legislative mosaic that comprises the US export control system is the Export Control Reform Act 2018 (ECRA). One reason for this is that in theory it can cover a significant part of the US exports —for example in 2019 96% of US exports by value—although only 0.4% of total exports in that year actually required licences.[8] The ECRA is implemented by the Export Administration Regulations.[9]

The US has given legislative lead in the field of export controls. Whilst hitherto several States have engaged in export controls through disparate measures, there is now a discernible movement towards a more strategic recalibration of national export control policy and practice. Thus, China enacted an Export Control Law in October 2020 that consolidated and advanced the patch work nature of its past involvement in this sphere. The Chinese legislation mirrors in its breadth the scope of the US legislation. In the same vein, the European Union reconfigured its export controls in May 2021.[10]

At the multilateral level, export controls concerning national and international security are set against the background of international arrangements, such as the Wassenaar Arrangement 1997; UN Security Council Resolutions; and national

6 Article I Section 9 (5) of the US Constitution.

7 The principal instruments being the Arms Export Control Act (AECA), the International Emergency Economic Powers Act (IEEPA), the Export Control Reform Act (ECRA).

8 See US CRS Report R46814: June 2021.

9 EAR:15 CFR 730.

10 Regulation (EU) 2021/821 of the European Parliament and of the Council of 20 May 2021 setting up a Union regime for the control of exports, brokering, technical assistance, transit and transfer of dual-use items (recast) EUR-Lex - 32021R0821 - EN - EUR-Lex (europa.eu) (last visited September 2021).

security exceptions to international commitments, for example Article XXI of GATT 1994 and Articles VIII and XIV of the IMF Articles of Agreements.[11] The Wassenaar Agreement[12] is a multilateral arrangement coordinating export controls amongst its 42 participating countries in conventional arms and dual-use goods and technologies. It is, however, a voluntary export control arrangement amongst a select group of countries, in which decisions are made by consensus under a soft law regime.[13] Increasingly, however, national export control regimes in the US, EU, and China are diverging from its dual list items for export controls.[14]

The bedrock of the historical development of US export controls has been fuelled mainly by national security concerns, as informed by international geopolitical circumstances. More recently these concerns have been enmeshed with economic interests including the concerns of US exporters opposed to such restrictions. The US controls date as far back as 1949—reflecting mainly national security concerns but also coupled with foreign policy and the protection of the domestic economy.[15] In 1969, however, the restrictions were constrained in response to domestic industry apprehensions with respect to their capacity to compete internationally.[16] ECRA 2018, however, introduced more controls, and is a culmination and consolidation of US responses to more recent geopolitical developments—embedded essentially in superpower rivalry, and the quest for technological superiority. It has further been buttressed by the United States Innovation and Competition Act of 2021, which has a strong expressly stated focus on China, whilst enhancing cooperation with US allies.

Issues

Contemporary discourse underlying US export controls has been US-centred—focusing on US defence and foreign and economic policy.[17] Thus, is it concerned whether dual-use sales impact negatively on the export competitiveness of US domestic industry in the sector? Whether a focus on dual use that is unilateral is effective? Whether similar export controls as applied with reference to technology should be extended to commodity products? How should the US work with its allies in coordinating/harmonising export control policies? Such a discourse

11 See also the Nuclear Suppliers Group, the Australia Group, and the Missile Technology Control Regime. For an interpretation of Articles VIII and XIV of IMF Articles see EB Decision 144-(52/51) August 14 1952.

12 See <https://www.wassenaar.org> (last visited February 2022).

13 <https://www.wassenaar.org/about-us/> (last visited February 2002). See also Whang, op. cit.

14 See Kim, op. cit.

15 ECA 1949 and US CRS Report 2021.

16 See EEA 1969.

17 See US CRS Report R46814: June 2021.

assumes the very propriety of export controls, focusing on specific issues from that standpoint.

In the same vein, the European response to recent US initiatives in export controls—namely the ECRA—has been broadly in alignment with the US worldview.[18] Thus, it is observed in a brief to the European Parliament:[19]

> Competition in technology has become a central component of the relationship between powerful international actors. Perhaps the most visible manifestation of this is the rising relevance of technological supremacy in the competition between the USA and China. China's ambition to be a world leader in certain technologies, as laid out in its Made in China 2025 (MIC2025) industrial policy, has led to concerns, including about the potential erosion of Western norms governing the use of emerging technologies. The proliferation of technology that can be used for both civilian and military purposes, terrorism, and/or weapons of mass destruction-related applications – known as dual-use technology – is a growing source of concern globally. Within this context, debate and regulation of export controls has come to the fore on both sides of the Atlantic.

A few observations need to be made here. First, competition in technology needs to be distinguished from seeking technological supremacy and seeking leadership in technological advancements. In the same vein, the means to achieve leadership is distinct from the goal of achieving it. Nations which seek supremacy or its maintenance, seek dominance. Nations which seek leadership are not necessarily seeking dominance. As such there is nothing sinister about seeking leadership. The way that leadership is sought to be achieved domestically may well be something of concern to foreign stakeholders in terms of fair competition. Equally far-reaching export controls specifically designed to inhibit that quest for leadership of another State are of concern when they go beyond countering an unfair advantage gained outside the setting of international disciplines. Second, the statement 'about the potential erosion of Western norms governing the use of emerging technologies' is unfortunate, West-centric, emotive, and empirically not substantiated. Third, the assertion that there has been a 'proliferation of technology that can be used for both civilian and military purposes' is a generalisation suggesting that this a recent phenomenon calling for concern. It does need some substantiation. Moreover, are the compendium of concerns not simply 'western' preoccupations? Is the dual use for military purposes not about non-western States playing catch up in military advancement? Are the concerns related to 'terrorism' and weapons of mass destruction not preoccupations relatively closer to western insecurities? This is of course not to deny that these concerns are justified

18 See Elena Lazarou with Nicholas Lokker, 'United States Export Control Reform Act,' European Parliamentary Research Service, PE 644.187 – November 2019.
19 Ibid.

and should be of universal concern. But what about export controls on items that lead to pollution or the destruction of other cultures? In sum, the concerns may well be shared globally but equally they may be said to reflect an agenda of 'West-centric' concerns. And finally, the authors confirm the knee-jerk West-centric alignment on both sides of the Atlantic—with the implicit suggestion that this 'global' issue can only be taken forward amongst such like-minded nations or at any rate primarily so. This European approach is now reflected in its recently enacted 2021 Regulation on Export Controls.[20] Alas the Chinese export control law of 2020[21] mirrors the underlying nationalistic approach to export controls set by the United States.

From a policy perspective it is not possible to delink export from import controls. Both are integral to the broader desideratum of a liberal international trading order, and the underlying rational it is based upon. By so bifurcating the discourse it is almost natural to come to export controls more from a sovereignty paradigm given its historical national security overtones. On the other hand, import controls generally can be conceived from the way other States restrict imports—and therefore here it is easier to adopt the liberal trade high ground, even if qualified by the notion of reciprocity—an argument itself that does not sit well with the underlying spirit of liberal trade. Indeed, GATT 1994[22] always had contextualised export controls as an integral part of the liberalisation of international trade— and this in stronger terms than GATT 1994—in the Chinese accession protocol.[23] Under the steer of national security, export controls have become the handmaiden of other objectives to embrace foreign and domestic economic policy, such that the relative neutrality in terms of non-trade issues that the international trading system strived for has now come under serious strain.

Export controls, as opposed to market access, are fundamentally about the conditions for sharing of goods, services, and technology with others. As such they raise a spectrum of concerns that go beyond the national/sovereignty lenses. These include distributive justice; sustainable development; the right to development of other nations; human rights of foreigners, for example the right to life, right to basic needs, the individual's freedom to engage in transnational economic relations; and the interests of others in terms of the heritage of mankind—for example, technological innovations have a background of accumulated knowledge of a combination of civilisations, raising questions of one State's absolute ownership of the decision relating to its export.

From a legal perspective, under customary international law there are few limitations on a State's ability to limit exports. In the same vein, there would be few obligations on a State to have export controls. It is not clear, however, what

20 Regulation (EU) 2021/821 of the European Parliament and the Council of 20 May 2021.

21 PRC Export Control Law of 17 October 2020.

22 See for example Article XI (1) of GATT 1994.

23 See Article 11 of Protocol on the Accession of the People's Republic of China (November 2011: WT/L/432)

the 'few' in either case are. Given the absence of direct authority and clear State practice the scope of what constitutes 'few' could be informed by decisions such as the Trail Smelter case, albeit in the field of environmental control. The Trail Smelter case itself is very specific, including a high threshold. In that case the Tribunal famously held as follows:[24]

> no State has the right to use or permit the use of its territory in such a manner as to cause injury by fumes in or to the territory of another or the properties or persons therein, when the case is of serious consequence and the injury is established by clear and convincing evidence.
>
> (Second Decision 1965)

This ruling has been developed in Principle 21 of the 1972 Stockholm Declaration of the United Nations Conference on the Human Environment (Stockholm Declaration [1972] and Rio Declaration [1992]) as follows:

> States have, in accordance with the Charter of the United Nations and the principles of international law, the sovereign right to exploit their own resources pursuant to their own environmental policies, and the responsibility to ensure that activities within their jurisdiction or control do not cause damage to the environment of other States or areas beyond the limits of national jurisdiction.

Given the treaty practice in the field of export controls with respect to international arms, along with national practice implementing those international obligations, this line of development in the field of environmental law has a relevance here—at any rate if not *de jure lex lata*. On the other hand, export controls grounded in national security do not escape the focus of international law just because they are so grounded.[25]

Furthermore, export controls need to be formulated within the normative framework of the WTO, the IMF, investment, and preferential trade agreements. The exceptions within which export controls may be set in these agreements need to be interpreted according to the disciplines integral to them. In particular, of note is the jurisprudence both in the WTO and investment sphere of limiting the scope of the self-judging character of a national security exception. Whether these normative regimes provide a coherent effective and comprehensive set of disciplines is, however, a question of note, although this does not detract from the fact that relevant disciplines do exist. In the same vein, principles set in the UN Charter are relevant in informing the normative

24 Trail Smelter Arbitration (U.S. v. Can.), 3 R.I.A.A. 1905 at p.1965 (1941), reprinted in *Am. J. Int'l L.* Vol. 35 (1941) 684.

25 See this author Chapter Four herein.

framework within which national export controls have international legitimacy.[26] First of note, the preamble to the UN refers in relevant parts to the 'equal rights of men and women and of nations large and small,' 'to promote social progress and better standards of life in larger freedom,' 'for the promotion of the economic and social advancement of all peoples.' This is a commitment of the international community of an endeavour to work towards the sharing of resources for the advancement of all people. Second, Article 1 of the UN refers to principles of justice and international law,' 'equal rights and self-determination of peoples.' Rawl's theory of justice speaks of a commitment to redistribute resources to the extent that those resources have been arbitrarily dispersed to those unequally so endowed as an obligation set in justice (contra charity or favour).[27] The notion of sustainable development embraces not only intragenerational but also intergenerational equity.[28] Article 2 affirms the 'sovereign equality' of States and enjoins nations to fulfil their obligations in good faith. There is no right of supremacy in international law. Articles 1 (3) and 2 (3) refer to the achievement of the resolution of international problems through international cooperation and to settle disputes by peaceful means—in a manner that international peace and security and justice are not endangered.

In sum, are export controls that violate the equal rights of individuals and nations—in justice and international law—of concern? Are export controls that violate the sovereign equality of nations problematic? Are export controls that unilaterally approach international problems rather than through international cooperation of concern? Are export controls that underpin an underlying dispute and that essentially are unilateral methods of resolving a dispute—a peaceful manner of resolving them? Should export controls that inhibit and distort the advancement of knowledge including its transmission in universities and centres of learning be of concern? The need to address these questions is not addressed by the argument that one nation's expansive interpretation of its national security concerns can be checked by other States similarly interpreting the scope of their national security, whilst buttressing that stand through national blocking statutes. Importantly this laissez-faire stance allows for the development of national approaches to export controls when in fact export controls call out for an international approach.

26 I am grateful to Professor Mark Feldman for asking me to elaborate on the meaning of legitimacy. Legitimacy is used here as a broader measure of validation that is not confined to legality. See for example Alexander P d'Entrèves, 'Legality and Legitimacy,' *The Review of Metaphysics* Vol. 16 No. 4 (1963) 687–702.

27 John Rawls, *A Theory of Justice* (Belknap Press: 1971)

28 See for example Justice Mensah, 'Sustainable Development: Meaning, History, Principles, Pillars, and Implications for Human Action: Literature Review,' *Cogent Social Sciences* Vol. 5 No. 1 (2019) 1653531, DOI: 10.1080/23311886.2019.1653531.

Analysis of ECRA 2018[29]

ECRA is the main legislative instrument under which the US Export Administration Regulations (EAR) are set. The EAR is a detailed set of rules and procedures, including licencing requirements for export control and a control list (CCL) of dual-use goods and technology, administered by the US Department of Commerce, through the Bureau of Industry and Security (BIS). As such, the EAR informs an important part of the legal framework of ECRA. ECRA itself has 41 sections, with three different parts, titled respectively as follows: Part 1—Authority and Administration of Controls. This part outlines the policy of the legislation, the authority of the President, the administration of the export controls viz., licencing, compliance, enforcement. Part II is titled the Anti-Boycott Act of 2018; and Part III—sets out the Administrative Authorities concerned with the management of the legislation. In what follows, is not a description of ECRA, nor a comprehensive exposition of it in its historical context.[30] Herein is a focus from two different perspectives viz., the scope of ECRA and its impact. This is based mainly on the policy outlined in ECRA and the considerations highlighted in Section 2 above.

The Scope of ECRA

The jurisdiction of the United States for the purposes of ECRA is defined mainly with reference to what is a 'controlled item.'[31] Thus, US jurisdiction is synonymous with what is defined as 'controlled.' However, there is no express elaboration as such of what is 'controlled' other than that it refers to 'an item subject to the jurisdiction of the United States.' In international law, as is well understood even in the United States, the limits of a State's jurisdiction is informed by international law, and not subject to an autonomous domestic remit.

The scope of ECRA is further expanded and problematic in several ways. First, the definition of export includes 'release or transfer of technology or source code relating to the item to a foreign person in the United States.'[32] Article 2 of the PCR Export Control Law can also be read to include such an intraterritorial scope of export as it refers to the 'provision of any Controlled Items by any citizens, legal persons or non-corporate organizations of the People's Republic of China to any foreign organizations and individuals.' In the EU Regulation 2021/821 export is defined to include the 'oral transmission of technology when the technology is described over a voice transmission medium.'

29 Public Law 115-232—Title XVII, Subtitle B referred to as the Export Control Reform Act of 2018—codified, as amended, at 50 U.S.C. Sections 4801–4852.

30 For a contextual exposition of ECRA set in its historical context against the background of multinational consensus on export controls see Whang, op. cit.

31 Section 1742.

32 Section 1742.

The US definition is a novel and somewhat stretched definition of 'export'; beyond the way it is understood in the WTO.[33] This is not an issue on its own but given its wide scope it could contribute to confusion in export trade; and/or inhibit cross border flows. In such circumstances therefore, it could come within the purview of the WTO, for example as an export restriction.[34] Moreover, there is an issue of clarity with respect to 'export controls' that is recognised in the legislation itself.[35] However, such a recognition on its own is not enough. As is implicit in the legislation the proof of clarity will be in the regulations and their administration.

Second, ECRA covers re-export—defined to include:[36]

(A) The shipment or transmission of the item from a foreign country to another foreign country, including the sending or taking of the item from the foreign country to the other foreign country, in any manner; and

(B) The release or transfer of technology or source code relating to the item to a foreign person outside the United States.

The PRC Export Control Law does not specifically refer to re-export. However, there are obligations placed on end-users.[37] On the other hand whereas the EU Regulations refers to re-export it does not seem to impose obligations out of the EU, preferring instead to rely on the knowledge of the exporter of a re-export to a prohibited place/end-user.[38]

The ECRA re-export obligations constitute a controversial exercise of extraterritorial legislative jurisdiction by the US.[39] It undermines the sovereignty of another State; and impinges on the transnational economic human rights of foreigners. It interferes in the international trade of another State thus potentially exposing it to violations of its obligations under the WTO.[40] Moreover, the focus is not only on re-exports from a foreign country but includes in-country transfers

33 Although not defined specifically it is understood as a cross border flow.

34 For example, Articles I and XI of GATT 1994. Article XI refers to 'restrictions' on exports. Article X of GATT requires the publication of laws 'promptly in such a manner as to enable governments and traders to become acquainted with them' and the administration of those laws 'in a uniform, impartial and reasonable manner.' See also Article 6 of TRIMs and Understanding Regarding Notification, Consultation, Dispute Settlement and Surveillance adopted on 28 November 1979 and in the Ministerial Decision on Notification Procedures adopted on 15 April 1994.

35 See Section 1752 (7) and (8).

36 Section 1742.

37 See Article 16.

38 See for example EU Regulation 2021/821 op. cit. Part 3 (c).

39 See for example Robert Jennings, Arthur Watts, Ronald Roxburgh (eds) *Oppenheim's International Law* (1996) 471; V Lowe, 'US Extraterritorial Jurisdiction: The Helms-Burton and D'Amota Acts,' *ICLQ* Vol. 46 (1997), 378; and C. Ryngart, 'Extraterritorial Export Controls (Secondary Boycotts)' *CJIL* Vol. 7 No. 3 (2008) 625–658.

40 For example, Articles I and XI of GATT 1994.

in a foreign country—defined to include 'a change in the end-use or end user of the item within the same foreign country.'[41]

Third, ECRA's definition of what constitutes an 'item' and 'technology' is wide. An item is defined as 'a commodity, software, or technology;'[42] and technology includes 'information, in tangible or intangible form, necessary for the development, production, or use of an item.'[43] Technology thus is defined so broadly that it includes 'information.' Information is a very broad notion, without further clarification. In addition, technology is not defined with reference to Intellectual Property Rights (IPRs). Moreover, the US State appears to be exercising ownership rights of private IPRs, to the extent that they fall under the scope of an item and/or technology—in the way these can be 'exported.' The PRC Export Control Law also has a wide definition of controlled items to include technical information and other data.[44] The same could be said of the EU Regulation which covers 'technology that can be described over a voice transmission medium.'[45]

Fourth, the definition in ECRA of a foreign person includes 'international organizations, foreign governments and any agency or subdivision of a foreign government (e.g., diplomatic mission).' The governance of international organizations is informed by their constitution not US dictates. Moreover, international organisations and diplomatic missions enjoy diplomatic immunity and foreign States State immunity.

And finally, and significantly, the wide-ranging tentacles of ECRA are reinforced by the extension of US controls beyond military items to include dual-use items. These are defined as items having 'civilian applications and military, terrorism, weapons of mass destruction, or law-enforcement-related applications.'[46] The dual use definition in the Chinese and European export controls does not include 'law-enforcement-related applications'[47] as such although in the case of China it includes 'services,'[48] and in the case of the EU export controls could be imposed for dual-use items for 'human rights considerations,'[49] and specifically in the case of cyber-surveillance items the use of these 'in connection with internal repression or the commission of serious violations of human rights and international human rights law.'[50] This breadth of coverage in the recent new generation

41 Section 1742.
42 Section 1742.
43 Section 1742.
44 Article 2 of PRC Export Control Law.
45 Article 2 (d) of the EU 2021/821 Regulation of May 2021.
46 Section 1742.
47 Article 2 of the PRC Control Law; and Article 2 (1) of the EU 2021/821 Regulation of May 2021.
48 See Article 2 of the PRC Control Law.
49 See Article 9 of EU 2021/821 Regulation of May 2021.
50 EU Regulation 2021/821 of May 2021 para 2 of preamble.

of national export control laws is fairly open ended. When exactly does an item become of dual use? Can there be an objective criterion for such a determination?

In sum, the scope of ECRA is wide in several respects. National security grounds as a basis for the justification of these excesses are not open-ended.[51] This legislation, the spirit of which is to enforce international law and contribute to international peace and security itself, needs to be considered for its conformity with international norms.

The Impact of ECRA on Foreign States, Foreign Persons, and the International Economy

Essentially ECRA does not concern itself with the impact it has on foreign persons, States, and the development of the international economy/community. It is only concerned with the impact on the US national security, economy, and the pursuits of its foreign policy goals. Thus, the legislation mandates export controls 'only after full consideration of the impact on the economy of the United States.'[52] In the same vein, the legislation is concerned with the impact resulting from exports on 'the military capabilities of the foreign country,' 'the relative military strengths of countries in the region,' and 'the relations of the United States with the countries in the region region.'[53] The US economy, its military, and foreign relations are prioritised over the economy of other States and the world economy. Ultimately export controls have an impact on individuals, foreign States, and the international community. This is not in the spirit of the multilateral economic institutions (viz. IMF and WTO), nor indeed with the UN Charter—in particular, the Security Council of which the US is a permanent member and whose mandate is to ensure '*international* peace and security' (emphasis added).

Several observations can be made in relation to the purposes of export control as set out in ECRA. First, the objective of furthering US foreign policy.[54] As has been stated already, the multilateral economic institutions eschew the integration of foreign policy in economic decision-making—a prime vehicle of which is the ubiquitous most-favoured-nation clause in many international economic agreements. Of course, US foreign policy serves laudable objectives as well—for example human rights. However, US focus here can be selective and in alignment with its overall strategic objectives. In sum, 'US foreign policy' is a wide mandate that can be the handmaiden for many purposes. This is the case also with the Chinese Export Control Law which is replete with references to 'national interests' as a policy underpinning export control.[55] In the same vein, the EU Regulation

51 See Asif H Qureshi on 'A Public International Law Perspective of Section 232 of the U.S. Trade Expansion Act,' *Kansas Journal of Law and Public Policy* Vol. XXX (2021), 3.

52 See Section 1752.

53 Section 1754 (2) (IV).

54 See Section 1752 (B) and then repeated in para (D) again!

55 See for example Article 1, 12 and 13.

enjoins the considering of national foreign policy in the administration of export controls.[56]

Second, in relation to the use of export controls with respect to items related to military/armament proliferation concerns.[57] This is the historical justification of arms control although in contemporary times this discourse is not a closed one. This is because it is tainted with the interests of those who are already armed and their need to preserve that lead. But there is here an important point albeit provocative that George Bernard Shaw made through the mouths of an arms manufacturer, albeit more than a century ago, in his play *Major Barbara*:[58]

> LADY BRITOMART. There is no moral question in the matter at all, Adolphus. You must simply sell cannons and weapons to people whose cause is right and just, and refuse them to foreigners and criminals.
>
> UNDERSHAFT. [determinedly] No: none of that. You must keep the true faith of an Armorer, or you don't come in here.
>
> CUSINS. What on earth is the true faith of an Armorer?
>
> UNDERSHAFT. To give arms to all men who offer an honest price for them, without respect of persons or principles: to aristocrat and republican, to Nihilist and Tsar, to Capitalist and Socialist, to Protestant and Catholic, to burglar and policeman, to black man, white man and yellow man, to all sorts and conditions, all nationalities, all faiths, all follies, all causes and all crimes. The first Undershaft wrote up in his shop IF GOD GAVE THE HAND, LET NOT MAN WITHHOLD THE SWORD. The second wrote up ALL HAVE THE RIGHT TO FIGHT: NONE HAVE THE RIGHT TO JUDGE. The third wrote up TO MAN THE WEAPON: TO HEAVEN THE VICTORY. The fourth had no literary turn; so he did not write up anything; but he sold cannons to Napoleon under the nose of George the Third. The fifth wrote up PEACE SHALL NOT PREVAIL SAVE WITH A SWORD IN HER HAND. The sixth, my master, was the best of all. He wrote up NOTHING IS EVER DONE IN THIS WORLD UNTIL MEN ARE PREPARED TO KILL ONE ANOTHER IF IT IS NOT DONE. After that, there was nothing left for the seventh to say. So he wrote up, simply, UNASHAMED.

In sum, the underlying discourse in *Major Barbara* is that the arms industry provides for employment, is a necessary means for bringing about important changes, and investment in its development leads to more precision in its delivery and in doing so saving lives by limiting the damages. To posit the question provocatively: do Americans want to be blown up completely or would they rather allow foreigners to develop precision-guided missiles that only obliterated vital organs

56 See EU Regulation 2021/821, op. cit., preamble para 2 and Article 15.

57 See Section 1752 (2) (a).

58 George Bernard Shaw, *Major Barbara* (1907).

of the US? After all, in the latter option there is a chance to live another day. This author is not advocating this line of argument here. What is being asserted is that export controls assume this discourse as being *passé*. In fact, these considerations do operate in the design of export controls; and indeed, this discourse is not foreclosed. It needs to be aired. Perhaps the resultant discourse may lead to a fairer objective and better purposed normative framework for export controls.

Third, export controls are to be availed to preserve the qualitative military superiority of the US.[59] But at what cost? Fairly or unfairly? Even in the quest for military 'superiority' by one State there are ethical restraints not to mention legal ones. Moreover, a goal for military superiority approximates to a desire for world dominance.

Fourth, the conclusion that the 'national security of the United States requires that it maintains its leadership in the science, technology, engineering, and manufacturing sectors, including foundational technology that is essential to innovation,'[60] is not necessarily self-evident. There are sound reasons for anyone to push for the advancement of these disciplines; and there are more laudable reasons for their advancement than the gratification of the US and its national security alone. Importantly, however, the national security of the US can be secured in other ways, for example through international cooperation and consensus. Indeed, as economists might point out, a State will be better off by trading in these disciplines and their fruits through the comparative advantage model. In short, access to these disciplines and their fruits may well contribute to enhancing US national security. But in the long run it nurtures a divisive world and creates for inefficiencies in the use of the world's resources. It does not follow, however, from this that national security requires leadership as suggested. Moreover, the legislation ensures through export controls this leadership to 'United States persons' so that such persons are competitive in global markets.[61] Are US persons under the umbrella of national security being given an unfair competitive advantage in these disciplines to acquire world leadership in these sectors?

Fifth, ECRA affects the release of critical technologies of concern to foreign persons involved in investment in the US.[62] Such a regulation would be discriminatory and as such would violate national treatment provisions in investment agreements. Moreover, export restrictions on foreign investors would be a restriction under Article XI of GATT 1994 and therefore considered under TRIMs[63] as prohibited. If the restriction is in furtherance of US foreign policy, it is possible it would not be a sufficient justification as a defence in the WTO. Article 2 of the PRC Export Control Law could be interpreted similarly as precluding the 'provision of any Controlled Items' to a foreign investor.

59 Section 1752 (B).
60 Section 1752 (3).
61 Second sentence of Section 1752 (3).
62 Section 1752 (10).
63 See Agreement on Trade-Related Investment Measures Article 2 and Annex Illustrative List para 2 (c).

Sixth, the legislation applies to 'academic institutions, scientific and research establishments.'[64] This is an intrusion in academic freedom and research. It will deter foreign interests in US research institutions; and inhibit the advancement of ideas that comes from diversity. As one education correspondent put it very aptly:[65]

> When does the defensive instinct morph into oppression? When does curiosity-driven research morph into malevolence? Difficult questions that aren't going anywhere. Somewhat in contrast the EU Regulation in its preamble is somewhat softer in its approach calling for the promotion of awareness of the risks involved in the provision of export-controlled items; whilst recognising the commitment to free exchange of ideas amongst researchers and consultants.[66]

In the same vein, ECRA overrides freely entered contracts, joint development agreements or similar collaborative agreements between US persons and US and foreign persons.[67] In sum, the legislation tramples on some dearly cherished individual and economic liberties that have been the hallmark of liberal democracies.

Seventh, not only is the concept of national security widely conceived but determinations of undesirable foreign persons, their activities, and those of foreign States is left to the determination of the US alone. Thus, it is the US Secretary of State who makes the determination if a country has 'repeatedly provided support for acts of international terrorism.'[68] In terms of the WTO the defence of national security is justiciable and not completely left to a national autonomous interpretation.[69] Moreover, the decision by the Secretary of State is unilateral. The WTO dispute settlement renders its dispute settlement system, despite its shortcomings, as the only method of resolving a dispute concerned with international trade.[70] Such unilateral determinations can be attributed also to the EU and China in their export control systems.

Eighth, it is understandable that export controls may be necessary to protect against negative impacts of items of exports in the advancement of national security. However, how that negative impact is ascertained is relevant. In this respect ECRA affords different measures. One concern, however, is the use of the word 'likely' in one of the exceptions of a general nature. Thus, reference is made to a 'reduction in the availability of an item produced in the United States that is likely

64 Section 1753 (b) (7).

65 See John Ross, 'China Facial Recognition Scholar "Ignored Questions", Went Home,' *Times Higher Education* (September 15, 2021).

66 Para 13 of the Preamble.

67 Section 1753 (c).

68 Section 1754 (C) (1) (A) (a) (i).

69 Russia—Measures Concerning Traffic in Transit (WTO DS512:2019).

70 See Article 23 of the WTO Dispute Settlement Understanding.

to be acquired.'[71] 'Likely' is a term of wide scope. It is for example different from 'necessary.' It can encompass items that may be likely but not necessary.

Ninth, ECRA has a very limited number of exceptions to the application of export controls.[72] There is surely room here for a consideration of more exceptions. Be that as it may, one exception of note is[73] export control over technology under section 203(b) of the International Emergency Economic Powers Act (50 U.S.C. 1702(b). This exception concerns an 'unusual and extraordinary threat' to the 'national security, foreign policy, or economy of the United States.' However, to the extent that it is grounded in the foreign policy or the economy of the US in a general way and can be proven to have a discriminatory impact on certain other like exports, it could be contrary to the non-discrimination provisions in the WTO.[74]

Tenth, there is nothing in the policy statement in Part I of ECRA that speaks about conformity with international obligations of the US export controls, although there is reference to multilateral export regimes set up to impose/enhance the efficacy of export controls.[75] The US is aware that its export controls need to be in conformity with its international obligations. There is not even lip service to this in contrast to Part II (see below). On the other hand, the EU Regulations call for the taking into account of international obligations and commitments although they do not refer to the WTO specifically.[76] In the same vein, there is no reference to WTO obligations in the PRC Regulations.[77]

Finally, Part II of ECRA is titled Anti-Boycott Act 2018. This is curious for an outsider, as it is not actually a separate piece of legislation but integral to ECRA. It is concerned essentially with prohibiting compliance of other countries' export controls directed at countries friendly to the US or any US persons. This is regardless of the reasons for the boycott imposed on the other US friendly countries, or the US persons. The right of other countries to police international norms, for example with reference to human rights and/or terrorism; or in furtherance of their foreign policy, national security, or their economy is denied, when it comes to US friendly nations and US persons. Moreover, the export controls of other countries in such circumstances are labelled as 'restrictive trade practices'[78]—and the US is enjoined to engage in international cooperation 'and the development of international rules and institutions to assure reasonable access to world supplies![79] The contrast and hypocrisy here cannot be understated. Further, ECRA directs for measures to counter and neutralise the other coun-

71 Section 1756 (3) (a).
72 Section 1758.
73 Section 1758 (4) (A).
74 For example, Sections I and III of GATT 1994.
75 See Section 1752 (5).
76 See para 2 of the Preamble to the EU Regulation, op. cit.
77 See Article 32 of the PRC Regulations, op. cit.
78 Section 1772.
79 Section 1772.

tries' export controls involving concerned US persons, whether in the US or in foreign territory, thus extending US regulation in this manner extraterritorially.

Conclusion

ECRA is so riddled with flaws from an international perspective that even an undergraduate international law student could unpack them. The flaws are in the policy consideration that it is underpinned with, in the manner of its administration, and its potential illegality in terms of international law, in particular WTO obligations. The challenge of course is to provide the constructive advice that could result in a better management of the issues. This legislation must be repealed. This must be stated even if it is an unrealistic suggestion. The setting under which it was conceived has now passed. It is bad legislation that has given the wrong leadership in the field.

Discourse on a new conception must take on board all relevant affected stakeholders, including foreign. Just because the legislation concerns national security is itself not reason not to reflect and consider the foreign standpoint. More inclusive methods need to be found to accommodate a fuller debate on the issues. The issues that underpin export controls are not the domain of one nation, an alliance, or a group of like-minded 'have got it all' States. Export controls implicate the distribution of the world's resources and the heritage of mankind. Those who have exports to control, those who have a need for those exports, and ultimately individuals who are impacted upon by such controls, have a legitimate interest in defining the agenda of problems that call for export controls. But beyond the respective interests there is the international community's interest and its collective advancement—which is implicated, and which nation States must be informed by in this discourse. In short, this is an international issue that should be on the international agenda—conceived from an international perspective. Finally, responsible nations need to engage in impact assessments that concern not just their own economy, foreign policy, and national security. They need to build impact assessments with respect to foreign countries, individuals, and the international community in the administration of their export controls. Moreover, national legislation that has an international impact must always be appraised for its conformity with international obligations before it is enacted.

Concluding Remarks

States need to cooperate more in building consensus for a normative framework that is universally acceptable. In this manner the human rights of the people who populate nations are maximally respected. International normative developments, whether in the form of international law, informed by the asymmetrical distribution of power amongst nations, or legislative changes in another nation, brought about unilaterally by a foreign State through its superior position, undermine the basic human rights of all individuals. Indeed, the human rights and basic dignity of individuals residing within the States who export norms through their mere weight can also be the subject of deprivation. This is because within these States there is a likelihood of the hijacking of the State apparatus by the powerful national rent-seekers in foreign policy-making. Such normative developments not only lack in legitimacy but also in their proper enforcement. Consequently, they are in terms of their relative lifespan short-lived. Empirical evidence is not required to substantiate the point that the more lasting and efficacious national and international norms are those that appeal universally to the rational self. Similarly, normative developments in the economic sphere that are informed by power can be self-serving and distortive of the overarching goal of serving the interests of the international community as a whole. Finally, normative impositions lack the contextual element that is necessary for law to have legitimacy in the locus where it operates.

In international economic relations, normative power i.e., the capacity to bring normative changes, takes different forms, and is exercised in different ways. In the colonial era, normative regimes were imposed by the use of force. In contemporary times that same model of unidirectional normative imparting is sugar-coated in the economics of giving. The measure of a civilised society is the degree to which it consciously abstains from engaging in unidirectional normative power. In all spheres of international economic relations, it is necessary to address upfront and at the outset how unidirectional normative power needs to be reined in. This is a challenging endeavour, possibly even impossible, but certainly one wherein a range of soft mechanisms can be institutionalised to minimise or inhibit it—in the framework within which such decisions have the potential of materialising. For example, there is a case for entrenching the right of self-determination of other nations in domestic constitutions; subjecting the right of the executive

DOI: 10.4324/9781003047575-8

of a State to exercise a veto in international economic organisations to domestic parliamentary approval and judicial review within the setting of the international institution.

In contemporary international economic relations, the increasing bilateral nature of its *modus operandi* has been accompanied by an admixture of non-economic conditions in packages of unidirectional norms. In part this reflects the sophistication of modern society. But the momentum of sophistication can also be blinding to its full impact. In the same vein, the economic discourse in such engagements comes with a level of conviction and under an apparatus that makes it difficult for rational dialogue. There is much to be said about the unlinking of economic engagement from political expectations in foreign economic relations that the Bretton Woods institutions have hitherto strived to promote—not least because it lends itself to the undermining of the economic foundations of the architecture of the international trading order.

Annex

Selected US Foreign Trade Law (Edited)

Chapter 1

Section 301 of the Trade Act 1974 (19 U.S.C.A Section 2411)

See Andres B. Schwarzenberg, Section 301 of Trade Act 1974 (Congressional Research Service, January 24, 2022); and WTO Panel Decision: United States — Sections 301–310 of the Trade Act 1974 (WTO: DS 152 – 1999).

19 U.S.C.A. § 2411

§ 2411. Actions by United States Trade Representative

(a) **Mandatory action**

(1) If the United States Trade Representative determines under section 2414(a)(1) of this title that—

(A) the rights of the United States under any trade agreement are being denied; or

(B) an act, policy, or practice of a foreign country—

i. violates, or is inconsistent with, the provisions of, or otherwise denies benefits to the United States under, any trade agreement, or

ii. is unjustifiable and burdens or restricts United States commerce;

the Trade Representative shall take action authorized in subsection (c), subject to the specific direction, if any, of the President regarding any such action, and shall take all other appropriate and feasible action within the power of the President that the President may direct the Trade Representative to take under this subsection, to enforce such rights or to obtain the elimination of such act, policy, or practice. Actions may be taken that are within the power of the President with respect to trade in any goods or services, or with respect to any other area of pertinent relations with the foreign country.

(2) The Trade Representative is not required to take action under paragraph (1) in any case in which—

(A) the Dispute Settlement Body (as defined in section 3531(5) of this title) has adopted a report, or a ruling issued under the formal dispute settlement proceeding provided under any other trade agreement finds, that—

i. the rights of the United States under a trade agreement are not being denied, or
ii. the act, policy, or practice—
    (I) is not a violation of, or inconsistent with, the rights of the United States, or
    (II) does not deny, nullify, or impair benefits to the United States under any trade agreement; or

(B) the Trade Representative finds that—

i. the foreign country is taking satisfactory measures to grant the rights of the United States under a trade agreement,
ii. the foreign country has—
    (I) agreed to eliminate or phase out the act, policy, or practice, or
    (II) agreed to an imminent solution to the burden or restriction on United States commerce that is satisfactory to the Trade Representative,
iii. it is impossible for the foreign country to achieve the results described in clause (i) or (ii), as appropriate, but the foreign country agrees to provide to the United States compensatory trade benefits that are satisfactory to the Trade Representative,
iv. in extraordinary cases, where the taking of action under this subsection would have an adverse impact on the United States economy substantially out of proportion to the benefits of such action, taking into account the impact of not taking such action on the credibility of the provisions of this subchapter, or
v. the taking of action under this subsection would cause serious harm to the national security of the United States.

(3) Any action taken under paragraph (1) to eliminate an act, policy, or practice shall be devised so as to affect goods or services of the foreign country in an amount that is equivalent in value to the burden or restriction being imposed by that country on United States commerce.

(b) **Discretionary action**

If the Trade Representative determines under section 2414(a)(1) of this title that—

(1) an act, policy, or practice of a foreign country is unreasonable or discriminatory and burdens or restricts United States commerce, and
(2) action by the United States is appropriate, the Trade Representative shall take all appropriate and feasible action authorized under subsection (c), subject to the specific direction, if any, of the Presi-

dent regarding any such action, and all other appropriate and feasible action within the power of the President that the President may direct the Trade Representative to take under this subsection, to obtain the elimination of that act, policy, or practice. Actions may be taken that are within the power of the President with respect to trade in any goods or services, or with respect to any other area of pertinent relations with the foreign country.

(c) **Scope of authority**

(1) For purposes of carrying out the provisions of subsection (a) or (b) or section 2416(c) of this title, the Trade Representative is authorized to—

(A) suspend, withdraw, or prevent the application of, benefits of trade agreement concessions to carry out a trade agreement with the foreign country referred to in such subsection;

(B) impose duties or other import restrictions on the goods of, and, notwithstanding any other provision of law, fees or restrictions on the services of, such foreign country for such time as the Trade Representative determines appropriate;

(C) in a case in which the act, policy, or practice also fails to meet the eligibility criteria for receiving duty-free treatment under subsections (b) and (c) of section 2462 of this title, subsections (b) and (c) of section 2702 of this title, or subsections (c) and (d) of section 3202 of this title, withdraw, limit, or suspend such treatment under such provisions, notwithstanding the provisions of subsection (a)(3) of this section; or

(D) enter into binding agreements with such foreign country that commit such foreign country to—

i. eliminate, or phase out, the act, policy, or practice that is the subject of the action to be taken under subsection (a) or (b),

ii. eliminate any burden or restriction on United States commerce resulting from such act, policy, or practice, or

iii. provide the United States with compensatory trade benefits that—

(I) are satisfactory to the Trade Representative, and

(II) meet the requirements of paragraph (4).

(2) —

(A) Notwithstanding any other provision of law governing any service sector access authorization, and in addition to the authority conferred in paragraph (1), the Trade Representative may, for purposes of carrying out the provisions of subsection (a) or (b)—

i. restrict, in the manner and to the extent the Trade Representative determines appropriate, the terms and conditions of any such authorization, or

ii. deny the issuance of any such authorization.

(B) Actions described in subparagraph (A) may only be taken under this section with respect to service sector access authorizations granted, or applications therefor pending, on or after the date on which—

i. a petition is filed under section 2412(a) of this title, or

ii. a determination to initiate an investigation is made by the Trade Representative under section 2412(b) of this title.

(C) Before the Trade Representative takes any action under this section involving the imposition of fees or other restrictions on the services of a foreign country, the Trade Representative shall, if the services involved are subject to regulation by any agency of the Federal Government or of any State, consult, as appropriate, with the head of the agency concerned.

(3) The actions the Trade Representative is authorized to take under subsection (a) or (b) may be taken against any goods or economic sector—

(A) on a nondiscriminatory basis or solely against the foreign country described in such subsection, and

(B) without regard to whether or not such goods or economic sector were involved in the act, policy, or practice that is the subject of such action.

(4) Any trade agreement described in paragraph (1)(D)(iii) shall provide compensatory trade benefits that benefit the economic sector which includes the domestic industry that would benefit from the elimination of the act, policy, or practice that is the subject of the action to be taken under subsection (a) or (b), or benefit the economic sector as closely related as possible to such economic sector, unless—

(A) the provision of such trade benefits is not feasible, or

(B) trade benefits that benefit any other economic sector would be more satisfactory than such trade benefits.

(5) If the Trade Representative determines that actions to be taken under subsection (a) or (b) are to be in the form of import restrictions, the Trade Representative shall—

(A) give preference to the imposition of duties over the imposition of other import restrictions, and

(B) if an import restriction other than a duty is imposed, consider substituting, on an incremental basis, an equivalent duty for such other import restriction.

(6) Any action taken by the Trade Representative under this section with respect to export targeting shall, to the extent possible, reflect the full benefit level of the export targeting to the beneficiary over the period during which the action taken has an effect.

(d) **Definitions and special rules**

For purposes of this subchapter—

(1) The term 'commerce' includes, but is not limited to—

(A) services (including transfers of information) associated with international trade, whether or not such services are related to specific goods, and

(B) foreign direct investment by United States persons with implications for trade in goods or services.

(2) An act, policy, or practice of a foreign country that burdens or restricts United States commerce may include the provision, directly or indirectly, by that foreign country of subsidies for the construction of vessels used in the commercial transportation by water of goods between foreign countries and the United States.

(3) —

(A) An act, policy, or practice is unreasonable if the act, policy, or practice, while not necessarily in violation of, or inconsistent with, the international legal rights of the United States, is otherwise unfair and inequitable.

(B) Acts, policies, and practices that are unreasonable include, but are not limited to, any act, policy, or practice, or any combination of acts, policies, or practices, which—

(i) denies fair and equitable—

(I) opportunities for the establishment of an enterprise,

(II) provision of adequate and effective protection of intellectual property rights notwithstanding the fact that the foreign country may be in compliance with the specific obligations of the Agreement on Trade-Related Aspects of Intellectual Property Rights referred to in section 3511(d)(15) of this title,

(III) nondiscriminatory market access opportunities for United States persons that rely upon intellectual property protection, or

(IV) market opportunities, including the toleration by a foreign government of systematic anticompetitive activities by enterprises or among enterprises in the foreign country that have the effect of restricting, on a basis that is inconsistent with commercial considerations, access of United States goods or services to a foreign market,

(ii) constitutes export targeting,

(iii) constitutes a persistent pattern of conduct that—

(I) denies workers the right of association,

(II) denies workers the right to organize and bargain collectively,

(III) permits any form of forced or compulsory labor,

(IV) fails to provide a minimum age for the employment of children, or

(V) fails to provide standards for minimum wages, hours of work, and occupational safety and health of workers, or

(iv) constitutes a persistent pattern of conduct by the government of a foreign country under which that government fails to effectively enforce commitments under agreements to which the foreign country and the United States are parties, including with respect to trade in goods, trade in services, trade in agriculture, foreign investment, intellectual property, digital trade in goods and services and cross-border data flows, regulatory practices, state-owned and state-controlled enterprises, localization barriers to trade, labor and the environment, anticorruption, trade remedy laws, textiles, and commercial partnerships.

(C) —

(i) Acts, policies, and practices of a foreign country described in subparagraph (B)(iii) shall not be treated as being unreasonable if the Trade Representative determines that—

(I) the foreign country has taken, or is taking, actions that demonstrate a significant and tangible overall advancement in providing throughout the foreign country (including any designated zone within the foreign country) the rights and other standards described in the subclauses of subparagraph (B)(iii), or

(II) such acts, policies, and practices are not inconsistent with the level of economic development of the foreign country.

(ii) The Trade Representative shall publish in the Federal Register any determination made under clause (i), together with a description of the facts on which such determination is based.

(D) For purposes of determining whether any act, policy, or practice is unreasonable, reciprocal opportunities in the United States for foreign nationals and firms shall be taken into account, to the extent appropriate.

(E) The term 'export targeting' means any government plan or scheme consisting of a combination of coordinated actions (whether carried out severally or jointly) that are bestowed on a specific enterprise, industry, or group thereof, the effect of which is to assist the enterprise, industry, or group to become more competitive in the export of a class or kind of merchandise.

(F) —

(i) For the purposes of subparagraph (B)(i)(II), adequate and effective protection of intellectual property rights includes adequate and effective means under the laws of the foreign country for persons who are not citizens or nationals of such country to secure, exercise, and enforce rights and enjoy commercial benefits relating to patents, trademarks, copyrights and related rights, mask works, trade secrets, and plant breeder's rights.

(ii) For purposes of subparagraph (B)(i)(IV), the denial of fair and equitable nondiscriminatory market access opportunities includes restrictions on market access related to the use, exploitation, or enjoyment of commercial benefits derived from exercising intellectual property rights in protected works or fixations or products embodying protected works.

(4) —

(A) An act, policy, or practice is unjustifiable if the act, policy, or practice is in violation of, or inconsistent with, the international legal rights of the United States.

(B) Acts, policies, and practices that are unjustifiable include, but are not limited to, any act, policy, or practice described in subparagraph (A) which denies national or most-favored-nation treatment or the right of establishment or protection of intellectual property rights.

(5) Acts, policies, and practices that are discriminatory include, when appropriate, any act, policy, and practice which denies national or most-favored-nation treatment to United States goods, services, or investment.

(6) The term 'service sector access authorization' means any license, permit, order, or other authorization, issued under the authority of Federal law, that permits a foreign supplier of services access to the United States market in a service sector concerned.

(7) The term 'foreign country' includes any foreign instrumentality. Any possession or territory of a foreign country that is administered separately for customs purposes shall be treated as a separate foreign country.

(8) The term 'Trade Representative' means the United States Trade Representative.

(9) The term 'interested persons', only for purposes of sections 2412(a)(4)(B), 2414(b)(1)(A), 2416(c)(2),[1] and 2417(a)(2) of this title, includes, but is not limited to, domestic firms and workers,

representatives of consumer interests, United States product exporters, and any industrial user of any goods or services that may be affected by actions taken under subsection (a) or (b).

(Footnotes omitted)

See Executive Orders No. 13155 (May 10, 2000, 65 F.R. 30521) with respect to application of Section 301 to Access to HIV/AIDS Pharmaceuticals and Medical Technologies

Chapter 2

Special 301

19 U.S.C.A. § 2241

§ 2241. Estimates of barriers to market access

(a) **National trade estimates**

(1) **In general**

For calendar year 1988, and for each succeeding calendar year, the United States Trade Representative, through the interagency trade organization established pursuant to section 1872(a) of this title and with the assistance of the interagency advisory committee established under section 2171(d)(2) of this title, shall—

(A) identify and analyze acts, policies, or practices of each foreign country which constitute significant barriers to, or distortions of—

(i) United States exports of goods or services (including agricultural commodities; and property protected by trademarks, patents, and copyrights exported or licensed by United States persons),

(ii) foreign direct investment by United States persons, especially if such investment has implications for trade in goods or services; and

(iii) United States electronic commerce,

(B) make an estimate of the trade-distorting impact on United States commerce of any act, policy, or practice identified under subparagraph (A); and

(C) make an estimate, if feasible, of—

(i) the value of additional goods and services of the United States,

(ii) the value of additional foreign direct investment by United States persons, and

(iii) the value of additional United States electronic commerce,

that would have been exported to, or invested in or transacted with,[3] each foreign country during such calendar year if each of such acts, policies, and practices of such country did not exist.

(2) **Certain factors taken into account in making analysis and estimate**

In making any analysis or estimate under paragraph (1), the Trade Representative shall take into account--

(A) the relative impact of the act, policy, or practice on United States commerce;

(B) the availability of information to document prices, market shares, and other matters necessary to demonstrate the effects of the act, policy, or practice;

(C) the extent to which such act, policy, or practice is subject to international agreements to which the United States is a party;

(D) any advice given through appropriate committees established pursuant to section 2155 of this title; and

(E) the actual increase in—

(i) the value of goods and services of the United States exported to,

(ii) the value of foreign direct investment made in, and

(iii) the value of electronic commerce transacted with,

the foreign country during the calendar year for which the estimate under paragraph (1)(C) is made.

(3) **Inclusion of certain discriminatory laws, policies, and practices of the Russian Federation**

For calendar year 2012 and each succeeding calendar year, the Trade Representative shall include in the analyses and estimates under paragraph (1) an identification and analysis of any laws, policies, or practices of the Russian Federation that deny fair and equitable market access to United States digital trade.

(4) **Annual revisions and updates**

The Trade Representative shall annually revise and update the analysis and estimate under paragraph (1).

(b) **Reports**

(1) **In general**

On or before April 30, 1989, and on or before March 31 of each succeeding calendar year, the Trade Representative shall submit a report on the analysis and estimates made under subsection (a) for the calendar year preceding such calendar year (which shall be known as the 'National Trade Estimate') to the President, the Committee on Finance of the Senate, and appropriate committees of the House of Representatives.

(2) **Reports to include information with respect to action being taken**

The Trade Representative shall include in each report submitted under paragraph (1) information with respect to any action taken (or the reasons for no action taken) to eliminate any act, policy, or practice identified under subsection (a), including, but not limited to—

(A) any action under section 2411 of this title,
(B) negotiations or consultations with foreign governments, or
(C) a section on foreign anticompetitive practices, the toleration of which by foreign governments is adversely affecting exports of United States goods or services.

(3) **Consultation with Congress on trade policy priorities**
The Trade Representative shall keep the committees described in paragraph (1) currently informed with respect to trade policy priorities for the purposes of expanding market opportunities. After the submission of the report required by paragraph (1), the Trade Representative shall also consult periodically with, and take into account the views of, the committees described in that paragraph regarding means to address the foreign trade barriers identified in the report, including the possible initiation of investigations under section 2412 of this title or other trade actions.

(c) **Assistance of other agencies**

(1) **Furnishing of information**
The head of each department or agency of the executive branch of the Government, including any independent agency, is authorized and directed to furnish to the Trade Representative or to the appropriate agency, upon request, such data, reports, and other information as is necessary for the Trade Representative to carry out his functions under this section. In preparing the section of the report required by subsection (b)(2)(C), the Trade Representative shall consult in particular with the Attorney General.

(2) **Restrictions on release or use of information**
Nothing in this subsection shall authorize the release of information to, or the use of information by, the Trade Representative in a manner inconsistent with law or any procedure established pursuant thereto.

(3) **Personnel and services**
The head of any department, agency, or instrumentality of the United States may detail such personnel and may furnish such services, with or without reimbursement, as the Trade Representative may request to assist in carrying out his functions.

(d) **Electronic commerce**
For purposes of this section, the term 'electronic commerce' has the meaning given that term in section 1104(3) of the Internet Tax Freedom Act.

Footnotes omitted

19 U.S.C.A. § 2242

§ 2242. Identification of countries that deny adequate protection, or market access, for intellectual property rights

(a) **In general**
By no later than the date that is 30 days after the date on which the annual report is submitted to Congressional committees under section 2241(b)

of this title, the United States Trade Representative (hereafter in this section referred to as the 'Trade Representative') shall identify—

(1) those foreign countries that—

(A) deny adequate and effective protection of intellectual property rights, or

(B) deny fair and equitable market access to United States persons that rely upon intellectual property protection, and

(2) those foreign countries identified under paragraph (1) that are determined by the Trade Representative to be priority foreign countries.

(b) **Special rules for identifications**

(1) In identifying priority foreign countries under subsection (a)(2), the Trade Representative shall only identify those foreign countries—

(A) that have the most onerous or egregious acts, policies, or practices that—

(i) deny adequate and effective intellectual property rights, or

(ii) deny fair and equitable market access to United States persons that rely upon intellectual property protection,

(B) whose acts, policies, or practices described in subparagraph (A) have the greatest adverse impact (actual or potential) on the relevant United States products, and

(C) that are not—

(i) entering into good faith negotiations, or

(ii) making significant progress in bilateral or multilateral negotiations,

to provide adequate and effective protection of intellectual property rights.

(2) In identifying priority foreign countries under subsection (a)(2), the Trade Representative shall—

(A) consult with the Register of Copyrights, the Under Secretary of Commerce for Intellectual Property and Director of the United States Patent and Trademark Office, other appropriate officers of the Federal Government, and

(B) take into account information from such sources as may be available to the Trade Representative and such information as may be submitted to the Trade Representative by interested persons, including information contained in reports submitted under section 2241(b) of this title and petitions submitted under section 2412 of this title.

(3) The Trade Representative may identify a foreign country under subsection (a)(1)(B) only if the Trade Representative finds that there is a factual basis for the denial of fair and equitable market access as a result of the violation of international law or agreement, or the existence of barriers, referred to in subsection (d)(3).

(4) In identifying foreign countries under paragraphs (1) and (2) of subsection (a), the Trade Representative shall take into account—
 (A) the history of intellectual property laws and practices of the foreign country, including any previous identification under subsection (a)(2), and
 (B) the history of efforts of the United States, and the response of the foreign country, to achieve adequate and effective protection and enforcement of intellectual property rights.

(c) **Revocations and additional identifications**

(1) The Trade Representative may at any time—
 (A) revoke the identification of any foreign country as a priority foreign country under this section, or
 (B) identify any foreign country as a priority foreign country under this section,

if information available to the Trade Representative indicates that such action is appropriate.

(2) The Trade Representative shall include in the semiannual report submitted to the Congress under section 2419(3) of this title a detailed explanation of the reasons for the revocation under paragraph (1) of the identification of any foreign country as a priority foreign country under this section.

(d) **Definitions**

For purposes of this section—

(1) The term 'persons that rely upon intellectual property protection' means persons involved in—
 (A) the creation, production or licensing of works of authorship (within the meaning of sections 102 and 103 of Title 17) that are copyrighted, or
 (B) the manufacture of products that are patented or for which there are process patents.

(2) A foreign country denies adequate and effective protection of intellectual property rights if the foreign country denies adequate and effective means under the laws of the foreign country for persons who are not citizens or nationals of such foreign country to secure, exercise, and enforce rights relating to patents, process patents, registered trademarks, copyrights, trade secrets, and mask works.

(3) A foreign country denies fair and equitable market access if the foreign country effectively denies access to a market for a product protected by a copyright or related right, patent, trademark, mask work, trade secret, or plant breeder's right, through the use of laws, procedures, practices, or regulations which—
 (A) violate provisions of international law or international agreements to which both the United States and the foreign country are parties, or

(B) constitute discriminatory nontariff trade barriers.

(4) A foreign country may be determined to deny adequate and effective protection of intellectual property rights, notwithstanding the fact that the foreign country may be in compliance with the specific obligations of the Agreement on Trade-Related Aspects of Intellectual Property Rights referred to in section 3511(d)(15) of this title.

(e) **Publication**

The Trade Representative shall publish in the Federal Register a list of foreign countries identified under subsection (a) and shall make such revisions to the list as may be required by reason of action under subsection (c).

(f) **Special rule for actions affecting United States cultural industries**

(1) **In general**

By no later than the date that is 30 days after the date on which the annual report is submitted to Congressional committees under section 2241(b) of this title, the Trade Representative shall identify any act, policy, or practice of Canada which—

(A) affects cultural industries,

(B) is adopted or expanded after December 17, 1992, and

(C) is actionable under article 32.6 of the USMCA (as defined in section 4502 of this title).

(2) **Special rules for identifications**

For purposes of section 2412(b)(2)(A) of this title, an act, policy, or practice identified under this subsection shall be treated as an act, policy, or practice that is the basis for identification of a country under subsection (a)(2), unless the United States has already taken action pursuant to article 32.6 of the USMCA in response to such act, policy, or practice. In deciding whether to identify an act, policy, or practice under paragraph (1), the Trade Representative shall—

(A) consult with and take into account the views of representatives of the relevant domestic industries, appropriate committees established pursuant to section 2155 of this title, and appropriate officers of the Federal Government, and

(B) take into account the information from such sources as may be available to the Trade Representative and such information as may be submitted to the Trade Representative by interested persons, including information contained in reports submitted under section 2241(b) of this title.

(3) **Cultural industries**

For purposes of this subsection, the term 'cultural industries' means persons engaged in any of the following activities:

(A) The publication, distribution, or sale of books, magazines, periodicals, or newspapers in print or machine readable form but not including the sole activity of printing or typesetting any of the foregoing.

(B) The production, distribution, sale, or exhibition of film or video recordings.

(C) The production, distribution, sale, or exhibition of audio or video music recordings.

(D) The publication, distribution, or sale of music in print or machine readable form.

(E) Radio communications in which the transmissions are intended for direct reception by the general public, and all radio, television, and cable broadcasting undertakings and all satellite programming and broadcast network services.

(g) **Special rules for foreign countries on the priority watch list**

(1) **Action plans**

(A) **In general**

Not later than 90 days after the date on which the Trade Representative submits the National Trade Estimate under section 2241(b) of this title, the Trade Representative shall develop an action plan described in subparagraph (C) with respect to each foreign country described in subparagraph (B).

(B) **Foreign country described**

The Trade Representative shall develop an action plan under subparagraph (A) with respect to each foreign country that—

(i) the Trade Representative has identified for placement on the priority watch list; and

(ii) has remained on such list for at least one year.

(C) **Action plan described**

An action plan developed under subparagraph (A) shall contain the benchmarks described in subparagraph (D) and be designed to assist the foreign country—

(i) to achieve—

(I) adequate and effective protection of intellectual property rights; and

(II) fair and equitable market access for United States persons that rely upon intellectual property protection; or

(ii) to make significant progress toward achieving the goals described in clause (i).

(D) **Benchmarks described**

The benchmarks contained in an action plan developed pursuant to subparagraph (A) are such legislative, institutional, enforcement, or other actions as the Trade Representative determines to be necessary for the foreign country to achieve the goals described in clause (i) or (ii) of subparagraph (C).

(2) **Failure to meet action plan benchmarks**

If, as of one year after the date on which an action plan is developed under paragraph (1)(A), the President, in consultation with the Trade Representative, determines that the foreign country to which the action plan applies has not substantially complied with the benchmarks described in paragraph (1)(D), the President may take appropriate action with respect to the foreign country.

(3) **Priority watch list defined**

In this subsection, the term 'priority watch list' means the priority watch list established by the Trade Representative pursuant to subsection (a).

(h) **Annual report**

Not later than 30 days after the date on which the Trade Representative submits the National Trade Estimate under section 2241(b) of this title, the Trade Representative shall submit to the Committee on Ways and Means of the House of Representatives and the Committee on Finance of the Senate a report on actions taken under this **section** during the **12** months preceding such report, and the reasons for such actions, including—

(1) a list of any foreign countries identified under subsection (a);

(2) a description of progress made in achieving improved intellectual property protection and market access for persons relying on intellectual property rights; and

(3) a description of the action plans developed under subsection (g) and any actions taken by foreign countries under such plans.

Footnoted omitted

Chapter 3

Sections 3004 & 3005 of the Omnibus Trade & Competitiveness Act 1988 &
701 – 702 of the Trade Facilitation & Trade Enforcement Act 2015

Section 3.1

Section 3004 OMNIBUS TRADE AND COMPETITIVENESS ACT OF 1988 (H.R. 3). 22 U.S.C.A. § 5304

§ 5304. International negotiations on exchange rate and economic policies

(a) **Multilateral negotiations**

The President shall seek to confer and negotiate with other countries—

(1) to achieve—

(A) better coordination of macroeconomic policies of the major industrialized nations; and

(B) more appropriate and sustainable levels of trade and current account balances, and exchange rates of the dollar and other currencies consistent with such balances; and

(2) to develop a program for improving existing mechanisms for coordination and improving the functioning of the exchange rate system to provide for long-term exchange rate stability consistent with more appropriate and sustainable current account balances.

(b) **Bilateral negotiations**

The Secretary of the Treasury shall analyze on an annual basis the exchange rate policies of foreign countries, in consultation with the International Monetary Fund, and consider whether countries manipulate the rate of exchange between their currency and the United States dollar for purposes of preventing effective balance of payments adjustments or gaining unfair competitive advantage in international trade. If the Secretary considers that such manipulation is occurring with respect to countries that (1) have material global current account surpluses; and (2) have significant bilateral trade surpluses with the United States, the Secretary of the Treasury shall take action to initiate negotiations with such foreign countries on an expedited basis, in the International Monetary Fund or bilaterally, for the purpose of ensuring that such countries regularly and promptly adjust the rate of exchange between their currencies and the United States dollar to permit effective balance of payments adjustments and to eliminate the unfair advantage. The Secretary shall not be required to initiate negotiations in cases where such negotiations would have a serious detrimental impact on vital national economic and security interests; in such cases, the Secretary shall inform the chairman and the ranking minority member of the Committee on Banking, Housing, and Urban Affairs of the Senate and of the Committee on Banking, Finance and Urban Affairs of the House of Representatives of his determination.

Section 3.2

Section 3005 OMNIBUS TRADE AND COMPETITIVENESS ACT OF 1988 (H.R. 3). 22 U.S.C.A § 5305

§ 5305. Reporting requirements

(a) **Reports required**

In furtherance of the purpose of this chapter, the Secretary, after consultation with the Chairman of the Board, shall submit to the Committee on Banking, Finance and Urban Affairs of the House of Representatives and the Committee on Banking, Housing, and Urban Affairs of the Senate, on or before October 15 of each year, a written report on international economic policy, including exchange rate policy. The Secretary shall provide a written update of developments six months after the initial report. In addition, the Secretary shall appear, if requested, before both committees to provide testimony on these reports.

(b) **Contents of report**

Each report submitted under subsection (a) shall contain—

(1) an analysis of currency market developments and the relationship between the United States dollar and the currencies of our major trade competitors;

(2) an evaluation of the factors in the United States and other economies that underlie conditions in the currency markets, including developments in bilateral trade and capital flows;
(3) a description of currency intervention or other actions undertaken to adjust the actual exchange rate of the dollar;
(4) an assessment of the impact of the exchange rate of the United States dollar on—
    (A) the ability of the United States to maintain a more appropriate and sustainable balance in its current account and merchandise trade account;
    (B) production, employment, and noninflationary growth in the United States;
    (C) the international competitive performance of United States industries and the external indebtedness of the United States;
(5) recommendations for any changes necessary in United States economic policy to attain a more appropriate and sustainable balance in the current account;
(6) the results of negotiations conducted pursuant to section 5304 of this title;
(7) key issues in United States policies arising from the most recent consultation requested by the International Monetary Fund under article IV of the Fund's Articles of Agreement; and
(8) a report on the size and composition of international capital flows, and the factors contributing to such flows, including, where possible, an assessment of the impact of such flows on exchange rates and trade flows.

Chapter 4

Trade Expansion Act of 1962 § 232, 19 U.S.C.A. § 1862.

19 U.S.C.A. § 1862

§ 1862. Safeguarding national security

(a) **Prohibition on decrease or elimination of duties or other import restrictions if such reduction or elimination would threaten to impair national security**

No action shall be taken pursuant to section 1821(a) of this title or pursuant to section 1351 of this title to decrease or eliminate the duty or other import restrictions on any article if the President determines that such reduction or elimination would threaten to impair the national security.

(b) **Investigations by Secretary of Commerce to determine effects on national security of imports of articles; consultation with Secretary of Defense and other officials; hearings; assessment of defense requirements; report to President; publication in Federal Register; promulgation of regulations**

(1) —

(A) Upon request of the head of any department or agency, upon application of an interested party, or upon his own motion, the Secretary of Commerce (hereafter in this section referred to as the 'Secretary') shall immediately initiate an appropriate investigation to determine the effects on the national security of imports of the article which is the subject of such request, application, or motion.

(B) The Secretary shall immediately provide notice to the Secretary of Defense of any investigation initiated under this section.

(2) —

(A) In the course of any investigation conducted under this subsection, the Secretary shall—

(i) consult with the Secretary of Defense regarding the methodological and policy questions raised in any investigation initiated under paragraph (1),

(ii) seek information and advice from, and consult with, appropriate officers of the United States, and

(iii) if it is appropriate and after reasonable notice, hold public hearings or otherwise afford interested parties an opportunity to present information and advice relevant to such investigation.

(B) Upon the request of the Secretary, the Secretary of Defense shall provide the Secretary an assessment of the defense requirements of any article that is the subject of an investigation conducted under this section.

(3) —

(A) By no later than the date that is 270 days after the date on which an investigation is initiated under paragraph (1) with respect to any article, the Secretary shall submit to the President a report on the findings of such investigation with respect to the effect of the importation of such article in such quantities or under such circumstances upon the national security and, based on such findings, the recommendations of the Secretary for action or inaction under this section. If the Secretary finds that such article is being imported into the United States in such quantities or under such circumstances as to threaten to impair the national security, the Secretary shall so advise the President in such report.

(B) Any portion of the report submitted by the Secretary under subparagraph (A) which does not contain classified information or proprietary information shall be published in the Federal Register.

(4) The Secretary shall prescribe such procedural regulations as may be necessary to carry out the provisions of this subsection.

(c) **Adjustment of imports; determination by President; report to Congress; additional actions; publication in Federal Register**

(1) —

(A) Within 90 days after receiving a report submitted under subsection (b)(3)(A) in which the Secretary finds that an article is being imported into the United States in such quantities or under such circumstances as to threaten to impair the national security, the President shall—

(i) determine whether the President concurs with the finding of the Secretary, and

(ii) if the President concurs, determine the nature and duration of the action that, in the judgment of the President, must be taken to adjust the imports of the article and its derivatives so that such imports will not threaten to impair the national security.

(B) If the President determines under subparagraph (A) to take action to adjust imports of an article and its derivatives, the President shall implement that action by no later than the date that is 15 days after the day on which the President determines to take action under subparagraph (A).

(2) By no later than the date that is 30 days after the date on which the President makes any determinations under paragraph (1), the President shall submit to the Congress a written statement of the reasons why the President has decided to take action, or refused to take action, under paragraph (1). Such statement shall be included in the report published under subsection (e).

(3) —

(A) If—

(i) the action taken by the President under paragraph (1) is the negotiation of an agreement which limits or restricts the importation into, or the exportation to, the United States of the article that threatens to impair national security, and

(ii) either—

(I) no such agreement is entered into before the date that is 180 days after the date on which the President makes the determination under paragraph (1)(A) to take such action, or

(II) such an agreement that has been entered into is not being carried out or is ineffective in eliminating the threat to the national security posed by imports of such article, the President shall take such other actions as the President deems necessary to adjust the imports of such article so that such imports will not threaten to impair the national security. The President shall publish in the Federal Register notice of any additional actions being taken under this section by reason of this subparagraph.

(B) If—

(i) clauses (i) and (ii) of subparagraph (A) apply, and

(ii) the President determines not to take any additional actions under this subsection,

the President shall publish in the Federal Register such determination and the reasons on which such determination is based.

(d) **Domestic production for national defense; impact of foreign competition on economic welfare of domestic industries**

For the purposes of this section, the Secretary and the President shall, in the light of the requirements of national security and without excluding other relevant factors, give consideration to domestic production needed for projected national defense requirements, the capacity of domestic industries to meet such requirements, existing and anticipated availabilities of the human resources, products, raw materials, and other supplies and services essential to the national defense, the requirements of growth of such industries and such supplies and services including the investment, exploration, and development necessary to assure such growth, and the importation of goods in terms of their quantities, availabilities, character, and use as those affect such industries and the capacity of the United States to meet national security requirements. In the administration of this section, the Secretary and the President shall further recognize the close relation of the economic welfare of the Nation to our national security, and shall take into consideration the impact of foreign competition on the economic welfare of individual domestic industries; and any substantial unemployment, decrease in revenues of government, loss of skills or investment, or other serious effects resulting from the displacement of any domestic products by excessive imports shall be considered, without excluding other factors, in determining whether such weakening of our internal economy may impair the national security.

(e) **Report by Secretary of Commerce**[1]

(1) Upon the disposition of each request, application, or motion under subsection (b), the Secretary shall submit to the Congress, and publish in the Federal Register, a report on such disposition.

(2) Omitted

(f) **Congressional disapproval of Presidential adjustment of imports of petroleum or petroleum products; disapproval resolution**[2]

(1) An action taken by the President under subsection (c) to adjust imports of petroleum or petroleum products shall cease to have force and effect upon the enactment of a disapproval resolution, provided for in paragraph (2), relating to that action.

(2) —

(A) This paragraph is enacted by the Congress—

(i) as an exercise of the rulemaking power of the House of Representatives and the Senate, respectively, and as such is deemed a part of the rules of each House, respectively, but applicable only with respect to the procedures to be followed in that House in the case of disapproval resolutions and such procedures supersede other rules only to the extent that they are inconsistent therewith; and

(ii) with the full recognition of the constitutional right of either House to change the rules (so far as relating to the procedure of that House) at any time, in the same manner, and to the same extent as any other rule of that House.

(B) For purposes of this subsection, the term 'disapproval resolution' means only a joint resolution of either House of Congress the matter after the resolving clause of which is as follows: 'That the Congress disapproves the action taken under section 232 of the Trade Expansion Act of 1962 with respect to petroleum imports under ______ dated ______.', the first blank space being filled with the number of the proclamation, Executive order, or other Executive act issued under the authority of subsection (c) of this section for purposes of adjusting imports of petroleum or petroleum products and the second blank being filled with the appropriate date.

(C) —

(i) All disapproval resolutions introduced in the House of Representatives shall be referred to the Committee on Ways and Means and all disapproval resolutions introduced in the Senate shall be referred to the Committee on Finance.

(ii) No amendment to a disapproval resolution shall be in order in either the House of Representatives or the Senate, and no motion to suspend the application of this clause shall be in order in either House nor shall it be in order in either House for the Presiding Officer to entertain a request to suspend the application of this clause by unanimous consent.

Chapter 5

Generalized System of Preferences

19 U.S.C.A. § 2461

§ 2461. Authority to extend preferences

The President may provide duty-free treatment for any eligible article from any beneficiary developing country in accordance with the provisions of this subchapter. In taking any such action, the President shall have due regard for—

(1) the effect such action will have on furthering the economic development of developing countries through the expansion of their exports;
(2) the extent to which other major developed countries are undertaking a comparable effort to assist developing countries by granting generalized preferences with respect to imports of products of such countries;
(3) the anticipated impact of such action on United States producers of like or directly competitive products; and
(4) the extent of the beneficiary developing country's competitiveness with respect to eligible articles.

19 U.S.C.A. § 2462

§ 2462. Designation of beneficiary developing countries

(a) **Authority to designate countries**

(1) **Beneficiary developing countries**

The President is authorized to designate countries as beneficiary developing countries for purposes of this subchapter.

(2) **Least-developed beneficiary developing countries**

The President is authorized to designate any beneficiary developing country as a least-developed beneficiary developing country for purposes of this subchapter, based on the considerations in section 2461 of this title and subsection (c) of this section.

(b) **Countries ineligible for designation**

(1) **Specific countries**

The following countries may not be designated as beneficiary developing countries for purposes of this subchapter:

(A) Australia.
(B) Canada.
(C) European Union member states.
(D) Iceland.
(E) Japan.
(F) Monaco.
(G) New Zealand.
(H) Norway.
(I) Switzerland.

(2) **Other bases for ineligibility**

The President shall not designate any country a beneficiary developing country under this subchapter if any of the following applies:

(A) Such country is a Communist country, unless—
(i) the products of such country receive nondiscriminatory treatment,
(ii) such country is a WTO Member (as such term is defined in section 3501(10) of this title) and a member of the International Monetary Fund, and
(iii) such country is not dominated or controlled by international communism.

(B) Such country is a party to an arrangement of countries and participates in any action pursuant to such arrangement, the effect of which is—

(i) to withhold supplies of vital commodity resources from international trade or to raise the price of such commodities to an unreasonable level, and

(ii) to cause serious disruption of the world economy.

(C) Such country affords preferential treatment to the products of a developed country, other than the United States, which has, or is likely to have, a significant adverse effect on United States commerce.

(D) --

(i) Such country—

(I) has nationalized, expropriated, or otherwise seized ownership or control of property, including patents, trademarks, or copyrights, owned by a United States citizen or by a corporation, partnership, or association which is 50 percent or more beneficially owned by United States citizens,

(II) has taken steps to repudiate or nullify an existing contract or agreement with a United States citizen or a corporation, partnership, or association which is 50 percent or more beneficially owned by United States citizens, the effect of which is to nationalize, expropriate, or otherwise seize ownership or control of property, including patents, trademarks, or copyrights, so owned, or

(III) has imposed or enforced taxes or other exactions, restrictive maintenance or operational conditions, or other measures with respect to property, including patents, trademarks, or copyrights, so owned, the effect of which is to nationalize, expropriate, or otherwise seize ownership or control of such property,

unless clause (ii) applies.

(ii) This clause applies if the President determines that—

(I) prompt, adequate, and effective compensation has been or is being made to the citizen, corporation, partnership, or association referred to in clause (i),

(II) good faith negotiations to provide prompt, adequate, and effective compensation under the applicable provisions of international law are in progress, or the country described in clause (i) is otherwise taking steps to discharge its obligations under international law with respect to such citizen, corporation, partnership, or association, or

(III) a dispute involving such citizen, corporation, partnership, or association over compensation for such a seizure has been submitted to arbitration under the provisions of the Convention for the Settlement of Investment Disputes, or in another mutually agreed upon forum,

and the President promptly furnishes a copy of such determination to the Senate and House of Representatives.

(E) Such country fails to act in good faith in recognizing as binding or in enforcing arbitral awards in favor of United States citizens or a corporation, partnership, or association which is 50 percent or more beneficially owned by United States citizens, which have been made by arbitrators appointed for each case or by permanent arbitral bodies to which the parties involved have submitted their dispute.

(F) Such country aids or abets, by granting sanctuary from prosecution to, any individual or group which has committed an act of international terrorism or the Secretary of State makes a determination with respect to such country under section 4605(j)(1)(A) of Title 50 or such country has not taken steps to support the efforts of the United States to combat terrorism.

(G) Such country has not taken or is not taking steps to afford internationally recognized worker rights to workers in the country (including any designated zone in that country).

(H) Such country has not implemented its commitments to eliminate the worst forms of child labor.

Subparagraphs (D), (E), (F), (G), and (H) (to the extent described in section 2467(6)(D) of this title) shall not prevent the designation of any country as a beneficiary developing country under this subchapter if the President determines that such designation will be in the national economic interest of the United States and reports such determination to the Congress with the reasons therefor.

(c) **Factors affecting country designation**

In determining whether to designate any country as a beneficiary developing country under this subchapter, the President shall take into account—

(1) an expression by such country of its desire to be so designated;

(2) the level of **economic** development of such country, including its per capita gross national product, the living standards of its inhab-

itants, and any other economic factors which the President deems appropriate;

(3) whether or not other major developed countries are extending generalized preferential tariff treatment to such country;

(4) the extent to which such country has assured the United States that it will provide equitable and reasonable access to the markets and basic commodity resources of such country and the extent to which such country has assured the United States that it will refrain from engaging in unreasonable export practices;

(5) the extent to which such country is providing adequate and effective protection of intellectual property rights;

(6) the extent to which such country has taken action to—

(A) reduce trade distorting investment practices and policies (including export performance requirements); and

(B) reduce or eliminate barriers to trade in services; and

(7) whether or not such country has taken or is taking steps to afford to workers in that country (including any designated zone in that country) internationally recognized worker rights.

(d) **Withdrawal, suspension, or limitation of country designation**

(1) **In general**

The President may withdraw, suspend, or limit the application of the duty-free treatment accorded under this subchapter with respect to any country. In taking any action under this subsection, the President shall consider the factors set forth in section 2461 of this title and subsection (c) of this section.

(2) **Changed circumstances**

The President shall, after complying with the requirements of subsection (f)(2), withdraw or suspend the designation of any country as a beneficiary developing country if, after such designation, the President determines that as the result of changed circumstances such country would be barred from designation as a beneficiary developing country under subsection (b)(2). Such country shall cease to be a beneficiary developing country on the day on which the President issues an Executive order or Presidential proclamation revoking the designation of such country under this subchapter.

(3) **Advice to Congress**

The President shall, as necessary, advise the Congress on the application of section 2461 of this title and subsection (c) of this section, and the actions the President has taken to withdraw, to suspend, or to limit the application of duty-free treatment with respect to any country which has failed to adequately take the actions described in subsection (c).

(e) **Mandatory graduation of beneficiary developing countries**

If the President determines that a beneficiary developing country has become a 'high income' country, as defined by the official statistics of the International Bank for Reconstruction and Development, then the President shall terminate the designation of such country as a beneficiary developing country for purposes of this subchapter, effective on January 1 of the second year following the year in which such determination is made.

(f) **Congressional notification**

(1) **Notification of designation**

(A) **In general**

Before the President designates any country as a beneficiary developing country under this subchapter, the President shall notify the Congress of the President's intention to make such designation, together with the considerations entering into such decision.

(B) **Designation as least-developed beneficiary developing country**

At least 60 days before the President designates any country as a least-developed beneficiary developing country, the President shall notify the Congress of the President's intention to make such designation.

(2) **Notification of termination**

If the President has designated any country as a beneficiary developing country under this subchapter, the President shall not terminate such designation unless, at least 60 days before such termination, the President has notified the Congress and has notified such country of the President's intention to terminate such designation, together with the considerations entering into such decision.

9 U.S.C.A. § 2463

§ 2463. Designation of eligible articles

(a) **Eligible articles**

(1) **Designation**

(A) **In general**

Except as provided in subsection (b), the President is authorized to designate articles as eligible articles from all beneficiary developing countries for purposes of this subchapter by Executive order or Presidential proclamation after receiving the advice of the International Trade Commission in accordance with subsection (e).

(B) **Least-developed beneficiary developing countries**

Except for articles described in subparagraphs (A), (B), and (E) of subsection (b)(1) and articles described in paragraphs (2) and (3) of subsection (b), the President may, in carrying out section 2462(d)(1) of this title and subsection (c)(1) of this section, designate articles as eligible articles only for countries designated as least-developed beneficiary developing countries under section 2462(a)(2) of this title if, after receiving the advice of the International Trade Commission in accordance with subsection (e) of this section, the President determines that such articles are not import-sensitive in the context of imports from least-developed beneficiary developing countries.

(C) **Three-year rule**

If, after receiving the advice of the International Trade Commission under subsection (e), an article has been formally considered for designation as an eligible article under this subchapter and denied such designation, such article may not be reconsidered for such designation for a period of 3 years after such denial.

(2) **Rule of origin**

(A) **General rule**

The duty-free treatment provided under this subchapter shall apply to any eligible article which is the growth, product, or manufacture of a beneficiary developing country if—

(i) that article is imported directly from a beneficiary developing country into the customs territory of the United States; and

(ii) the sum of—

(I) the cost or value of the materials produced in the beneficiary developing country or any two or more such countries that are members of the same association of countries and are treated as one country under section 2467(2) of this title, plus

(II) the direct costs of processing operations performed in such beneficiary developing country or such member countries, is not less than 35 percent of the appraised value of such article at the time it is entered.

(B) **Exclusions**

An article shall not be treated as the growth, product, or manufacture of a beneficiary developing country by virtue of having merely undergone—

(i) simple combining or packaging operations, or

(ii) mere dilution with water or mere dilution with another substance that does not materially alter the characteristics of the article.

(3) **Regulations**

The Secretary of the Treasury, after consulting with the United States Trade Representative, shall prescribe such regulations as may be necessary to carry out paragraph (2), including, but not limited to, regulations providing that, in order to be eligible for duty-free treatment under this subchapter, an article—

(A) must be wholly the growth, product, or manufacture of a beneficiary developing country, or

(B) must be a new or different article of commerce which has been grown, produced, or manufactured in the beneficiary developing country.

(b) **Articles that may not be designated as eligible articles**

(1) **Import-sensitive articles**

The President may not designate any article as an eligible article under subsection (a) if such article is within one of the following categories of import-sensitive articles:

(A) Except as provided in paragraphs (4) and (5),[1] textile and apparel articles which were not eligible articles for purposes of this subchapter on January 1, 1994, as this subchapter was in effect on such date.

(B) Watches, except those watches entered after June 30, 1989, that the President specifically determines, after public notice and comment, will not cause material injury to watch or watch band, strap, or bracelet manufacturing and assembly operations in the United States or the United States insular possessions.

(C) Import-sensitive electronic articles.

(D) Import-sensitive steel articles.

(E) Except as provided in paragraph (5),[1] footwear, handbags, luggage, flat goods, work gloves, and leather wearing apparel which were not eligible articles for purposes of this subchapter on January 1, 1995, as this subchapter was in effect on such date.

(F) Import-sensitive semi manufactured and manufactured glass products.

(G) Any other articles which the President determines to be import-sensitive in the context of the Generalized System of Preferences.

(2) **Articles against which other actions taken**

An article shall not be an eligible article for purposes of this subchapter for any period during which such article is the subject of any action proclaimed pursuant to section 2253 of this title or section 1862 or 1981 of this title.

(3) **Agricultural products**

No quantity of an agricultural product subject to a tariff-rate quota that exceeds the in-quota quantity shall be eligible for duty-free treatment under this subchapter.

(4) **Certain hand-knotted or hand-woven carpets**

Notwithstanding paragraph (1)(A), the President may designate as an eligible article or articles under subsection (a) carpets or rugs which are hand-loomed, hand-woven, hand-hooked, hand-tufted, or hand-knotted, and classifiable under subheading 5701.10.16, 5701.10.40, 5701.90.10, 5701.90.20, 5702.10.90, 5702.42.20, 5702.49.10, 5702.51.20, 5702.91.30, 5702.92.00, 5702.99.10, 5703.10.00, 5703.20.10, or 5703.30.00 of the Harmonized Tariff Schedule of the United States.

(5) **Certain cotton articles**[2]

Notwithstanding paragraph (3), the President may designate as an eligible article or articles under subsection (a)(1)(B) only for countries designated as least-developed beneficiary developing countries under section 2462(a)(2) of this title cotton articles classifiable under subheading 5201.00.18, 5201.00.28, 5201.00.38, 5202.99.30, or 5203.00.30 of the Harmonized Tariff Schedule of the United States.

(6) **Certain luggage and travel articles**[2]

Notwithstanding subparagraph (A) or (E) of paragraph (1), the President may designate the following as eligible articles under subsection (a):

(A) Articles classifiable under subheading 4202.11.00, 4202.12.40, 4202.21.60, 4202.21.90, 4202.22.15, 4202.22.45, 4202.31.60, 4202.32.40, 4202.32.80, 4202.92.15, 4202.92.20, 4202.92.45, or 4202.99.90 of the Harmonized Tariff Schedule of the United States.

(B) Articles classifiable under statistical reporting number 4202.12.2020, 4202.12.2050, 4202.12.8030, 4202.12.8070, 4202.22.8050, 4202.32.9550, 4202.32.9560, 4202.91.0030, 4202.91.0090, 4202.92.3020, 4202.92.3031, 4202.92.3091, 4202.92.9026, or 4202.92.9060 of the Harmonized Tariff Schedule of the United States, as such statistical reporting numbers are in effect on June 29, 2015.

(c) **Withdrawal, suspension, or limitation of duty-free treatment; competitive need limitation**

(1) **In general**

The President may withdraw, suspend, or limit the application of the duty-free treatment accorded under this subchapter with respect to any article, except that no rate of duty may be established with respect to any article pursuant to this subsection other than the rate which would apply but for this subchapter. In taking any action under this subsection, the President shall consider the factors set forth in sections 2461 and 2462(c) of this title.

(2) **Competitive need limitation**

(A) Basis **for withdrawal of duty-free treatment**

(i) **In general**

Except as provided in clause (ii) and subject to subsection (d), whenever the President determines that a beneficiary developing country has exported (directly or indirectly) to the United States during any calendar year beginning after December 31, 1995—

(I) a quantity of an eligible article having an appraised value in excess of the applicable amount for the calendar year, or

(II) a quantity of an eligible article equal to or exceeding 50 percent of the appraised value of the total imports of that article into the United States during any calendar year, the President shall, not later than November 1 of the next calendar year, terminate the duty-free treatment for that article from that beneficiary developing country.

(ii) **Annual adjustment of applicable amount**

For purposes of applying clause (i), the applicable amount is—

(I) for 1996, $75,000,000, and

(II) for each calendar year thereafter, an amount equal to the applicable amount in effect for the preceding calendar year plus $5,000,000.

(B) **'Country' defined**

For purposes of this paragraph, the term 'country' does not include an association of countries which is treated as one country under section 2467(2) of this title, but does include a country which is a member of any such association.

(C) **Redesignations**

A country which is no longer treated as a beneficiary developing country with respect to an eligible article by reason of subparagraph (A) may, subject to the considerations set forth in sections 2461 and 2462 of this title, be redesignated a beneficiary developing country with respect to such article if imports of such article from such country did not exceed the limitations in subparagraph (A) during the preceding calendar year.

(D) **Least-developed beneficiary developing countries and beneficiary sub-Saharan African countries**

Subparagraph (A) shall not apply to any least-developed beneficiary developing country or any beneficiary sub-Saharan African country.

(E) **Articles not produced in the United States excluded**

Subparagraph (A)(i)(II) shall not apply with respect to any eligible article if a like or directly competitive article was not produced in the United States in any of the preceding 3 calendar years.

(F) **De minimis waivers**

(i) **In general**

The President may disregard subparagraph (A)(i)(II) with respect to any eligible article from any beneficiary developing country if the aggregate appraised value of the imports of such article into the United States during the preceding calendar year does not exceed the applicable amount for such preceding calendar year.

(ii) **Applicable amount**

For purposes of applying clause (i), the applicable amount is—

(I) for calendar year 1996, $13,000,000, and

(II) for each calendar year thereafter, an amount equal to the applicable amount in effect for the preceding calendar year plus $500,000.

(d) **Waiver of competitive need limitation**

(1) **In general**

The President may waive the application of subsection (c)(2) with respect to any eligible article of any beneficiary developing country if, before November 1 of the calendar year beginning after the calendar year for which a determination described in subsection (c)(2)(A) was made with respect to such eligible article, the President—

(A) receives the advice of the International Trade Commission under section 1332 of this title on whether any industry in the United States is likely to be adversely affected by such waiver,

(B) determines, based on the considerations described in sections 2461 and 2462(c) of this title and the advice described in subparagraph (A), that such waiver is in the national economic interest of the United States, and

(C) publishes the determination described in subparagraph (B) in the Federal Register.

(2) **Considerations by the President**

In making any determination under paragraph (1), the President shall give great weight to—

(A) the extent to which the beneficiary developing country has assured the United States that such country will provide equitable and reasonable access to the markets and basic commodity resources of such country, and

(B) the extent to which such country provides adequate and effective protection of intellectual property rights.

(3) **Other bases for waiver**

The President may waive the application of subsection (c)(2) if, before November 1 of the calendar year beginning after the calendar year for which a determination described in subsection (c)(2) was made with respect to a beneficiary developing country, the President determines that—

(A) there has been a historical preferential trade relationship between the United States and such country,

(B) there is a treaty or trade agreement in force covering economic relations between such country and the United States, and

(C) such country does not discriminate against, or impose unjustifiable or unreasonable barriers to, United States commerce, and the President publishes that determination in the Federal Register.

(4) **Limitations on waivers**

(A) **In general**

The President may not exercise the waiver authority under this subsection with respect to a quantity of an eligible article entered during any calendar year beginning after 1995, the aggregate appraised value of which equals or exceeds 30 percent of the aggregate appraised value of all articles that entered duty-free under this subchapter during the preceding calendar year.

(B) **Other waiver limits**

(i) The President may not exercise the waiver authority provided under this subsection with respect to a quantity of an eligible article entered during any calendar year beginning after 1995, the aggregate appraised value of which exceeds 15 percent of the aggregate appraised value of all articles that have entered duty-free under this subchapter during the preceding calendar year from those beneficiary developing countries which for the preceding calendar year—

(I) had a per capita gross national product (calculated on the basis of the best available information, including that of the International Bank for Reconstruction and Development) of $5,000 or more; or

(II) had exported (either directly or indirectly) to the United States a quantity of articles that was duty-free under this subchapter that had an aggregate appraised value of more than 10 percent of the aggregate appraised value of all articles that entered duty-free under this subchapter during that year.

(ii) Not later than November 1 of each year, the President should revoke any waiver that has then been in effect with respect to an article for 5 years or more if the beneficiary developing country has exported to the United States (directly or indirectly) during the preceding calendar year a quantity of the article—

(I) having an appraised value in excess of 1.5 times the applicable amount set forth in subsection (c)(2)(A)(ii) for that calendar year; or

(II) exceeding 75 percent of the appraised value of the total imports of that article into the United States during that calendar year.

(C) **Calculation of limitations**

There shall be counted against the limitations imposed under subparagraphs (A) and (B) for any calendar year only that value of any eligible article of any country that—

(i) entered duty-free under this subchapter during such calendar year; and

(ii) is in excess of the value of that article that would have been so entered during such calendar year if the limitations under subsection (c)(2)(A) applied.

(5) **Effective period of waiver**

Any waiver granted under this subsection shall remain in effect until the President determines that such waiver is no longer warranted due to changed circumstances.

(e) **International Trade Commission advice**

Before designating articles as eligible articles under subsection (a)(1), the President shall publish and furnish the International Trade Commission with lists of articles which may be considered for designation as eligible articles for purposes of this subchapter. The provisions of sections 2151, 2152, 2153, and 2154 of this title shall be complied with as though action under section 2461 of this title and this section were action under section 2133 of this title to carry out a trade agreement entered into under section 2133 of this title.

(f) **Special rule concerning Puerto Rico**

No action under this subchapter may affect any tariff duty imposed by the Legislature of Puerto Rico pursuant to section 1319 of this title on coffee imported into Puerto Rico.
Footnoted omitted

19 U.S.C.A. § 2464

§ 2464. Review and report to Congress
The President shall submit an annual report to the Congress on the status of internationally recognized worker rights within each beneficiary developing country, including the findings of the Secretary of Labor with respect to the beneficiary country's implementation of its international commitments to eliminate the worst forms of child labor.

19 U.S.C.A. § 2465

§ 2465. Date of termination
No duty-free treatment provided under this subchapter shall remain in effect after December 31, 2020.

19 U.S.C.A. § 2466

§ 2466. Agricultural exports of beneficiary developing countries
The appropriate agencies of the United States shall assist beneficiary developing countries to develop and implement measures designed to assure that the agricultural sectors of their economies are not directed to export markets to the detriment of the production of foodstuffs for their citizenry.

Chapter 6

Export Control Reform Act of 2018

Note: This legislation needs to be understood alongside the detailed regulations contained in the Export Administration Regulations (EAR).
SECTION 1. SHORT TITLE; TABLE OF CONTENTS.

(a) Short Title.—This Act may be cited as the 'Export Control Reform Act of 2018'.

SEC. 2. DEFINITIONS.

In this Act:

(1) CONTROLLED.—The term 'controlled', with respect to an item, means the export, reexport, or transfer of the item is controlled under title I.

(2) DUAL-USE.—The term 'dual-use', with respect to an item, means the item has civilian applications and military, terrorism, or weapons of mass destruction-related applications.

(3) EXPORT.—The term 'export', with respect to an item subject to controls under title I, includes—

- (A) the shipment or transmission of the item out of the United States, including the sending or taking of the item out of the United States, in any manner; and
- (B) the release or transfer of technology or source code relating to the item to a foreign person in the United States.

(4) EXPORT ADMINISTRATION REGULATIONS.—The term 'Export Administration Regulations' means—

- (A) the Export Administration Regulations as promulgated, maintained, and amended under the authority of the International Emergency Economic Powers Act and codified, as of the date of the enactment of this Act, in subchapter C of chapter VII of title 15, Code of Federal Regulations; or
- (B) regulations that are promulgated, maintained, and amended under the authority of title I on or after the date of the enactment of this Act.

(5) FOREIGN PERSON.—The term 'foreign person' means a person that is not a United States person.

(6) ITEM.—The term 'item' means a commodity, software, or technology.

(7) PERSON.—

- (A) IN GENERAL.—The term 'person' means—
  - (i) a natural person;
  - (ii) a corporation, business association, partnership, society, trust, financial institution, insurer, underwriter, guarantor, and any other business organization, any other nongovernmental entity, organization, or group, and any governmental entity operating as a business enterprise; and
  - (iii) any successor to any entity described in clause (ii).
- (B) APPLICATION TO GOVERNMENTAL ENTITIES.—The term 'person' does not include a government or governmental entity that is not operating as a business enterprise.

(8) REEXPORT.—The term 'reexport', with respect to an item subject to controls under title I, includes—

(A) the shipment or transmission of the item from a foreign country to another foreign country, including the sending or taking of the item from the foreign country to the other foreign country, in any manner; and

(B) the release or transfer of technology or source code relating to the item to a foreign person outside the United States.

(9) TECHNOLOGY.—The term 'technology'—

(A) includes—

(i) information necessary for the development, production, use, operation, installation, maintenance, repair, overhaul or refurbishing of an item; and

(ii) information at whatever stage of its creation, such as foundational information and know-how, as further defined by regulations; and

(B) does not include published information, including prerecorded records, printed books, pamphlets, miscellaneous publications, or other information, that—

(i) arises during, or results from, fundamental research and is intended to be published;

(ii) is released by instruction in a catalog course or associated teaching laboratory of an academic institution;

(iii) appears in patents or open (published) patent publications available from or at any patent office, unless covered by an invention secrecy order;

(iv) is non-proprietary system descriptions;

(v) is telemetry data; or

(vi) is any other category or type of information, as determined by the President for purposes of national security or foreign policy concerns.

(10) TRANSFER.—The term 'transfer', with respect to an item subject to controls under title I, means a change in the end-use or end user of the item within the same foreign country.

(11) UNITED STATES.—The term 'United States' means the several States, the District of Columbia, the Commonwealth of Puerto Rico, the Commonwealth of the Northern Mariana Islands, American Samoa, Guam, the United States Virgin Islands, and any other territory or possession of the United States.

(12) UNITED STATES PERSON.—The term 'United States person' means—

(A) any individual who is a citizen or national of the United States or who is an individual described in subparagraph (B) of section 274B(a)(3) of the Immigration and Nationality Act (8 U.S.C. 1324b(a)(3)); and

(B) a corporation or other legal entity which is organized under the laws of the United States, any State or territory thereof, or the District of Columbia, if natural persons described in subparagraph (A) own, directly or indirectly, more than 50 percent of the outstanding capital stock or other beneficial interest in such legal entity.

(13) WEAPONS OF MASS DESTRUCTION.—The term 'weapons of mass destruction' means nuclear, radiological, chemical, and biological weapons and delivery systems for such weapons.

TITLE I—AUTHORITY AND ADMINISTRATION OF CONTROLS

SEC. 101. SHORT TITLE.

This title may be cited as the 'Export Controls Act of 2018'.

SEC. 102. STATEMENT OF POLICY.

The following is the policy of the United States:

(1) The national security and foreign policy of the United States require that the export, reexport, and transfer of items, and specific activities of United States persons, wherever located, be controlled for the following purposes:
   (A) To control the access to items for use in—
      (i) the proliferation of weapons of mass destruction or of conventional weapons;
      (ii) the acquisition of destabilizing numbers or types of conventional weapons;
      (iii) acts of terrorism;
      (iv) military programs that could pose a threat to the security of the United States or its allies; or
      (v) activities undertaken specifically to cause significant interference with or disruption of critical infrastructure.
   (B) To preserve the qualitative military superiority of the United States.
   (C) To strengthen the United States industrial base.
   (D) To carry out the foreign policy of the United States, including the protection of human rights and the promotion of democracy.
   (E) To carry out obligations and commitments under international agreements and arrangements, including multilateral export control regimes.
   (F) To facilitate military interoperability between the United States and its North Atlantic Treaty Organization (NATO) and other close allies.
   (G) To ensure national security controls are tailored to focus on those core technologies and other items that are capable of being used to pose a serious national security threat to the United States.

(2) The national security of the United States requires that the United States maintain its leadership in the science, technology, en-

gineering, and manufacturing sectors. Such leadership requires that United States persons are competitive in global markets. The impact of the implementation of this title on such leadership and competitiveness must be evaluated on an ongoing basis and applied in imposing controls under sections 103 and 104 to avoid negatively affecting such leadership.

(3) The national security and foreign policy of the United States require that the United States participate in multilateral organizations and agreements regarding export controls on items that are consistent with the policy of the United States, and take all the necessary steps to secure the adoption and consistent enforcement, by the governments of such countries, of export controls on items that are consistent with such policy.

(4) Export controls should be fully coordinated with the multilateral export control regimes. Export controls that are multilateral are most effective, and should be tailored to focus on those core technologies and other items that are capable of being used to pose a serious national security threat to the United States and its allies.

(5) Export controls applied unilaterally to items widely available from foreign sources generally are less effective in preventing end-users from acquiring those items.

(6) The effective administration of export controls requires a clear understanding both inside and outside the United States Government of which technologies and other items are controlled and an efficient process should be created to update the controls, such as by removing and adding technologies and other items.

(7) The export control system must ensure that it is transparent, predictable, and timely, has the flexibility to be adapted to address new threats in the future, and allows seamless access to and sharing of export control information among all relevant United States national security and foreign policy agencies.

(8) Implementation and enforcement of United States export controls require robust capabilities in monitoring, intelligence, and investigation, appropriate penalties for violations, and the ability to swiftly interdict unapproved transfers.

(9) Export controls should be balanced with United States counterterrorism, information security, and cyber-security policies to ensure the ability to export, reexport, and transfer technology and other items in support of counterterrorism, critical infrastructure, and other homeland security priorities, while effectively preventing malicious cyber terrorists from obtaining items that threaten the United States and its interests, including the protection of and safety of United States citizens abroad.

(10) Export controls complement and are a critical element of the national security policies underlying the laws and regulations gov-

erning foreign direct investment in the United States, including controlling the transfer of critical technologies to certain foreign persons. Thus, the President, in close coordination with the Department of Commerce, the Department of Defense, the Department of State, the Department of Energy, and other agencies responsible for export controls, should have a regular and robust process to identify the emerging and other types of critical technologies of concern, as defined in United States foreign direct investment laws, and regulate their release to foreign persons as warranted regardless of the nature of the underlying transaction. Such identification efforts should draw upon the resources and expertise of all relevant parts of the United States Government, industry, and academia. These efforts should be in addition to traditional efforts to modernize and update the lists of controlled items under the multilateral export control regimes.

(11) The authority under this title may be exercised only in furtherance of all of the objectives set forth in paragraphs (1) through (10).

SEC. 103. AUTHORITY OF THE PRESIDENT.

(a) Authority.—In order to carry out the policy set forth in paragraphs (1) through (10) of section 102, the President shall control—
- (1) the export, reexport, and transfer of items, whether by United States persons, wherever located, or by foreign persons, wherever located; and
- (2) the activities of United States persons, wherever located, relating to specific—
  - (A) nuclear explosive devices;
  - (B) missiles;
  - (C) chemical or biological weapons;
  - (D) whole plants for chemical weapons precursors;
  - (E) foreign maritime nuclear projects; and
  - (F) foreign intelligence services.

(b) Requirements.—In exercising authority under this title, the President shall impose controls to achieve the following objectives:

- (1) To regulate the export, reexport, and transfer of items described in subsection (a)(1) of United States persons, wherever located, or foreign persons, wherever located.
- (2) To regulate the activities described in subsection (a)(2) of United States persons, wherever located.
- (3) To secure the cooperation of other governments and multilateral organizations to impose control systems that are consistent, to the extent possible, with the controls imposed under subsection (a).
- (4) To maintain the leadership of the United States in science, engineering, technology research and development, and manufacturing.

(5) To enhance the viability of commercial firms, academic institutions, and research establishments, and maintain the skilled workforce of such firms, institutions, and establishments, that are necessary to preserving the leadership of the United States described in paragraph (4).

(6) To strengthen the United States industrial base, both with respect to current and future defense requirements.

(7) To enforce the controls through means such as regulations, requirements for compliance, lists of controlled items, lists of foreign persons who threaten the national security or foreign policy of the United States, and guidance in a form that facilitates compliance by United States persons and foreign persons, in particular academic institutions, scientific and research establishments, and small- and medium-sized businesses.

SEC. 104. ADDITIONAL AUTHORITIES.

(a) In General.—In carrying out this title, the President shall—

(1) establish and maintain lists published by the Secretary of Commerce of items that are controlled under this title;

(2) establish and maintain lists published by the Secretary of Commerce of foreign persons and end-uses that are determined to be a threat to the national security and foreign policy of the United States pursuant to the policy set forth in section 102(1)(A) and to whom exports, reexports, and transfers of items are controlled;

(3) prohibit unauthorized exports, reexports, and transfers of controlled items;

(4) restrict exports, reexports, and transfers of any controlled items to any foreign person or end-use listed under paragraph (2);

(5) require licenses or other authorizations, as appropriate, for exports, reexports, and transfers of controlled items, including imposing conditions or restrictions on United States persons and foreign persons with respect to such licenses or other authorizations;

(6) establish a process by which the Secretary of Commerce or a license applicant requests an assessment that a foreign item is comparable in quality to an item controlled under this title, and is available in sufficient quantities to render the United States export control of that item or the denial of a license ineffective;

(7) require measures for compliance with the export controls established under this title;

(8) require and obtain such information from United States persons and foreign persons as is necessary to carry out this title;

(9) require, as appropriate, advance notice before an item is exported, reexported, or transferred, as an alternative to requiring a license;

(10) require, to the extent feasible, identification of items subject to controls under this title in order to facilitate the enforcement of such controls;

(11) inspect, search, detain, seize, or impose temporary denial orders with respect to items, in any form, that are subject to controls under this title, or conveyances on which it is believed that there are items that have been, are being, or are about to be exported, reexported, or transferred in violation of this title;
(12) monitor shipments, or other means of transfer;
(13) keep the public fully apprised of changes in policy, regulations, and procedures established under this title;
(14) appoint technical advisory committees in accordance with the Federal Advisory Committee Act;
(15) create, as warranted, exceptions to licensing requirements in order to further the objectives of this title; and
(16) undertake any other action as is necessary to carry out this title and is not otherwise prohibited by law.

(b) Relationship To IEEPA.—The authority under this title may not be used to regulate or prohibit under this title the export, reexport, or transfer of any item that may not be regulated or prohibited under section 203(b) of the International Emergency Economic Powers Act (50 U.S.C. 1702(b)).

(c) Countries Supporting International Terrorism.—
(1) LICENSE REQUIREMENT.—
(A) IN GENERAL.—A license shall be required for the export, reexport, or transfer of items to a country if the Secretary of State has made the following determinations:
(i) The government of such country has repeatedly provided support for acts of international terrorism.
(ii) The export, reexport, or transfer of such items could make a significant contribution to the military potential of such country, including its military logistics capability, or could enhance the ability of such country to support acts of international terrorism.
(B) DETERMINATION UNDER OTHER PROVISIONS OF LAW.—A determination of the Secretary of State under section 620A of the Foreign Assistance Act of 1961 (22 U.S.C. 2371), section 40 of the Arms Export Control Act (22 U.S.C. 2780), or any other provision of law that the government of a country described in subparagraph (A) has repeatedly provided support for acts of international terrorism shall be deemed to be a determination with respect to such government for purposes of clause (i) of subparagraph (A).
(2) NOTIFICATION TO CONGRESS.—The Secretary of State and the Secretary of Commerce shall notify the Committee on Foreign Affairs of the House of Representatives and the Committee on Banking, Housing, and Urban Affairs and the Committee on

Foreign Relations of the Senate at least 30 days before issuing any license required by paragraph (1).

(3) PUBLICATION IN FEDERAL REGISTER.—Each determination of the Secretary of State under paragraph (1)(A) shall be published in the Federal Register, except that the Secretary of State may exclude confidential information and trade secrets contained in such determination.

(4) RESCISSION OF DETERMINATION.—A determination of the Secretary of State under paragraph (1)(A) may not be rescinded unless the President submits to the Speaker of the House of Representatives, the chairman of the Committee on Foreign Affairs, and the chairman of the Committee on Banking, Housing, and Urban Affairs and the chairman of the Committee on Foreign Relations of the Senate—

(A) before the proposed rescission would take effect, a report certifying that—

(i) there has been a fundamental change in the leadership and policies of the government of the country concerned;

(ii) that government is not supporting acts of international terrorism; and

(iii) that government has provided assurances that it will not support acts of international terrorism in the future; or

(B) at least 90 days before the proposed rescission would take effect, a report justifying the rescission and certifying that—

(i) the government concerned has not provided any support for acts international terrorism during the preceding 24-month period; and

(ii) the government concerned has provided assurances that it will not support acts of international terrorism in the future.

(5) DISAPPROVAL OF RESCISSION.—No rescission under paragraph (4)(B) of a determination under paragraph (1)(A) with respect to the government of a country may be made if Congress, within 90 days after receipt of a report under paragraph (4)(B), enacts a joint resolution described in subsection (f)(2) of section 40 of the Arms Export Control Act with respect to a rescission under subsection (f)(1) of such section with respect to the government of such country.

(6) NOTIFICATION AND BRIEFING.—Not later than—

(A) ten days after initiating a review of the activities of the government of the country concerned within the 24-month period referred to in paragraph (4)(B)(i), the Secretary of State shall notify the Committee on Foreign Affairs of the House of Representatives and the Committee on Foreign Relations of the Senate of such initiation; and

(B) 20 days after the notification described in paragraph (1), the Secretary of State shall brief the congressional committees described in paragraph (1) on the status of such review.

(7) CONTENTS OF NOTIFICATION OF LICENSE.—The Secretary of State shall include in the notification required by paragraph (2)—

(A) a detailed description of the items to be offered, including a brief description of the capabilities of any item for which a license to export, reexport, or transfer the items is sought;

(B) the reasons why the foreign country, person, or entity to which the export, reexport, or transfer is proposed to be made has requested the items under the export, reexport, or transfer, and a description of the manner in which such country, person, or entity intends to use such items;

(C) the reasons why the proposed export, reexport, or transfer is in the national interest of the United States;

(D) an analysis of the impact of the proposed export, reexport, or transfer on the military capabilities of the foreign country, person, or entity to which such transfer would be made;

(E) an analysis of the manner in which the proposed export, reexport, or transfer would affect the relative military strengths of countries in the region to which the items that are the subject of such export, reexport, or transfer would be delivered and whether other countries in the region have comparable kinds and amounts of items; and

(F) an analysis of the impact of the proposed export, reexport, or transfer on the relations of the United States with the countries in the region to which the items that are the subject of such export, reexport, or transfer would be delivered.

(d) Enhanced Proliferation Controls.—

(1) IN GENERAL.—In furtherance of section 103(a) of this title, the President shall, except to the extent authorized by a statute or regulation administered by a Federal department or agency other than the Department of Commerce, require a United States person, wherever located, to apply for and receive a license from the Department of Commerce for the export, reexport, or transfer of items described in paragraph (2) or for the performance of services relating to such items.

(2) ITEMS DESCRIBED.—The items described in this paragraph are—

(A) nuclear explosive devices;

(B) missiles;

(C) chemical or biological weapons;

(D) whole plants for chemical weapons precursors; and
(E) foreign maritime nuclear projects that would pose a risk to the national security or foreign policy of the United States.

(e) Additional Prohibitions.—The Secretary of Commerce may inform United States persons, either individually by specific notice or through amendment to any regulation or order issued under this title, that a license from the Bureau of Industry and Security of the Department of Commerce is required to engage in any activity if the activity involves the types of movement, service, or support described in subsection (d). The absence of any such notification does not excuse the United States person from compliance with the license requirements of subsection (d), or any regulation or order issued under this title.

(f) License Review Standards.—The Secretary of Commerce shall deny an application to engage in any activity that involves the types of movement, service, or support described in subsection (d) if the activity would make a material contribution to any of the items described in subsection (d)(2).

SEC. 105. ADMINISTRATION OF EXPORT CONTROLS.

(a) In General.—The President shall delegate to the Secretary of Commerce, the Secretary of Defense, the Secretary of State and, as appropriate, the Director of National Intelligence and the heads of other appropriate Federal departments and agencies, the authority to carry out the purposes set forth in subsection (b).

(b) Purposes.—

(1) IN GENERAL.—The purpose of the delegations of authority pursuant to subsection (a) are—

to advise the President with respect to—

(i) identifying specific threats to the national security and foreign policy that the authority of this title may be used to address; and
(ii) exercising the authority under this title to implement policies, regulations, procedures, and actions that are necessary to effectively counteract those threats;

to review and approve—

(i) criteria for including items on, and removing such an item from, a list of controlled items established under this title;
(ii) an interagency procedure for compiling and amending any list described in clause (i);
(iii) criteria for including a person on a list of persons to whom exports, reexports, and transfers of items are prohibited or restricted under this title;
(iv) standards for compliance by persons subject to controls under this title; and

(v) policies and procedures for the end-use monitoring of exports, reexports, and transfers of items controlled under this title;

to obtain independent evaluations, including from Inspectors General of the relevant departments or agencies, on a periodic basis on the effectiveness of the implementation of this title in carrying out the policy set forth in section 102; and

to benefit from the inherent equities, experience, and capabilities of the Federal officials described in subsection (a), including—

(i) the views of the Department of Defense with respect to the national security implications of a particular control or decision;

(ii) the views of the Department of State with respect to the foreign policy implications of a particular control or decision;

(iii) the views of the Department of Energy with respect to the implications for nuclear proliferation of a particular control or decision; and

(iv) the views of the Department of Commerce with respect to the administration of an efficient, coherent, reliable, enforceable, and predictable export control system, and the resolution of competing views or policy objectives described in section 102.

(2) AUTHORITY TO SEEK INFORMATION.—The Federal officials described in subsection (a) may, in carrying out the purposes set forth in paragraph (1), seek information and advice from experts who are not officers or employees of the Federal Government.

TRANSMITTAL AND IMPLEMENTATION OF EVALUATIONS.—The results of the independent evaluations conducted pursuant to paragraph (1)(D) shall be transmitted to the President and the Congress, in classified form if necessary. Subject to the delegation of authority by the President, the Federal officials described in subsection (a) shall determine, direct, and ensure that improvements recommended in the evaluations are implemented.

SEC. 106. CONTROL LISTS.

The President shall, pursuant to the delegation of authority in section 105, ensure that—

(1) a process is established for regular interagency review of each list established under section 104(a)(1), that pursuant to such review the Secretary of Commerce regularly updates such lists to ensure that new items (including emerging critical technologies) are appropriately controlled, and that the level of control of items on the lists are adjusted as conditions change;

(2) information and expertise is obtained from officers and employees from relevant Federal departments, agencies, and offices and

persons outside the Federal Government who have technical expertise, with respect to the characteristics of the items considered for each list established under section 104(a)(1) and the effect of controlling the items on addressing the policy set forth in section 102;

(3) each list established under section 104(a)(1) appropriately identifies each entry that has been included by virtue of the participation of the United States in a multilateral regime, organization, or group the purpose of which is consistent with and supports the policy of the United States under this title relating to the control of exports, reexports, and transfers of items; and

each list established under section 104(a)(1) is published by the Secretary of Commerce in a form that facilitates compliance with it and related requirements, particularly by small- and medium-sized businesses, and academic institutions.

SEC. 107. LICENSING.

(a) In General.—The President shall, pursuant to the delegation of authority in section 105, establish a procedure for the Department of Commerce to license or otherwise authorize the export, reexport, and transfer of items controlled under this title in order to carry out the policy set forth in section 102 and the requirements set forth in section 103(b). The procedure shall ensure that—

(i) license applications, other requests for authorization, and related dispute resolution procedures are considered and decisions made with the participation of appropriate departments, agencies, and offices that have delegated functions under this title; and

(ii) licensing decisions are made in an expeditious manner, with transparency to applicants on the status of license and other authorization processing and the reason for denying any license or request for authorization.

(b) Sense Of Congress.—It is the sense of Congress that the President should make best efforts to ensure that an accurate, consistent, and timely evaluation and processing of licenses or other requests for authorization to export, reexport, or transfer items controlled under this title is accomplished within 30 days from the date of such license request.

(c) Fees.—No fee may be charged in connection with the submission, processing, or consideration of any application for a license or other authorization or other request made in connection with any regulation in effect under the authority of this title.

SEC. 108. COMPLIANCE ASSISTANCE.

(a) System For Seeking Assistance.—The President may establish a system to provide United States persons with assistance in complying with this title, which may include a mechanism for providing information, in classified form as appropriate, who are potential customers, suppliers, or business partners with respect to items controlled under this title, in order to further ensure the prevention of the export, reexport, or transfer of items that may pose a threat to the national security or foreign policy of the United States.

(b) Security Clearances.—In order to carry out subsection (a), the President may issue appropriate security clearances to persons described in that subsection who are responsible for complying with this title.

(c) Assistance For Certain Businesses.—

(1) IN GENERAL.—Not later than 120 days after the date of the enactment of this Act, the President shall develop and submit to Congress a plan to assist small- and medium-sized United States in export licensing and other processes under this title.

CONTENTS.—The plan shall include, among other things, arrangements for the Department of Commerce to provide counseling to businesses described in paragraph (1) on filing applications and identifying items controlled under this title, as well as proposals for seminars and conferences to educate such businesses on export controls, licensing procedures, and related obligations.

SEC. 109. REQUIREMENTS TO IDENTIFY AND CONTROL EMERGING CRITICAL TECHNOLOGIES IN EXPORT CONTROL REGULATIONS.

(a) In General.—The President shall, pursuant to the delegation of authority in section 105, establish and, in coordination with the Department of Commerce, the Department of Defense, the Department of State, the Department of Energy, and other departments determined to be necessary, lead a regular, ongoing interagency process to identify emerging critical technologies that are not identified in any list of items controlled for export under United States law or regulations, but that nonetheless could be essential for maintaining or increasing the technological advantage of the United States over countries that pose a significant threat to the national security of the United States with respect to national defense, intelligence, or other areas of national security, or gaining such an advantage over such countries in areas where such an advantage may not currently exist.

(b) Requirements.—The interagency process required under subsection (a) shall—

(1) draw upon the expertise, resources, and equities of all relevant United States Government agencies, industries, and academic institutions to identify and describe such emerging critical technologies;

(2) require the relevant export control authority to publish proposed regulations for public comment that would control heretofore unlisted emerging critical technologies identified pursuant to subsection (a) and control the release of each such technology to destinations, end uses, or end users as determined by the President;

(3) require the Secretary of Commerce, the Secretary of State, and the Secretary of Defense to propose to the relevant multilateral export control regimes in the following year that such emerging critical technologies be added to the list of technologies controlled by such regimes;

(4) determine whether national security concerns warrant continued unilateral export controls over technologies identified pursuant to subsection (a) if the relevant multilateral export control regime does not agree to list such technologies on its control list within three years; and

(5) require the agencies responsible for administering the export controls identified in subsection (a) to remove or revise, as appropriate, existing controls determined to warrant removal or revision as a result of insight or information obtained during efforts undertaken to comply with the requirements of this section.

SEC. 110. PENALTIES.

(a) Unlawful Acts.—

(1) IN GENERAL.—It shall be unlawful for a person to violate, attempt to violate, conspire to violate, or cause a violation of this title or of any regulation, order, license, or other authorization issued under this title, including any of the unlawful acts described in paragraph (2).

(2) SPECIFIC UNLAWFUL ACTS.—The unlawful acts described in this paragraph are the following:

(A) No person may engage in any conduct prohibited by or contrary to, or refrain from engaging in any conduct required by this title, the Export Administration Regulations, or any order, license or authorization issued thereunder.

(B) No person may cause or aid, abet, counsel, command, induce, procure, or approve the doing of any act prohibited, or the omission of any act required by this title, the Export Administration Regulations, or any order, license or authorization issued thereunder.

(C) No person may solicit or attempt a violation of this Act, the Export Administration Regulations, or any order, license or authorization issued thereunder.

(D) No person may conspire or act in concert with one or more other persons in any manner or for any purpose to bring about or to do any act that constitutes a violation of this title, the Export Administration Regulations, or any order, license or authorization issued thereunder.

(E) No person may order, buy, remove, conceal, store, use, sell, loan, dispose of, transfer, transport, finance, forward, or otherwise service, in whole or in part, any item exported or to be exported from the United States, or that is otherwise subject to the Export Administration Regulations, with knowledge that a violation of this title, the Export Administration Regulations, or any order, license or authorization issued thereunder, has occurred, is about to occur, or is intended to occur in connection with the item unless valid authorization is obtained therefor.

(F) No person may make any false or misleading representation, statement, or certification, or falsify or conceal any material fact, either directly to the Department of Commerce, or an official of any other United States agency, or indirectly through any other person—

 (i) in the course of an investigation or other action subject to the Export Administration Regulations;

 (ii) in connection with the preparation, submission, issuance, use, or maintenance of any export control document or any report filed or required to be filed pursuant to the Export Administration Regulations; or

 (iii) for the purpose of or in connection with effecting any export, reexport, or transfer of an item subject to the Export Administration Regulations or a service or other activity of a United States person described in section 104.

(G) No person may engage in any transaction or take any other action with intent to evade the provisions of this title, the Export Administration Regulations, or any order, license, or authorization issued thereunder.

(H) No person may fail or refuse to comply with any reporting or recordkeeping requirements of the Export Administration Regulations or of any order, license, or authorization issued thereunder.

(I) Except as specifically authorized in the Export Administration Regulations or in writing by the Department of Commerce, no person may alter any license, authorization, export control document, or order issued under the Export Administration Regulations.

(J) No person may take any action that is prohibited by a denial order issued by the Department of Commerce to prevent imminent violations of this title, the Export Administration Regulations, or any order, license or authorization issued thereunder.

(3) ADDITIONAL REQUIREMENTS.—For purposes of subparagraph (G), any representation, statement, or certification made by any person shall be deemed to be continuing in effect. Each person who has made a representation, statement, or certification to the Department of Commerce relating to any order, license, or other

authorization issued under this title shall notify the Department of Commerce, in writing, of any change of any material fact or intention from that previously represented, stated, or certified, immediately upon receipt of any information that would lead a reasonably prudent person to know that a change of material fact or intention had occurred or may occur in the future.

(b) Criminal Penalty.—

(1) KNOWING VIOLATIONS.—Except as provided in paragraph (2), a person who knowingly violates or conspires or attempts to violate subsection (a) shall be fined not more than 5 times the amount or value of the exports, reexports, or transfers involved, or $500,000, whichever is greater, and, in the case of an individual, imprisoned not more than 5 years, or both.

(2) WILLFUL VIOLATIONS.—A person who willfully violates or conspires to or attempts to violate any provision of subsection (a) shall be fined not more than 5 times the amount or value of the exports, reexports, or transfers involved, or $1,000,000, whichever is greater, and, in the case of an individual, shall be fined not more than $250,000, or imprisoned not more than 10 years, or both.

(c) Civil Penalties.—

(1) AUTHORITY.—The President may impose the following civil penalties on a person for each violation by that person of this title or any regulation, order, or license issued under this title, for each violation:

(A) A fine of not more than $250,000 or an amount that is twice the value of the transaction that is the basis of the violation with respect to which the penalty is imposed, whichever is greater.

(B) Revocation of a license issued under this title to the person.

(C) A prohibition on the person's ability to export, reexport, or transfer any items, whether or not subject to controls under this title.

(2) PROCEDURES.—Any civil penalty under this subsection may be imposed only after notice and opportunity for an agency hearing on the record in accordance with sections 554 through 557 of title 5, United States Code.

(3) STANDARDS FOR LEVELS OF CIVIL PENALTY.—The President may by regulation provide standards for establishing levels of civil penalty under this subsection based upon factors such as the seriousness of the violation, the culpability of the violator, and such mitigating factors as the violator's record of cooperation with the Government in disclosing the violation.

(d) Criminal Forfeiture Of Property Interest And Proceeds.—

(1) FORFEITURE.—Any person who is convicted under subsection (b) of a violation of a control imposed under section 103 (or

any regulation, order, or license issued with respect to such control) shall, in addition to any other penalty, forfeit to the United States—

(A) any of that person's interest in, security of, claim against, or property or contractual rights of any kind in the tangible items that were the subject of the violation;

(B) any of that person's interest in, security of, claim against, or property or contractual rights of any kind in tangible property that was used in the violation; and

(C) any of that person's property constituting, or derived from, any proceeds obtained directly or indirectly as a result of the violation.

(2) PROCEDURES.—The procedures in any forfeiture under this subsection, and the duties and authority of the courts of the United States and the Attorney General with respect to any forfeiture action under this subsection or with respect to any property that may be subject to forfeiture under this subsection, shall be governed by the provisions of section 1963 of title 18, United States Code.

(e) Prior Convictions.—

(1) LICENSE BAR.—

(A) IN GENERAL.—The President may—

(i) deny the eligibility of any person convicted of a criminal violation described in subparagraph (B) to export, reexport, or transfer outside the United States any item, whether or not subject to controls under this title, for a period of up to 10 years beginning on the date of the conviction; and

(ii) revoke any license or other authorization to export, reexport, or transfer items that was issued under this title and in which such person has an interest at the time of the conviction.

(B) VIOLATIONS.—The violations referred to in subparagraph (A) are any criminal violations of, or criminal attempt or conspiracy to violate—

(i) this title (or any regulation, license, or order issued under this title);

(ii) any regulation, license, or order issued under the International Emergency Economic Powers Act;

(iii) section 793, 794, or 798 of title 18, United States Code;

(iv) section 4(b) of the Internal Security Act of 1950 (50 U.S.C. 783(b)); or

(v) section 38 of the Arms Export Control Act (22 U.S.C. 2778).

(2) APPLICATION TO OTHER PARTIES.—The President may exercise the authority under paragraph (1) with respect to any person related, through affiliation, ownership, control, or position of responsibility, to any person convicted of any violation of law set forth in paragraph (1), upon a showing of such relationship with the convicted party, and subject to the procedures set forth in subsection (c)(2).

(f) Other Authorities.—Nothing in subsection (c), (d), or (e) limits—

(1) the availability of other administrative or judicial remedies with respect to violations of this title, or any regulation, order, license or other authorization issued under this title;

(2) the authority to compromise and settle administrative proceedings brought with respect to violations of this title, or any regulation, order, license, or other authorization issued under this title; or

(3) the authority to compromise, remit or mitigate seizures and forfeitures pursuant to section 1(b) of title VI of the Act of June 15, 1917 (22 U.S.C. 401(b)).

SEC. 111. ENFORCEMENT.

(a) Authorities.—In order to enforce this title, the President may—

(1) issue regulations, orders, and guidelines;

(2) require, inspect, and obtain books, records, and any other information from any person subject to the provisions of this title;

(3) administer oaths or affirmations and by subpoena require any person to appear and testify or to appear and produce books, records, and other writings, or both;

(4) conduct investigations (including undercover) in the United States and in other countries, including intercepting any wire, oral, and electronic communications, conducting electronic surveillance, using pen registers and trap and trace devices, and carrying out acquisitions, to the extent authorized under chapters 119, 121, and 206 of title 18, United States Code, and other applicable laws of the United States;

(5) inspect, search, detain, seize, or issue temporary denial orders with respect to items, in any form, that are subject to controls under this title, or conveyances on which it is believed that there are items that have been, are being, or are about to be exported, reexported, or transferred in violation of this title, or any regulations, order, license, or other authorization issued thereunder;

(6) conduct prelicense inspections and post-shipment verifications; and

(7) execute warrants and make arrests.

(b) Enforcement Of Subpoenas.—In the case of contumacy by, or refusal to obey a subpoena issued to, any person under subsection (a)(3), a district court of the United States, after notice to such person and a hearing, shall have jurisdiction to issue an order requiring such person to appear and give testimony or to appear and produce books, records, and other writings, regardless of format, that are the subject of the subpoena. Any failure to obey such order of the court may be punished by such court as a contempt thereof.

(c) Best Practice Guidelines.—

(1) IN GENERAL.—The President, in consultation with the Secretary of Commerce and other Federal officials described in section 105(a), should publish and update 'best practices' guidelines to assist persons in developing and implementing, on a voluntary basis, effective export control programs in compliance with the regulations issued under this title.

(2) EXPORT COMPLIANCE PROGRAM.—The implementation by a person of an effective export compliance program and a high quality overall export compliance effort by a person should ordinarily be given weight as mitigating factors in a civil penalty action against the person under this title.

(d) Reference To Enforcement.—For purposes of this section, a reference to the enforcement of, or a violation of, this title includes a reference to the enforcement or a violation of any regulation, order, license or other authorization issued pursuant to this title.

(e) Immunity.—A person shall not be excused from complying with any requirements under this section because of the person's privilege against self-incrimination, but the immunity provisions of section 6002 of title 18, United States Code, shall apply with respect to any individual who specifically claims such privilege.

(f) Confidentiality Of Information.—

(1) EXEMPTIONS FROM DISCLOSURE.—

(A) IN GENERAL.—Information obtained under this title may be withheld from disclosure only to the extent permitted by statute, except that information described in subparagraph (B) shall be withheld from public disclosure and shall not be subject to disclosure under section 552(b)(3) of title 5, United States Code, unless the release of such information is determined by the President to be in the national interest.

(B) INFORMATION DESCRIBED.—Information described in this subparagraph is information submitted or obtained in connection with an application for a license or other authorization to export, reexport, or transfer items, engage in other activities, a recordkeeping or reporting requirement, enforcement activity, or other operations under this title, including—

(i) the license application, license, or other authorization itself;

(ii) classification or advisory opinion requests, and the response thereto;
(iii) license determinations, and information pertaining thereto;
(iv) information or evidence obtained in the course of any investigation; and
(v) information obtained or furnished in connection with any international agreement, treaty, or other obligation.

(2) INFORMATION TO THE CONGRESS AND GAO.—
(A) IN GENERAL.—Nothing in this section shall be construed as authorizing the withholding of information from the Congress or from the Government Accountability Office.
(B) AVAILABILITY TO THE CONGRESS.—
(i) IN GENERAL.—Any information obtained at any time under any provision of the Export Administration Act of 1979 (as in effect on the day before the date of the enactment of this Act and as continued in effect pursuant to the International Emergency Economic Powers Act), under the Export Administration Regulations, or under this title, including any report or license application required under any such provision, shall be made available to a committee or subcommittee of Congress of appropriate jurisdiction, upon the request of the chairman or ranking minority member of such committee or subcommittee.
(ii) PROHIBITION ON FURTHER DISCLOSURE.—No such committee or subcommittee, or member thereof, may disclose any information made available under clause (i), that is submitted on a confidential basis unless the full committee determines that the withholding of that information is contrary to the national interest.
(C) AVAILABILITY TO GAO.—
(i) IN GENERAL.—Information described in clause (i) of subparagraph (B) shall be subject to the limitations contained in section 716 of title 31, United States Code.
(ii) PROHIBITION ON FURTHER DISCLOSURE.—An officer or employee of the Government Accountability Office may not disclose, except to the Congress in accordance with this paragraph, any such information that is submitted on a confidential basis or from which any individual can be identified.

(3) INFORMATION SHARING.—
(A) IN GENERAL.—Any Federal official described in section 105(a) who obtains information that is relevant to

the enforcement of this title, including information pertaining to any investigation, shall furnish such information to each appropriate department, agency, or office with enforcement responsibilities under this section to the extent consistent with the protection of intelligence, counterintelligence, and law enforcement sources, methods, and activities.

(B) EXCEPTIONS.—The provisions of this paragraph shall not apply to information subject to the restrictions set forth in section 9 of title 13, United States Code, and return information, as defined in subsection (b) of section 6103 of the Internal Revenue Code of 1986 (26 U.S.C. 6103(b)), may be disclosed only as authorized by that section.

(C) EXCHANGE OF INFORMATION.—The President shall ensure that the heads of departments, agencies, and offices with enforcement authorities under this title, consistent with protection of law enforcement and its sources and methods—

(i) exchange any licensing and enforcement information with one another that is necessary to facilitate enforcement efforts under this section; and

(ii) consult on a regular basis with one another and with the head of other departments, agencies, and offices that obtain information subject to this paragraph, in order to facilitate the exchange of such information.

(D) INFORMATION SHARING WITH FEDERAL AGENCIES.—Licensing or enforcement information obtained under this title may be shared with heads of departments, agencies, and offices that do not have enforcement authorities under this title on a case-by-case basis at the discretion of the President. Such information may be shared only when the President makes a determination that the sharing of this information is in the national interest.

(g) Reporting Requirements.—In the administration of this section, reporting requirements shall be designed so as to reduce the cost of reporting, recordkeeping, and documentation to the extent consistent with effective enforcement and compilation of useful trade statistics. Reporting, recordkeeping, and documentation requirements shall be periodically reviewed and revised in the light of developments in the field of information technology.

(h) Civil Forfeiture.—

(1) IN GENERAL.—Any tangible items seized under subsection (a) by designated officers or employees shall be subject to forfeiture to the United States in accordance with applicable law, except that property seized shall be returned if the property owner is not found guilty of a civil or criminal violation under section 109.

PROCEDURES.—Any seizure or forfeiture under this subsection shall be carried out in accordance with the procedures set forth in section 981 of title 18, United States Code.

SEC. 112. ADMINISTRATIVE PROCEDURE.

(a) In General.—The functions exercised under this title shall be subject to sections 551, 553 through 559, and 701 through 706 of title 5, United States Code.

(b) Amendments To Regulations.—The President shall notify in advance the Committee on Banking, Housing, and Urban Affairs of the Senate and the Committee on Foreign Affairs of the House of Representatives of any proposed amendments to the Export Administration Regulations with an explanation of the intent and rationale of such amendments.

SEC. 113. ANNUAL REPORT TO CONGRESS.

(a) In General.—The President shall submit to Congress, by December 31 of each year, a report on the implementation of this title during the preceding fiscal year. The report shall include an analysis of—

(1) the effect of controls imposed under this title on exports, reexports, and transfers of items in addressing threats to the national security or foreign policy of the United States, including a description of licensing processing times;

(2) the impact of such controls on the scientific and technological leadership of the United States;

(3) the consistency with such controls of export controls imposed by other countries;

(4) efforts to provide exporters with compliance assistance, including specific actions to assist small- and medium-sized businesses;

(5) a summary of regulatory changes from the prior fiscal year;

(6) a summary of export enforcement actions, including of actions taken to implement end-use monitoring of dual-use, military, and other items subject to the Export Administration Regulations;

(7) a summary of approved license applications to proscribed persons; and

(8) efforts undertaken within the previous year to comply with the requirements of section 109, including any 'critical technologies' identified under such section and how or whether such critical technologies were controlled for export.

(b) Form.—The report required under subsection (a) shall be submitted in unclassified form, but may contain a classified annex.

SEC. 114. REPEAL.

(a) In General.—The Export Administration Act of 1979 (50 U.S.C. App. 2401 et seq.) (as continued in effect pursuant to the International Emergency Economic Powers Act) is repealed.

(b) Implementation.—The President shall implement the amendment made by subsection (a) by exercising the authorities of the President under the International Emergency Economic Powers Act (50 U.S.C. 1701 et seq.).

SEC. 115. EFFECT ON OTHER ACTS.

(a) In General.—Except as otherwise provided in this title, nothing contained in this title shall be construed to modify, repeal, supersede, or otherwise affect the provisions of any other laws authorizing control over exports, reexports, or transfers of any item, or activities of United States persons subject to the Export Administration Regulations.

(b) Coordination Of Controls.—

(1) IN GENERAL.—The authority granted to the President under this title shall be exercised in such manner so as to achieve effective coordination with all export control and sanctions authorities exercised by Federal departments and agencies delegated with authority under this title, particularly the Department of State, the Department of the Treasury, and the Department of Energy.

(2) SENSE OF CONGRESS.—It is the sense of Congress that in order to achieve effective coordination described in paragraph (1), such Federal departments and agencies—

(A) should continuously work to create enforceable regulations with respect to the export, reexport, and transfer by United States and foreign persons of commodities, software, technology, and services to various end uses and end users for foreign policy and national security reasons;

(B) should regularly work to reduce complexity in the system, including complexity caused merely by the existence of structural, definitional, and other non-policy based differences between and among different export control and sanctions systems; and

(C) should coordinate controls on items exported, reexported, or transferred in connection with a foreign military sale under chapter 2 of the Arms Export Control Act or a commercial sale under section 38 of the Arms Export Control Act to reduce as much unnecessary administrative burden as possible that is a result of differences between the exercise of those two authorities.

(c) Nonproliferation Controls.—Nothing in this title shall be construed to supersede the procedures published by the President pursuant to section 309(c) of the Nuclear Non-Proliferation Act of 1978.

SEC. 116. TRANSITION PROVISIONS.

(a) In General.—All delegations, rules, regulations, orders, determinations, licenses, or other forms of administrative action that have been made, issued, conducted, or allowed to become effective under the Export Administration Act of 1979 (as in effect on the day before the date of the enactment of this Act and as continued in effect pursuant to the International Emergency Economic Powers Act), or the Export Administration Regulations, and are in effect as of the date of the enactment of this Act, shall continue in effect according to their terms until modified, superseded, set aside, or revoked under the authority of this title.

(b) Administrative And Judicial Proceedings.—This title shall not affect any administrative or judicial proceedings commenced, or any applications for licenses made, under the Export Administration Act of 1979 (as in effect on the day before the date of the enactment of this Act and as continued in effect pursuant to the International Emergency Economic Powers Act), or the Export Administration Regulations.

(c) Certain Determinations And References.—

(1) STATE SPONSORS OF TERRORISM.—Any determination that was made under section 6(j) of the Export Administration Act of 1979 (as in effect on the day before the date of the enactment of this Act and as continued in effect pursuant to the International Emergency Economic Powers Act) shall continue in effect as if the determination had been made under section 104(c) of this Act.

(2) REFERENCE.—Any reference in any other provision of law to a country the government of which the Secretary of State has determined, for purposes of section 6(j) of the Export Administration Act of 1979 (as in effect on the day before the date of the enactment of this Act and as continued in effect pursuant to the International Emergency Economic Powers Act), is a government that has repeatedly provided support for acts of international terrorism shall be deemed to refer to a country the government of which the Secretary of State has determined, for purposes of section 104(c) of this Act, is a government that has repeatedly provided support for acts of international terrorism.

TITLE II—ANTI-BOYCOTT ACT OF 2018

SEC. 201. SHORT TITLE.

This Act may be cited as the 'Anti-Boycott Act of 2018'.

SEC. 202. STATEMENT OF POLICY.

Congress declares it is the policy of the United States—

(1) to oppose restrictive trade practices or boycotts fostered or imposed by any foreign country, or requests to impose restrictive trade practices or boycotts by any foreign country, against other countries friendly to the United States or against any United States person;

(2) to encourage and, in specified cases, require United States persons engaged in the export of goods or technology or other informa-

tion to refuse to take actions, including furnishing information or entering into or implementing agreements, which have the effect of furthering or supporting the restrictive trade practices or boycotts fostered or imposed by any foreign country, or requests to impose restrictive trade practices or boycotts by any foreign country against a country friendly to the United States or against any United States person; and

(3) to foster international cooperation and the development of international rules and institutions to assure reasonable access to world supplies.

SEC. 203. FOREIGN BOYCOTTS.

(a) Prohibitions And Exceptions.—

(1) PROHIBITIONS.—For the purpose of implementing the policies set forth in section 202, the President shall issue regulations prohibiting any United States person, with respect to that person's activities in the interstate or foreign commerce of the United States, from taking or knowingly agreeing to take any of the following actions with intent to comply with, further, or support any boycott fostered or imposed by any foreign country, or request to impose any boycott by any foreign country, against a country which is friendly to the United States and which is not itself the object of any form of boycott pursuant to United States law or regulation:

(A) Refusing, or requiring any other person to refuse, to do business with or in the boycotted country, with any business concern organized under the laws of the boycotted country, with any national or resident of the boycotted country, or with any other person, pursuant to an agreement with, a requirement of, or a request from or on behalf of the boycotting country. The mere absence of a business relationship with or in the boycotted country with any business concern organized under the laws of the boycotted country, with any national or resident of the boycotted country, or with any other person, does not indicate the existence of the intent required to establish a violation of regulations issued to carry out this subparagraph.

(B) Refusing, or requiring any other person to refuse, to employ or otherwise discriminating against any United States person on the basis of race, religion, sex, or national origin of that person or of any owner, officer, director, or employee of such person.

(C) Furnishing information with respect to the race, religion, sex, or national origin of any United States person or of any owner, officer, director, or employee of such person.

(D) Furnishing information, or requesting the furnishing of information, about whether any person has, has had, or proposes to have any business relationship (including a relationship by way of sale, purchase, legal or commercial representation, shipping or other transport, insurance, investment, or supply) with or in the boycotted country, with any business concern organized under the laws of the boycotted country, with any national or resident of the boycotted country, or with any other person which is known or believed to be restricted from having any business relationship with or in the boycotting country. Nothing in this subparagraph shall prohibit the furnishing of normal business information in a commercial context as defined by the Secretary.

(E) Furnishing information about whether any person is a member of, has made contributions to, or is otherwise associated with or involved in the activities of any charitable or fraternal organization which supports the boycotted country.

(F) Paying, honoring, confirming, or otherwise implementing a letter of credit which contains any condition or requirement compliance with which is prohibited by regulations issued pursuant to this paragraph, and no United States person shall, as a result of the application of this paragraph, be obligated to pay or otherwise honor or implement such letter of credit.

(2) EXCEPTIONS.—Regulations issued pursuant to paragraph (1) shall provide exceptions for—

(A) complying or agreeing to comply with requirements—

(i) prohibiting the import of goods or services from the boycotted country or goods produced or services provided by any business concern organized under the laws of the boycotted country or by nationals or residents of the boycotted country; or

(ii) prohibiting the shipment of goods to the boycotting country on a carrier of the boycotted country, or by a route other than that prescribed by the boycotting country or the recipient of the shipment;

(B) complying or agreeing to comply with import and shipping document requirements with respect to the country of origin, the name of the carrier and route of shipment, the name of the supplier of the shipment or the name of the provider of other services, except that no information knowingly furnished or conveyed in response to such requirements may be stated in negative, blacklisting, or similar exclusionary terms, other than with respect to carriers or route of shipment as may be permitted by such regulations in order to comply with precautionary requirements protecting against war risks and confiscation;

(C) complying or agreeing to comply in the normal course of business with the unilateral and specific selection by a boycotting country, or national or resident thereof, of carriers, insurers, suppliers of services to be performed within the boycotting country or specific goods which, in the normal course of business, are identifiable by source when imported into the boycotting country;

(D) complying or agreeing to comply with export requirements of the boycotting country relating to shipments or transshipments of exports to the boycotted country, to any business concern of or organized under the laws of the boycotted country, or to any national or resident of the boycotted country;

(E) compliance by an individual or agreement by an individual to comply with the immigration or passport requirements of any country with respect to such individual or any member of such individual's family or with requests for information regarding requirements of employment of such individual within the boycotting country; and

(F) compliance by a United States person resident in a foreign country or agreement by such person to comply with the laws of that country with respect to his activities exclusively therein, and such regulations may contain exceptions for such resident complying with the laws or regulations of that foreign country governing imports into such country of trademarked, trade named, or similarly specifically identifiable products, or components of products for his own use, including the performance of contractual services within that country, as may be defined by such regulations.

(3) SPECIAL RULES.—Regulations issued pursuant to paragraphs (2)(C) and (2)(F) shall not provide exceptions from paragraphs (1)(B) and (1)(C).

(4) RULE OF CONSTRUCTION.—Nothing in this subsection may be construed to supersede or limit the operation of the antitrust or civil rights laws of the United States.

(5) APPLICATION.—This section shall apply to any transaction or activity undertaken, by or through a United States person or any other person, with intent to evade the provisions of this section as implemented by the regulations issued pursuant to this subsection, and such regulations shall expressly provide that the exceptions set forth in paragraph (2) shall not permit activities or agreements (expressed or implied by a course of conduct, including a pattern of responses) otherwise prohibited, which are not within the intent of such exceptions.

(b) Foreign Policy Controls.—

(1) IN GENERAL.—In addition to the regulations issued pursuant to subsection (a), regulations issued under title I of this Act to carry out the policies set forth in section 102(1)(D) shall implement the policies set forth in this section.

(2) REQUIREMENTS.—Such regulations shall require that any United States person receiving a request for the furnishing of information, the entering into or implementing of agreements, or the taking of any other action referred to in subsection (a) shall report that fact to the Secretary, together with such other information concerning such request as the Secretary may require for such action as the Secretary considers appropriate for carrying out the policies of that section. Such person shall also report to the Secretary whether such person intends to comply and whether such person has complied with such request. Any report filed pursuant to this paragraph shall be made available promptly for public inspection and copying, except that information regarding the quantity, description, and value of any goods or technology to which such report relates may be kept confidential if the Secretary determines that disclosure thereof would place the United States person involved at a competitive disadvantage. The Secretary shall periodically transmit summaries of the information contained in such reports to the Secretary of State for such action as the Secretary of State, in consultation with the Secretary, considers appropriate for carrying out the policies set forth in section 202.

(c) Preemption.—The provisions of this section and the regulations issued pursuant thereto shall preempt any law, rule, or regulation of any of the several States or the District of Columbia, or any of the territories or possessions of the United States, or of any governmental subdivision thereof, which law, rule, or regulation pertains to participation in, compliance with, implementation of, or the furnishing of information regarding restrictive trade practices or boycotts fostered or imposed by foreign countries, or requests to impose restrictive trade practices or boycotts by any foreign country, against other countries friendly to the United States.

SEC. 204. ENFORCEMENT.

(a) Civil Penalties.—The President may impose the following civil penalties on a person who violates section 203 or any regulation issued under this title:

(1) A fine of not more than $250,000 or an amount that is twice the amount of the transaction that is the basis of the violation with respect to which the penalty is imposed.

(2) Revocation of a license issued under title I to the person.

(3) A prohibition on the person's ability to export, reexport, or transfer any items, whether or not subject to controls under this title.

(b) Procedures.—Any civil penalty under this section may be imposed only after notice and opportunity for an agency hearing on the record in accordance with sections 554 through 557 of title 5, United States Code, and shall be subject to judicial review in accordance with chapter 7 of such title.

(c) Standards For Levels Of Civil Penalty.—The President may by regulation provide standards for establishing levels of civil penalty under this section based upon factors such as the seriousness of the violation, the culpability of the violator, and the violator's record of cooperation with the Government in disclosing the violation.

TITLE III—SANCTIONS REGARDING MISSILE PROLIFERATION AND CHEMICAL AND BIOLOGICAL WEAPONS PROLIFERATION

SEC. 301. MISSILE PROLIFERATION CONTROL VIOLATIONS.

(a) Violations By United States Persons.—

(1) SANCTIONS.—

(A) SANCTIONABLE ACTIVITY.—The President shall impose the applicable sanctions described in subparagraph (B) if the President determines that a United States person knowingly—

(i) exports, reexports, or transfers of any item on the MTCR Annex, in violation of the provisions of section 38 (22 U.S.C. 2778) or chapter 7 of the Arms Export Control Act, title I of this Act, or any regulations or orders issued under any such provisions; or

(ii) conspires to or attempts to engage in such export, reexport, or transfer.

(B) SANCTIONS.—The sanctions that apply to a United States person under subparagraph (A) are the following:

(i) If the item on the MTCR Annex involved in the export, reexport, or transfer is missile equipment or technology within category II of the MTCR Annex, then the President shall deny to such United States person, for a period of 2 years, licenses for the transfer of missile equipment or technology controlled under title I.

(ii) If the item on the MTCR Annex involved in the export, reexport, or transfer is missile equipment or technology within category I of the MTCR Annex, then the President shall deny to such United States person, for a period of not less than 2 years, all licenses for items the transfer of which is controlled under title I.

(2) DISCRETIONARY SANCTIONS.—In the case of any determination referred to in paragraph (1), the President may pursue any other appropriate penalties under section 109 of this Act.

(3) WAIVER.—The President may waive the imposition of sanctions under paragraph (1) on a person with respect to a product or service if the President certifies to the Congress that—

(A) the product or service is essential to the national security of the United States; and

(B) such person is a sole source supplier of the product or service, the product or service is not available from any alternative reliable supplier, and the need for the product or service cannot be met in a timely manner by improved manufacturing processes or technological developments.

(b) Transfers Of Missile Equipment Or Technology By Foreign Persons.—

(1) SANCTIONS.—

(A) SANCTIONABLE ACTIVITY.—Subject to paragraphs (3) through (7), the President shall impose the applicable sanctions under subparagraph (B) on a foreign person if the President—

(i) determines that a foreign person knowingly—

(I) exports, reexports, or transfers any MTCR equipment or technology that contributes to the design, development, or production of missiles in a country that is not an MTCR adherent and would be, if it were United States-origin equipment or technology, subject to the jurisdiction of the United States under title I;

(II) conspires to or attempts to engage in such export, reexport, or transfer; or

(III) facilitates such export, reexport, or transfer by any other person; or

(ii) has made a determination with respect to the foreign person under section 73(a) of the Arms Export Control Act.

(B) SANCTIONS.—The sanctions that apply to a foreign person under subparagraph (A) are the following:

(i) If the item involved in the export, reexport, or transfer is within category II of the MTCR Annex, then the President shall deny, for a period of 2 years, licenses for the transfer to such foreign person of missile equipment or technology the transfer of which is controlled under title I.

(ii) If the item involved in the export, reexport, or transfer is within category I of the MTCR Annex, then the President shall deny, for a period of not less than 2 years, licenses for the transfer to such foreign person of items the transfer of which is controlled under title I.

(2) INAPPLICABILITY WITH RESPECT TO MTCR ADHERENTS.—Paragraph (1) does not apply with respect to—
  (A) any export, reexport, or transfer that is authorized by the laws of an MTCR adherent, if such authorization is not obtained by misrepresentation or fraud; or
  (B) any export, reexport, or transfer of an item to an end user in a country that is an MTCR adherent.

(3) EFFECT OF ENFORCEMENT ACTIONS BY MTCR ADHERENTS.—Sanctions set forth in paragraph (1) may not be imposed under this subsection on a person with respect to acts described in such paragraph or, if such sanctions are in effect against a person on account of such acts, such sanctions shall be terminated, if an MTCR adherent is taking judicial or other enforcement action against that person with respect to such acts, or that person has been found by the government of an MTCR adherent to be innocent of wrongdoing with respect to such acts.

(4) WAIVER AND REPORT TO CONGRESS.—
  (A) WAIVER AUTHORITY.—The President may waive the application of paragraph (1) to a foreign person if the President determines that such waiver is essential to the national security of the United States.
  (B) NOTIFICATION AND REPORT TO CONGRESS.—In the event that the President decides to apply the waiver described in subparagraph (A), the President shall so notify the appropriate congressional committees not less than 20 working days before issuing the waiver. Such notification shall include a report fully articulating the rationale and circumstances which led the President to apply the waiver.

(5) ADDITIONAL WAIVER.—The President may waive the imposition of sanctions under paragraph (1) on a person with respect to a product or service if the President certifies to the appropriate congressional committees that—
  (A) the product or service is essential to the national security of the United States; and
  (B) such person is a sole source supplier of the product or service, the product or service is not available from any alternative reliable supplier, and the need for the product or service cannot be met in a timely manner by improved manufacturing processes or technological developments.

(6) EXCEPTIONS.—The President shall not apply the sanction under this subsection prohibiting the importation of the products of a foreign person—
  (A) in the case of procurement of defense articles or defense services—

(i) under existing contracts or subcontracts, including the exercise of options for production quantities to satisfy requirements essential to the national security of the United States;

(ii) if the President determines that the person to which the sanctions would be applied is a sole source supplier of the defense articles or defense services, that the defense articles or defense services are essential to the national security of the United States, and that alternative sources are not readily or reasonably available; or

(iii) if the President determines that such articles or services are essential to the national security of the United States under defense coproduction agreements or NATO Programs of Cooperation;

(B) to products or services provided under contracts entered into before the date on which the President publishes his intention to impose the sanctions; or

(C) to—

(i) spare parts;

(ii) component parts, but not finished products, essential to United States products or production;

(iii) routine services and maintenance of products, to the extent that alternative sources are not readily or reasonably available; or

(iv) information and technology essential to United States products or production.

(c) Definitions.—In this section:

(1) APPROPRIATE CONGRESSIONAL COMMITTEES.—The term 'appropriate congressional committees' means—

(A) the Committee on Foreign Affairs of the House of Representatives; and

(B) the Committee on Foreign Relations and the Committee on Banking, Housing, and Urban Affairs of the Senate.

(2) DEFENSE ARTICLES; DEFENSE SERVICES.—The terms 'defense articles' and 'defense services' mean those items on the United States Munitions List as defined in section 47(7) of the Arms Export Control Act (22 U.S.C. 2794 note).

(3) MISSILE.—The term 'missile' means a category I system as defined in the MTCR Annex.

(4) MISSILE TECHNOLOGY CONTROL REGIME; MTCR.—The term 'Missile Technology Control Regime' or 'MTCR' means the policy statement, between the United States, the United Kingdom, the Federal Republic of Germany, France, Italy, Canada, and Japan, announced on April 16, 1987, to restrict sensitive missile-

relevant transfers based on the MTCR Annex, and any amendments thereto.

(5) MTCR ADHERENT.—The term 'MTCR adherent' means a country that participates in the MTCR or that, pursuant to an international understanding to which the United States is a party, controls MTCR equipment or technology in accordance with the criteria and standards set forth in the MTCR.

(6) MTCR ANNEX.—The term 'MTCR Annex' means the Guidelines and Equipment and Technology Annex of the MTCR, and any amendments thereto.

(7) MISSILE EQUIPMENT OR TECHNOLOGY; MTCR EQUIPMENT OR TECHNOLOGY.—The terms 'missile equipment or technology' and 'MTCR equipment or technology' mean those items listed in category I or category II of the MTCR Annex.

SEC. 302. CHEMICAL AND BIOLOGICAL WEAPONS PROLIFERATION SANCTIONS.

(a) Imposition Of Sanctions.—

(1) DETERMINATION BY THE PRESIDENT.—Except as provided in subsection (b)(2), the President shall impose the sanction described in subsection (c) if the President determines that a foreign person has knowingly and materially contributed—

(A) through the export from the United States of any item that is subject to the jurisdiction of the United States under this title; or

(B) through the export from any other country of any item that would be, if they were United States goods or technology, subject to the jurisdiction of the United States under this title,

to the efforts by any foreign country, project, or entity described in paragraph (2) to use, develop, produce, stockpile, or otherwise acquire chemical or biological weapons.

(2) COUNTRIES, PROJECTS, OR ENTITIES RECEIVING ASSISTANCE.—Paragraph (1) applies in the case of—

(A) any foreign country that the President determines has, at any time after January 1, 1980—

(i) used chemical or biological weapons in violation of international law;

(ii) used lethal chemical or biological weapons against its own nationals; or

(iii) made substantial preparations to engage in the activities described in clause (i) or (ii);

(B) any foreign country whose government is determined for purposes of section 104(c) of this Act to be a government that has repeatedly provided support for acts of international terrorism; or

(C) (C) any other foreign country, project, or entity designated by the President for purposes of this section.

(3) PERSONS AGAINST WHICH SANCTIONS ARE TO BE IMPOSED.—A sanction shall be imposed pursuant to paragraph (1) on—

(A) the foreign person with respect to which the President makes the determination described in that paragraph;

(B) any successor entity to that foreign person; and

(C) any foreign person that is a parent, subsidiary, or affiliate of that foreign person if that parent, subsidiary, or affiliate knowingly assisted in the activities which were the basis of that determination.

(b) Consultations With And Actions By Foreign Government Of Jurisdiction.—

(1) CONSULTATIONS.—If the President makes the determinations described in subsection (a)(1) with respect to a foreign person, the Congress urges the President to initiate consultations immediately with the government with primary jurisdiction over that foreign person with respect to the imposition of a sanction pursuant to this section.

(2) ACTIONS BY GOVERNMENT OF JURISDICTION.—In order to pursue such consultations with that government, the President may delay imposition of a sanction pursuant to this section for a period of up to 90 days. Following such consultations, the President shall impose the sanction unless the President determines and certifies to the appropriate congressional committees that the Government has taken specific and effective actions, including appropriate penalties, to terminate the involvement of the foreign person in the activities described in subsection (a)(1). The President may delay imposition of the sanction for an additional period of up to 90 days if the President determines and certifies to the Congress that the government is in the process of taking the actions described in the preceding sentence.

(3) REPORT TO CONGRESS.—The President shall report to the appropriate congressional committees, not later than 90 days after making a determination under subsection (a)(1), on the status of consultations with the appropriate government under this subsection, and the basis for any determination under paragraph (2) of this subsection that such government has taken specific corrective actions.

(c) Sanction.—

(1) DESCRIPTION OF SANCTION.—The sanction to be imposed pursuant to subsection (a)(1) is, except as provided that the United States Government shall not procure, or enter into any contract

for the procurement of, any goods or services from any person described in subsection (a)(3).

(2) EXCEPTIONS.—The President shall not be required to apply or maintain a sanction under this section—

(A) in the case of procurement of defense articles or defense services—

(i) under existing contracts or subcontracts, including the exercise of options for production quantities to satisfy United States operational military requirements;

(ii) if the President determines that the person or other entity to which the sanctions would otherwise be applied is a sole source supplier of the defense articles or defense services, that the defense articles or defense services are essential, and that alternative sources are not readily or reasonably available; or

(iii) if the President determines that such articles or services are essential to the national security under defense coproduction agreements;

(B) to products or services provided under contracts entered into before the date on which the President publishes his intention to impose sanctions;

(C) to—

(i) spare parts;

(ii) component parts, but not finished products, essential to United States products or production; or

(iii) routine servicing and maintenance of products, to the extent that alternative sources are not readily or reasonably available;

(D) to information and technology essential to United States products or production; or

(E) to medical or other humanitarian items.

(d) Termination Of Sanctions.—A sanction imposed pursuant to this section shall apply for a period of at least 12 months following the imposition of one sanction and shall cease to apply thereafter only if the President determines and certifies to the appropriate congressional committees that reliable information indicates that the foreign person with respect to which the determination was made under subsection (a)(1) has ceased to aid or abet any foreign government, project, or entity in its efforts to acquire chemical or biological weapons capability as described in that subsection.

(e) Waiver.—

(1) CRITERION FOR WAIVER.—The President may waive the application of any sanction imposed on any person pursuant to this section, after the end of the 12-month period beginning on the date on which that sanction was imposed on that person, if the

President determines and certifies to the appropriate congressional committees that such waiver is important to the national security interests of the United States.

(2) NOTIFICATION OF AND REPORT TO CONGRESS.—If the President decides to exercise the waiver authority provided in paragraph (1), the President shall so notify the appropriate congressional committees not less than 20 days before the waiver takes effect. Such notification shall include a report fully articulating the rationale and circumstances which led the President to exercise the waiver authority.

(f) Definitions.—In this section:

(1) APPROPRIATE CONGRESSIONAL COMMITTEES.—The term 'appropriate congressional committees' means—

(A) the Committee on Foreign Affairs of the House of Representatives; and

(B) the Committee on Foreign Relations and the Committee on Banking, Housing, and Urban Affairs of the Senate.

(2) DEFENSE ARTICLES; DEFENSE SERVICES.—The terms 'defense articles' and 'defense services' mean those items on the United States Munitions List or are otherwise controlled under the Arms Export Control Act.

Index

Note: Page numbers followed by "n" indicate footnotes.

Taylor & Francis Group
an informa business

For Product Safety Concerns and Information please contact our EU representative GPSR@taylorandfrancis.com
Taylor & Francis Verlag GmbH, Kaufingerstraße 24, 80331 München, Germany

www.ingramcontent.com/pod-product-compliance
Ingram Content Group UK Ltd.
Pitfield, Milton Keynes, MK11 3LW, UK
UKHW020008200926
475702UK00015B/2549
* 9 7 8 0 3 6 7 4 9 8 3 6 8 *